PAUL S. ENDY JR.

Las Vegas Casino Gaming Legend

ERIC P. ENDY MBA

Fulton Books
Meadville, PA

Published by Fulton Books 2022

ISBN 978-1-63710-238-1 (paperback)
ISBN 978-1-63710-239-8 (digital)

Printed in the United States of America

CHAPTER 1

T. R. King & Co. "Gaming in His Blood"

It was November of 1963, the year President John F. Kennedy was assassinated, when Paul Endy Jr. decided to leave Los Angeles and move our family to Las Vegas, Nevada. The gaming supply business was in his blood just like his father's, Paul Endy Sr. (affectionately known as Gramps) whom he worked for. My father would bring integrity to the gaming supply business, which would become one of his greatest assets to the growing gaming industry in the United States. In the early 1920s, Milton C. Anderson started a gaming supply company in Kansas City, Missouri. It was the roaring '20s, the Great Depression was over, and things were looking up. Anderson named his company T. R. King after his favorite president, Teddy Roosevelt, and the "king" crown molds on his casino chips. In 1931, Anderson relocated their business to Los Angeles, California. In 1956 Anderson sold his company to George Davies and his salesman Paul Endy Sr., who adored Teddy Roosevelt because he was an avid poker player. Poker has always been a favored game among US presidents, perhaps in part because of the many ways the strategies and challenges afforded by the game tend to overlap with those of politics. Stories of poker-playing presidents are well known, despite the efforts by some of them not to let their interest in the game become publicized because of the potential political damage. While being a cardplayer certainly can help a president connect with some citizens, moral objections to gambling by others can make being associated with poker a potential deficit. Still, many have argued persuasively that the skills one develops as a poker player can serve a president particularly well. Being able to weigh risk and reward, to be calculating enough to think several steps ahead, and to read others' bluffs are all part of both poker and being a president. Many presidents in US history are known to have been poker players even though the game really didn't begin to spread until the early- to mid-nineteenth century.

Theodore Roosevelt Jr. (/ˈroʊzəvɛlt/ *ROH-zə-velt*; October 27, 1858–January 6, 1919), often referred to as Teddy Roosevelt or his initials TR, was an American statesman, politician, conservationist, naturalist, and writer who served as the twenty-sixth president of the United States from 1901 to 1909. He served as the twenty-fifth vice president from March to September 1901 and as the thirty-third governor of New York from 1899 to 1900. Roosevelt emerged as a leader of the Republican Party and became a driving force for the antitrust policy while supporting Progressive-Era policies in the United States in the early twentieth century. His face is depicted on Mount Rushmore alongside George Washington, Thomas Jefferson, and Abraham Lincoln. He is generally ranked in polls of historians and political scientists as one of the five best presidents. Roosevelt got his foot in the door of the Republican Party through private poker games at smoky New York saloons. A polymath, he was considered one of the most intellectual and well-read presidents to be elected along with Thomas Jefferson. His sporting talents were similarly impressive—a keen swimmer, horse rider, hiker, boxer and, no doubt, quite the card sharp. Roosevelt would embody the image of one who dabbles in poker semiprofessionally, extremely successful in other areas of life and proving a force to be reckoned with at the tables too. A Nobel Peace Prize winner who lived by way of his signature "big stick diplomacy," Teddy definitely "walked lightly and carried a big stick" when it came to poker. The politician, who hadn't had any fear of stepping into the boxing ring, loved playing poker with his friends and political opponents in his free time. Considered a savvy poker player, Teddy's outgoing attitude and overt masculinity made him one of the more popular presidents in US history and gambling news history. After leading the Union to victory in the Civil War, Ulysses S. Grant became the country's eighteenth president and, while in office, enjoyed poker. So did numerous other politicians as the nineteenth century came to a close. Among that group was Theodore Roosevelt who used poker as a way to gain entry into social circles while moving up through the ranks to the vice presidency. Much as poker had been dominated by cheating, particularly in the saloons and on the steamboats of the Old West, more games were being played "on the square" as the new century began. Similarly, Teddy Roosevelt's "square deal" sought to protect consumers against overly powerful businesses, creating a level playing field for all. "All I ask is a square deal for every man," he wrote. "Give him a fair chance. Do not let him wrong anyone, and do not let him be wronged."

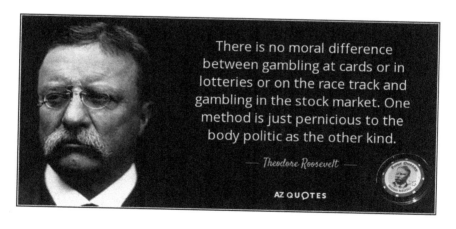

There is no moral difference between gambling at cards or in lotteries or on the race track and gambling in the stock market. One method is just pernicious to the body politic as the other kind.

— *Theodore Roosevelt* —

AZ QUOTES

Clarifying his position in a 1905 speech after being elected on his own, Teddy Roosevelt was even more explicit about the poker analogy. "When I say I believe in a square deal I do not mean... [It's] possible to give every man the best hand," he said, revealing a keen understanding of poker's chance element. "All I mean is that there shall not be any crookedness in the dealing." Delano Roosevelt followed Hoover as the nation's thirty-second president, bringing back the poker-playing tradition with low-stakes games several times a week, often nickel-ante stud. Some claim even to have heard FDR riffling chips during his famous radio *Fireside Chats*. Following the footsteps of his fifth cousin, Theodore, FDR likewise employed a poker metaphor to describe his "New Deal" series of programs aimed at fostering recovery from the Depression. FDR hosted games on the final night of each congressional session, and whoever led when the session adjourned was declared the winner. Once FDR was down when the call came but didn't let on to the others, the session was over. Hours later he was ahead, then had a phone brought to him and reported the session had ended, making him the winner. Gramps once told my father the story of how he met President Teddy Roosevelt in 1954 and delivered a personalized poker chip set with his name, Teddy Roosevelt, engraved on both sides of the chips. President Roosevelt was so impressed that he gave Gramps a special accommodation as an exchange gift. Gramps proudly hung the accommodation in his home on Electric Avenue in Monterey Park. My dad would tell me later that Gramps "always smiled ear to ear" bragging about the accommodation to anyone that came in his front door. Among the other presidents who played poker were Ulysses S. Grant, Abraham Lincoln, Franklin D. Roosevelt, John Kennedy, Harry Truman, and Barack Obama. Harding's advisers played so often with the boss they were known as "the Poker Cabinet."

My dad made a special collection of presidential chips.

Our house on Electric Avenue in the 1960s was simple but comfortable. It was built in 1951 and had three bedrooms and two bathrooms, which my brothers and I had to share. The highlight of our house was an outdoor adobe-elevated pop-up swimming pool in the back yard, which kept me and my two brothers mostly entertained in the warm Los Angeles summers.

159 South Electric Avenue, Monterey Park, California

We lived in a middle-class neighborhood, but I don't think we were, at least not until much later in life! It was my mother, Jean, who would be my brothers and my early mentor. Even though we lived a simple life, my mother always cooked healthy food for us even when we were young, refusing to buy precooked, prepared baby food. I don't remember much about my father's involvement in my early life; all I know is that he was the hardest worker I had ever met. Dad got up early in the morning before I woke up and didn't get home until I was fast asleep. If he wasn't manufacturing gaming supplies during the day, calling on customers and selling to them during the night, then he was next door in Gramps's extended garage, "marking" cards sold to illegal proprietors.

My dad wasn't a fan of the illegal gaming market and once told my mother, "I won't do this illegal shit much longer," and soon he wouldn't have to! It was the first and last time my mother ever heard my dad swear.

"Marking cards" and "crooked dice"

Marking is the process of altering playing cards in a method only apparent to a marker or conspirator, such as by bending or adding visible marks to a card. This allows different methods for card sharps to cheat or may be used for magic tricks. For as long as card games have been played for real money, people have tried to get an advantage. There have been some creative ways to mark cards over the years with the latest technological advances used along the way. In blackjack, you would not have to mark very many cards to gain a significant advantage. To be effective, the distinguishing mark or marks must be visible on the obverse sides of the cards, which are normally uniform. Card marking is often used to cheat in gambling. Marked cards can be used regardless of who shuffles and deals the cards. Some more sophisticated marked-cards scams involve additional manipulative skills to steer the cards into the correct positions once the desired cards have been identified. Marked cards can be used regardless of who shuffles and deals the cards. The first attempts to mark playing cards involved bends, crimps, and tiny pinprick bumps known as "blisters" resembling the Braille script.

Later, when the first designs appeared on the backs of playing cards, cheats began altering the designs on the backs of cards. Hustlers or "card markers" have used various inks, pigments, and scratches to add or remove lines or patterns from the back of the card designs. Some varieties of card marking include block-out work, cutout work, scrollwork, shade work, and tint work. Blocking is the most common method of marking cards. This involves making changes to the pattern on the back of a card by adding a colored section where the card was previously white. This could be as simple as filling in a single petal on a rose or just making one line thicker than the others. In blackjack, if you can see the dealer's down card is a 5 (for example), then you can adjust your own betting to account for this. Cutting is the opposite of blocking; this involves removing some of the patterns from the back of a card, usually with a razor. This can be a minor component for example the wing of a bird. Only people knowing what to look for would spot this during normal play. Physical changes to the back of cards do require that the cheats have access to the deck before the game begins. This is also easy to spot by 'riffing' the deck.

If you flick through all the cards quickly, then any pattern changes should jump out since the backs of the cards will jump around. Invisible ink has been a favorite way of marking cards for many years. There are several types of this ink available with the most common varieties requiring special sunglasses or contact lenses to see the marks. There are now more modern inks that can only be seen by computers; these are more likely to be used to catch cheats than for cheating by individuals. Other methods of daubing cards include dusting them or adding citrus type substances, which would only be seen by someone who knew what they were looking for. Lastly, marking cards is illegal, and you could be indicted and even jailed if caught doing this in a casino.

The method my grandfather used to mark cards, as described to me by my dad, was both wax and later correction fluid, which was invented in 1956 by Secretary Bette Nesmith Graham, founder of Liquid Paper. Correction fluid or Wite-Out is an opaque, usually white, fluid applied to paper to mask errors in the text. Once dried, it can be written over. It is typically packaged in small transparent bottles, and the lid has an attached brush (or a triangular piece of foam) that dips into the bottle. The brush is used to apply the fluid onto the paper. It can be used for many purposes, including "marking playing cards and changing spots on dice." T. R. King was historically known as a source for making and selling "marked" cards and "crooked" dice at their store in Los Angeles. Even though T. R. King wasn't selling illegal gaming supplies to Nevada, the Nevada Gaming Commission was watching T. R. King, and they didn't like that they saw. One example of card marking is by subtly tinting different body parts of this small "angel" feature on the back of a playing card (the head for an ace, the left wing for a king, etc.) so the card's rank can be discerned.

A subtler variation on blocking, card backs can be marked by lightly tinting certain areas of detail. Rather than blocking out the entire petal on a flower detail, the petal is washed with a light ink of a similar color to the card ink. It was suspected that after my dad left the company, the Nevada Gaming Board prohibited T. R. King from selling chips to Nevada casinos because they refused to stop dealing in items like marked cards and crooked dice to the public. T. R. King product catalogs from the 1930s and 1940s did feature gaming "enhancement" devices like these.

In 1963, Monterey Park was a small bedroom community of Los Angeles, which was a relatively quiet city with a bowling alley and the Monterey movie theater on Garfield as its entertainment venues. Originally opened in 1924 as the Mission Theatre, by 1941 it had been renamed Monterey Theatre. The theater appears in the Ed Wood film *Jailbait,* and though the marquee is not visible, its interior is. In the early 1950s it was operated by the Edwards Circuit, which ran it until around 1980. My dad said he enjoyed going to watch movies at the Monterey Theatre with my mother when they were teenagers. My dad's favorite movies were any with John Wayne in them, and he would later surprise his friends in Las Vegas with an unusual movie-theater surprise.

CHAPTER 2

Monterey Park, California— Birthplace of Paul Endy Jr. and Laura Scudder's Potato Chips

The original inhabitants of Monterey Park were Shoshone Indians, later renamed the Gabrielino Indians by the Spaniards; however, Chinese settlers eventually followed. When Fathers Angel Somero and Pedro Canbon led the first parties of soldiers into the San Gabriel Valley in 1771, there were more than four thousand Gabrielino residents. By the early 1800s, the area, now called Monterey Park, was part of the Mission San Gabriel de Archangel and later the Rancho San Antonio. The area first received a separate identity when Alessandro Repetto purchased five thousand acres of the rancho and built his home not far from where the Edison Substation is now located on Garfield Avenue. Some years later, Richard Garvey, a mail rider for the US Army whose route took him through Monterey Pass (a trail that is now Garvey Avenue) settled down in the King's Hills. Garvey began developing the land by bringing in spring water from near the Hondo River and by constructing a fifty-four-foot-high dam to form Garvey Lake located where Garvey Ranch Park is now. The community voted itself into cityhood on May 29, 1916, by a vote of 455 to 33. In the early 1900s, Monterey Park was a truck-farming community with no paved roads. Coyote Pass, now known as Monterey Pass Road, was the way to downtown Los Angeles before the great bridges and paved roads were constructed. The first subdivisions in 1906 were north of Garvey and east of Garfield along with the exclusive Midwick Country Club.

My dad's favorite snack food was Laura Scudder's potato chips. I never knew the reason that he had to have her potato chips, but now I think I know the real reason why he liked them. They were born in the same place he was. He always kept some Laura Scudder's potato chips in the top drawer of his desk at Paul-Son just in case he got hungry.

Potato chip queen Laura Scudder started her empire in Monterey Park with a service station on the southwest corner of Garvey and Atlantic back in the 1920s when the land was almost completely undeveloped. A documentary on Scudder in the museum reveals that part of the reason she started her business was that people's cars kept breaking down on Garvey near their property. While there, she became the first female attorney in Ukiah, California (but she never practiced law), before moving south in 1920 to Monterey Park, California, where Charles ran a gas station (a garage and attached-brick building at the northeast corner of Atlantic and Garvey) until he was disabled repairing a car. Laura took over the gas station and branched out into the potato chips in 1926 and later peanut butter in 1931.

Her station was one of the first on the emerging artery. A plaque on the northeast corner of the intersection commemorates Scudder and her legacy on Monterey Park.

By 1920, the White and Spanish-surname settlers in Monterey Park were joined by Asian residents who began farming potatoes and flowers and developing nurseries in the Monterey Highlands area. They improved the Monterey Pass Trail with a road to aid in shipping their produce to Los Angeles. The nameless pass, which had been a popular location for Western movies, was called Coyote Pass by pioneer Masami Abe.

Real estate became a thriving industry during the 1920s with investors attracted to the many subdivisions under development and increasing commercial opportunities.

Monterey Park is part of a cluster of cities (Alhambra, Arcadia, Temple City, Rosemead, San Marino, and San Gabriel in the west San Gabriel Valley) with a growing Asian American population. Beginning in the 1970s, well-educated and affluent Asian Americans and Asian immigrants began settling in the West San Gabriel Valley, primarily to Monterey Park. The city council subsequently tried and failed to pass English-only ordinances. In 1985 the city council of Monterey Park approved the drafting of a proposal that would require all businesses in Monterey Park to display English language identification on business signs.

In the last three decades, Monterey Park became known as the first city and suburb in America to have an Asian majority. Advertised in Asia as "the Chinese Beverly Hills," the city's unique social history has made it the subject of several books in the last two decades.

In the 1980s, Monterey Park was referred to as "Little Taipei." Frederic Hsieh, a local realtor who bought land in Monterey Park and sold it to newly arrived immigrants, is credited with engendering Monterey Park's Chinese American community. Many businesses from the Chinatown in downtown Los Angeles began to open up stores in Monterey Park. In the 1970s and 1980s, many affluent Taiwanese Waishengren immigrants moved abroad from Taiwan and began settling into Monterey Park. Mandarin Chinese became the most widely spoken language in many Chinese businesses of the city during that time. It displaced Cantonese that had been common previously. Cantonese has dominated the Chinatowns of North America for decades, but Mandarin is the most common language of Chinese immigrants in the past few decades. In 1983, Lily Lee Chen became the first Chinese American woman to be elected mayor of a US city. By the late 1980s, immigrants from Mainland China and Vietnam began moving into Monterey Park; and in the 1990 census, Monterey Park became the first city with an Asian descent majority population in the continental United States.

According to the 2009 American Community Survey, Monterey Park is 43.7 percent Chinese American and is the city in the United States with the largest concentration of people of Chinese descent. The Chinese American population in Monterey Park and San Gabriel Valley is relatively diverse in socioeconomics and region of origin. The city has attracted immigrants from Taiwan as well as Mainland Chinese, Japanese, and overseas Chinese from Southeast Asia. There are also Vietnamese, Korean, and Filipino communities living within Monterey Park. While the multigenerational American-born Latino population was generally declining in Monterey Park, there has been a small new influx of Mexican immigrants (about one percent increase in the population).

I believe there was a reason that I was born in Monterey Park, now a predominately Chinese community, and I married Hsiaochin (Cathy) Endy in Las Vegas on October 7, 1989. In the 1950s however, it was the poker clubs, Elks Lodges, and Las Vegas charity gaming nights held in Southern California that my father was interested in. He, in particular, had his eye on the growth of gambling in Las

Vegas since he was T. R. King's Nevada salesman. Beginning every month without exception, Gramps and my dad after him would travel in a truck and trailer loaded with gaming supplies. Every month they would head toward Las Vegas and then Reno (known as "the gambling capital" in 1920) and deliver cards, dice, and chips to legal gaming customers in Nevada. They would then complete their 1,500-mile trip by driving down the California coast from San Francisco and finally to Los Angeles, selling cards and chips to every Elks Lodge, California card rooms, and illegal poker clubs without exception. My dad would take the order by phone and then personally deliver it to them. His customers appreciated that they didn't have to pay for shipping and would place reorders with him for the next month. Customer service was always important to my dad. As he would always say, "The customer is always right even if he's wrong." He would continue the tradition of calling on and delivering gaming supplies to his customers every month even though it was a long and tiring trip for him. However, he would never complain but rather complimented his customer's great food quality for the ten days he was on the road. My dad is also credited with being the first salesman to provide gaming equipment to Southern California organizations that conducted charity casino nights. My father and his brother Charles would deliver the tables and gaming supplies to the California charity fundraiser in a Ford pickup truck and trailer and fill them up with chips then deal whatever game was needed that night. These fundraisers typically lasted very late into the night until the winners grabbed their prizes, and the raffle was over. Finally, my dad was there even later at night, collapsing the portable gaming tables, loading the chips, playing cards, the roulette wheel, and all the accessories back into the trailer, arriving back home as late as 2:00 or 3:00 a.m. to catch a few hours of sleep.

I don't remember if he was more tired after working the late charity casino nights or from the monthly long sales trips he made. I never heard him ever complain about working, and once in a while he would tell a funny joke. I will never forget the joke my father would later tell me after each trip about "the sign" on one of his customers' poker rooms front door that read, "Liquor Up Front and Poker in the Rear."

Eldorado Bar, Grill and Club, Sacramento, California

If I didn't hear my father repeat that proverb after every trip home, I knew he was tired—dead tired—from the road trip. He loved to drive no matter where; as a matter of fact, he had such an intense fear of flying that he wouldn't fly anywhere. As long as he was driving, he was in control, and soon he would control his own destiny.

CHAPTER 3

The Early Years

Paul Endy (1928–1999), "the Gaming Legend,"
founded one of the gaming industry's most
important casino products companies.

Born on July 12, 1928, in Monterey Park, California, Paul S. Endy
Jr. learned the gaming business from his father at T. R. King & Co.

My dad was a husky, handsome four-year letterman in baseball and football at Mark Keppel High School and played both sports while attending Long Beach City College. Paul S. Endy Jr. learned the gaming business from his father at T. R. King & Co. His good looks remind me of Elvis Presley when he was a teenager, don't you think so?

Paul Endy, tackle, 5'10", 185 pounds, 46 (*left*). Jean Marie Doyle (*right*).

After graduation from college, he worked as an electrician for Bethlehem Steel and then took a job with T. R. King & Co., a gaming-supply distributorship and dice-manufacturing operation in Los Angeles. In 1946, my dad met my mother, Jean Marie Doyle, his high school sweetheart, and a majorite at Mark Keppel High School. He married her at the tender age of sixteen in 1948.

He eventually purchased a home next door to his father in Monterey Park, California, only seven miles from downtown Los Angeles and the location of T. R. King & Co. In 1955 Paul Endy Jr. went to work for his father just as my brothers and I would do for him, all starting on the bottom rung and working their way up the ladder. My mom was an attractive bleached-blonde stay-at-home woman who exercised daily by practicing yoga. I often had to tell my friends or anyone who came over to our house that they couldn't date her and she wasn't my sister but was really my mother! My mom and dad raised three boys (Patrick, Tommy, and me), and my mom miscarried a baby girl to near term. I understand this forever scarred my mom as she would tell us later that her life with my dad would have been "easier" if she would have had a baby girl, but it was not to be.

Left to right: Patrick, Tommy, and me.

Even though my dad and mom were married in 1948, they were later divorced in 1978, the year I went away to college at UNR.

It would be one of my father's saddest days when he wrote a heartfelt letter to his wife begging her to reconsider the divorce. Unfortunately, my mother filed for divorce anyway. She would later confess to me and my two brothers that even though she kept herself "busy" painting and decorating, she was lonely, while my dad attended to his gaming customers both day and night. He would also often fundraise for the Optimist Club or voluntarily referee baseball on the weekends for the city of Monterey Park. It was something Dad would find enjoyment in from his early days of playing baseball in high school and college. He was also cubmaster for the local Boy Scout troop. I don't ever remember hearing my parents argue except about how many hours dad worked and his lack of sleep. However, my dad was strong as a bull, and recently my aunt Jackie (Mother's sister) explained to me that he was determined to give his family a better life than his family had when his dad was working at the steel mill before joining T. R. King. Even though my mother eventually remarried, the divorce would be something she would regret the rest of her life. Maybe a baby girl would have made a difference?

During the 1940s and 1950s, T. R. King was the leading supplier of cards and chips to California's legal and illegal card rooms. However, in 1963, Paul Endy Sr. and his partner, George Davies, had conflicting business visions for the company. Their business differences were always about the continuation of making illegal "marked cards" and "crooked dice," which my grandfather no longer wanted to sell. Since they were unable to settle their differences, they ended up in a courtroom where the judge told them that one partner needed to sell his half and the other needed to buy it. In the end, Gramps sold his half to George Davies.

My dad emerged as his father's top salesman, but when his father retired, Dad didn't get along with his partner, George Davies, either and knew his future wasn't to be at T. R. King & Co. George Davies was a man of short stature and a dark-haired "shifty" man with wide wire-rimmed glasses and a black beard. His background was secretive, and he had more questions than he had answers for. George Davies liked the sales of "marked cards" and "crooked dice" at T. R. King & Co. since they commanded a higher selling price. My dad wanted to discontinue making and selling illegal gaming supplies and was concerned that the company would eventually get into trouble and didn't want to be any part of it. He would let Davies take the "heat" if he was gone. In my dad's words, "Anyone with a beard is hiding something." And he believed George Davies had plenty to hide in his past but didn't want to know about it. Why should he? It was his father's partner, not his! The general manager at T. R. King & Co. at that time was Charles Endy (affectionately known as Uncle Charlie, my father's younger brother) who left when his father sold to Davies. Eventually, George Davies took on a partner, Roy Osterhault; and they together owned and operated T. R. King & Co. As predicted by my father, in 1974 T. R. King & Co. had to stop selling gaming supplies in Nevada. It was believed that the Nevada Gaming Board prohibited T. R. King from selling chips to its casinos because they refused to stop dealing in items like marked cards and crooked dice to the public. Shortly around the time of the Nevada ban, Roy Osterhaut's son-in-law, Dennis O'Neill, joined the team at T. R. King. According to the T. R. King Tribute Site, because of his hard work, O'Neill became the general manager and eventually the new owner. Under this leadership, the custom chip concept for home games really took off.

O'Neill's company's latter years were spent filling California and international casino orders as well as stock and custom orders from their website. Frustrated with the way things turned out with his dad's partner, my dad's destiny would not be to succeed his father at T. R. King. He decided to move our family to Utah in 1963 where he would work on a ranch. My dad traveled ahead of our family, but when he stopped at Las Vegas he noticed in the local newspaper, *The Las Vegas Sun*, an ad for a bankrupt dice company. My dad quickly changed his plans, borrowed $40,000 from his father, bought the bankrupt dice manufacturer, and moved it to Industrial Road. Uncle Charlie would later team up with my dad and move his Top Hat and Cane Company to Las Vegas and, in 1981, become part of Paul-Son Dice & Card Co. Top Hat and Cane Company manufactured chips in a totally different manner than T. R. King produced. For the first time, my father had his own gaming chips; and that was important for delivery, security, and confidence in the product from the casino bosses. The management from various casinos would often visit our factories to see how their chips were manufactured but primarily for security reasons. Whether the tour was in Las Vegas, Mexico, or later in France, the casino managers and the gaming commissions were always pleased with what they saw as my dad always referred to Paul-Son as "Fort Knox." Since we treated chips the same as money, we operated our chip-manufacturing plant similar to a bank. In addition to security cameras, security guards, and RFID-detection devices in the factory, each employee was responsible for their count of chips until they were counted in and out of the "chip bank." Once a chip order was complete, it was securely packed in Mexico, driven to Las Vegas by our own drivers, and/or shipped to a branch office to be delivered to the casino.

My father believed that there was an additional security benefit by our chips being made in Mexico. After the chips were produced, they had to be accounted for by both the factory and Mexico border security. According to maquiladora law, everything brought into Mexico from the United States had to be returned to the United States, and Paul-Son Mexican was formed as a maquiladora. A maquiladora is a company that allows factories to be largely duty-free and tariff-free. These factories take raw materials and assemble, manufacture, or process them and export the finished product. These factories and systems are present throughout Latin America, including Mexico, Paraguay, and El Salvador. Maquiladoras date back to 1964 when the Mexican government introduced the Programa de Industrialización Fronteriza ("Border Industrialization Program"). Specific programs and laws have made Mexico's maquila industry grow rapidly. My dad believed there were several advantages to manufacturing in Mexico including eventual sales to legalized Mexico casinos.

The first Paul-Son Mexicana factory, San Luis, Mexico

There were security guards and security cameras both inside and outside the factory for protection. Also, my father believed the distance from Las Vegas and other gaming jurisdictions added a layer of security. Paul-Son customers appreciated the company's commitment to protecting their money, and many even said, "They could sleep better at night," knowing their products were secure with us. And they were.

CHAPTER 4

A Brief History of Paul-Son Gaming Chips

Although the first recorded casino was legalized in Venice in 1626, gambling can be traced as far back as ancient civilizations of Mesopotamia and early China. The casino chip or cheque is relatively new. Casino tokens (also known as casino or gaming chips, checks, or cheques) are small discs used in place of currency in casinos. Colored metal, injection-molded plastic, or compression molded clay tokens of various denominations are used primarily in table games as opposed to metal token coins that were used primarily in slot machines. Gaming chips are treated as money because that's what they mean for the casino. Casino tokens are also widely used as

24

play money in casual or tournament games. One of the biggest misconceptions is that the standard weight of official casino poker chips is 11.5 grams. It is not. Although there is no single standard weight, all official casino chips are between 8.5 and 10 grams. Another misconception with casino chip weight is that heavier chips are of higher quality.

This is not actually true. While the super light chips (two to three ounces) are very cheap, there is no difference in quality within the eight- to fourteen-ounce weight range. It is simply a matter of preference. The chips that are in the lower end of this range (nine to ten ounces) are actually considered by most people to be the higher quality chips according to Pokerchipmania.com. Money is exchanged for chips at a casino at the casino cage, at the gaming tables, or at a cashier station. The chips are interchangeable with money at the casino. Generally, they have no value outside of the casino. Virtually all casinos have eliminated the use of metal tokens (and coins) in their slot machines in favor of paper receipts or prepaid cards. The ancestors of modern casino tokens were the counters used to keep score in the card games ombre and quadrille. In 1752, French quadrille sets contained several different counters known as jetons, fiches, and mils. Unlike modern casino chips, they were colored differently only to determine player ownership for purposes of settling payments at the end of the game with different denominations differentiated by different shapes that each counter type had. In the early history of poker during the nineteenth century, players seemed to use any small valuable object imaginable according to David Parlett in "Quadrille and Médiateur: Courtly ladies' game of 18th-century France" (retrieved January 28, 2009). Back in the nineteenth century, chips didn't even exist. Instead, the great poker players of the world brought strange objects to the table to gamble with. Early players sometimes used jagged gold pieces, gold nuggets, gold dust, or coins as well as "chips" primarily made of ivory, bone, wood, paper, and a composition made from clay and shellac. Several companies between the 1880s and the late 1930s made clay-composite poker chips.

In the early history of poker, during the nineteenth century, players seemed to use any small valuable object imaginable. Needless to say, some sort of standardization was desperately needed. So the saloons and gaming houses that offered poker games created their own standardized substitutes—pieces of ivory, bones, and clay. Unfortunately, these "standards" were easy to forge; so the gambling houses began to brand those pieces of ivory, bones, and clay with unique symbols and attributes. Forging remained a problem, so by the 1880s companies started creating clay composition poker chips, giving birth to an entire industry and ultimately changing the way several companies between the 1880s and the late 1930s made clay-composite casino chips. Most chips were white, red, blue, and yellow; but they could be made in almost any color desired. These chips, made of 100 percent clay, are the direct ancestors of the casino chips that are used today. The downside to using these 100 percent clay chips was that they were very fragile and broke easily when handled roughly by the players. This was an issue that casinos would struggle with up until the early 1950s when the companies that produced them started to add other materials to the clay to increase the durability of the chips. That was when the companies started to add earthen materials such as sand, chalk, and clay material similar to the material found in cat litter that the modern clay-composite chip that we know today was truly born. The process to make these modern "clay-composite" chips is a trade secret, and each manufacturer uses their own recipe of ingredients when making their chips. The vast majority of casino chips are "clay" chips but can be more accurately described as compression-molded chips.

Contrary to popular belief, no gaming chip going as far back as the 1950s has been 100 percent clay. Modern clay chips are a composition of materials more durable than clay alone. At least some percentage of the chips is of an earthen material such as sand, chalk, and clay.

In the mid-twentieth century, the large casinos had already been established in several parts of the US and these casinos became the hot spot for gamblers from all over the world. There was a need for manufacturing thousands of casino chips. The process used to make

Paul-Son casino chips is a trade secret and labor-intensive. Paul-Son edge spots or inserts are not painted on. To achieve this effect, this area of the clay is removed and then replaced with the clay of a different color. This can be done to each chip individually, or a strip can be taken out of a cylindrical block of material and replaced with the alternate color before the block is cut into chips. Then each Paul-Son chip receives a mid-inlay if desired and is placed in a special mold that heats and compresses the chip at approximately 10152.6 psi (70 MPa) at 302°F (150°C), hence the term *compression-molded chips*. The printed graphics on clay chips is called an inlay. Inlays are typically made of paper and are then covered with a plastic film applied to the chip before the compression molding process. During the molding process, the inlay becomes permanently fastened to the chip and cannot be removed from the chip without destroying the inlay. We developed a special process at Paul-Son of printing directly on a plastic inlay that was not removable from the chip.

Ceramic chips were introduced in the mid-1980s as an alternative to clay chips and are also used in casinos as well as being readily available to the home market.

Ceramic chips are sometimes also referred to as clay or clay composite; but they are, in fact, an injection-molded chip made with a special plastic or resin formula that approximates the feel and sound of ceramic or porcelain. There are less expensive chips for the home market made from various forms of plastic and plastic covered metal slugs as well. Each casino has a unique set of chips even if the casino is part of a greater company. This distinguishes a casino's chips from others since each chip and token on the gaming floor must be backed with the appropriate amount of cash. Also, except Nevada, casinos are not permitted to honor another casino's chips.

The security features of casino chips are numerous. The artwork is of a very high resolution or photographic quality. Custom color combinations on the chip edge spots are always distinctive to a particular casino. UV markings can be made on the inlay. One security feature being used is an audible taggant incorporated into the ceramic chip blank. A simple handheld reader will beep if the gaming chip is authentic. Counterfeit chips are rare but happen from time to time. High levels of surveillance, along with staff familiarity with chip design and coloring, make passing counterfeit chips difficult. Casinos, though, are somewhat prepared for this in case it happens. During the 1970s, Paul-Son worked with the gaming commissions, particularly in Nevada, to standardize the base colors of our gaming chips. At first, I understand the casinos were reluctant to standardize the chip base colors since each casino wanted to look different and have chips unique to the property.

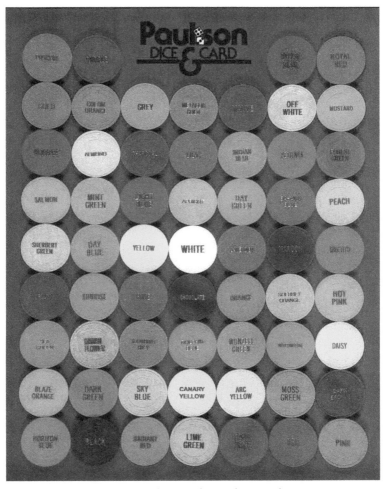

Paul-Son's original sixty chip color combinations

Before Paul-Son standardizing the base chip color.

Paul-Son standardized the base chip color.

We eventually convinced the state of Nevada to standardize the base color. So a $1 chip was blue or white, a $5 chip was red, a $25 chip was green, and a $100 chip was black. Paul-Son color-coded the edge spots so each casinos' color combinations were different from each other. At the time, we estimated that we could produce more than 150,000 different edge-spot color combinations. Also, all state gaming commissions require that casinos have an additional (second rack) set of casino chips in reserve with alternate markings. Several casinos such as the Hard Rock Hotel and Casino in Las Vegas issue "limited edition" varied-designed chips commemorating various events though retaining a common color scheme. This encourages customers to keep them for souvenirs at a profit to the casino.

$25 Hard Rock Hotel grand-opening Jimi Hendrix gaming chips in 1995

In certain casinos such as the Bellagio and Wynn Las Vegas, chips are embedded with RFID tags to help casinos keep better track of them, determine gamblers' average bet sizes, and make them harder for counterfeiters to reproduce. In less than 150 years, casino chips have come from the crude easy-to-forge chips made of makeshift materials to the modern chips we know today that boast enhanced security features such as radio frequency identification (RFID), UV markings only visible under a black light, and other security features.

Only the future knows what is in store for the casino chip of tomorrow.

Today casinos are testing using digital chips that are usually part of an electronic video game, usually poker. However, my dad always told me, "Gamblers prefer to feel their chips and stack them in front of them." You can't do that with digital chips. Over time, security devices were constantly improved and inserted into Paul-Son gaming chips. My dad constantly explored new technologies, including high-tech security features and improved graphics applications to the Paul-Son gaming chips.

Paul-Son's top hat and cane in blacklight

Back in January 2014, the Borgata Winter Poker Open $2-million guarantee was suspended and ultimately cancelled after counterfeit chips were introduced into the tournament. Christian Lusardi, forty-two, was ultimately charged with the crime. In preparation for the 2014 Borgata Spring Poker Open, the Borgata Casino Hotel & Spa had introduced new, state-of-the-art chips for the seventeen-event series that ran from April 8 to 26 and culminates with the $5-million-guarantee World Poker Tour Championship. Paul-Son Top Hat and Cane chips are compression molded, ten grams in weight, and have more of a clay composition than the ceramic chips that T. R. King produced.

Casino patrons preferred the feel and weight of clay composition chips, and eventually the Top Hat and Cane chips would end up being the chip of choice for gamblers in the United States. Paul-Son would sell a commemorative or collectible chip, usually a $5 or $10 denomination, to the casino for approximately $1. Every time a casino patron would walk out the casino's front door, the casino would make the difference of either $4 or $9 per chip. My father liked to call casinos "America's real bank" and that Paul-Son chips were "played the world over."

The first Paul-Son Dice & Card Co. color catalog.

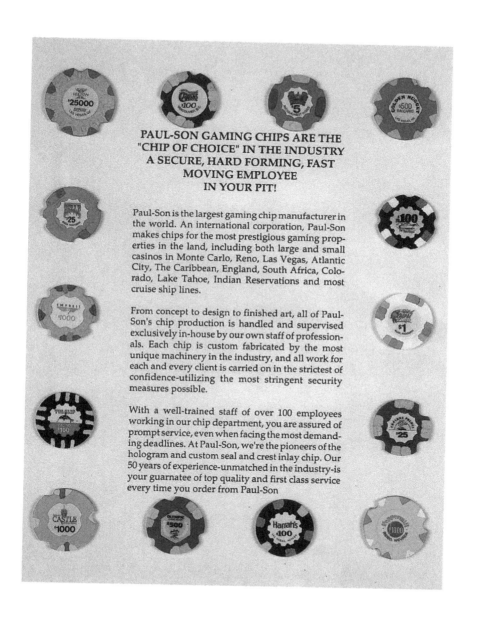

PAUL-SON GAMING CHIPS ARE THE "CHIP OF CHOICE" IN THE INDUSTRY A SECURE, HARD FORMING, FAST MOVING EMPLOYEE IN YOUR PIT!

Paul-Son is the largest gaming chip manufacturer in the world. An international corporation, Paul-Son makes chips for the most prestigious gaming properties in the land, including both large and small casinos in Monte Carlo, Reno, Las Vegas, Atlantic City, The Caribbean, England, South Africa, Colorado, Lake Tahoe, Indian Reservations and most cruise ship lines.

From concept to design to finished art, all of Paul-Son's chip production is handled and supervised exclusively in-house by our own staff of professionals. Each chip is custom fabricated by the most unique machinery in the industry, and all work for each and every client is carried on in the strictest of confidence-utilizing the most stringent security measures possible.

With a well-trained staff of over 100 employees working in our chip department, you are assured of prompt service, even when facing the most demanding deadlines. At Paul-Son, we're the pioneers of the hologram and custom seal and crest inlay chip. Our 50 years of experience-unmatched in the industry-is your guarnatee of top quality and first class service every time you order from Paul-Son

PAUL-SON'S CHIPS ARE PLAYED AROUND THE WORLD

HIGH SECURITY CHIP CONTROL POLICY

Maximum precautions safeguard chips at all times! We at Paul-Son are well aware of the need for 100% effective security measures in casino operations and we assign the highest priority to this most important aspect of your business. All of our gaming chips are made and handled in very stringent security conditions. Our time-tested, experienced procedures provide a reliable assurance that the color-code used for one customer's chips is registered and protected against the possibility that it might ever be used for another. Special molds and registered color combinations make your chips unique to your casino property.

Personalized logos are created with your artwork or designed by our in-house artist, at no charge.

Our custom seal and crest or hologram chips are compression molded for permance and security. A special analizer and security implants provide maximum protection against counterfeiting.

P.O. Box 18400 • Las Vegas, Nevada 89114 • U.S.A.
2121 Industrial Road • Las Vegas, Nevada 89102 • U.S.A.
TELEPHONE (702) 384-2425 • FAX (702) 384-1965

The Facts & Faults Of Making Chips For 65 Years

"A Chip Is A Chip."
Fact Or Fallacy?

FACT: A chip or "cheque" as it is referred to in the industry, is the "House's" or establishment's money. These chips or cheques are backed by a sufficient bank of currency or legal tender.

FACT: A chip or cheque must be fabricated utilizing a special plastic formula conducive to only this product.

FACT: A chip or cheque must "stack" properly and correctly so that it can be dealt in a professional manner, so as to prevent slipping and avoid spilling

FACT: A chip or cheque must be fabricated using techniques of exacting tolerances as to color, size and shape including both internal and external controls.

FACT: A chip or cheque should be fabricated by an establishment that is duly licensed, registered, reputable, reliable and utilizes all of the above techniques.

FALLACY: A chip or cheque that is rapidly produced using inferior components is sufficient as a chip or cheque.

FALLACY: A chip or cheque that utilizes components that are not "tried and true" and have not stood the "test of time" are acceptable.

FALLACY: A chip or cheque only because of its cosmetic appearance is acceptable as an instrument, and a representitive of an establishment.

FALLACY: A chip or cheque can be fabricated and utilized by an establishment when it is attractive, slippery and its components are not wholly fabricated "in house."

FALLACY: "A chip is a chip."

Foxwoods Casino's Paul-Son commemorative chip program was so successful that they would hold a birthday celebration every year in December for Frank Sinatra with $5, $25, and $100 commemorative chips that sell out every year.

Foxwoods Resort Casino is a hotel and casino complex owned and operated by the Mashantucket Pequot Tribal Nation on their reservation located in Mashantucket, Connecticut. Including six casinos, the resort covers an area of nine million square feet. The casinos have more than 250 gaming tables for blackjack, craps, roulette, and poker and have more than 5,500 slot machines. The Mashantucket Pequot Tribe gained legal control over their reservation and federal recognition by an act of Congress in 1983. The tribe moved forward with development, and Foxwoods was founded in 1986 as a high-stakes bingo hall on their reservation.

November 12, 2015 03:25 PM Eastern Standard Time

MASHANTUCKET, Conn.—(BUSINESS WIRE)— "The best is yet to come" never rang so true as Foxwoods® Resort Casino prepares to honor "Ol' Blue Eyes" throughout the property during the month of December. Highlighting the festivities will be a full-scale, property-wide birthday party during "Sinatra Weekend," December 11th–13th, culminating with a special not-to-miss performance of Sinatra songs by Robert Davi on Saturday, December 12th, 2015. A limited number of Frank Sinatra commemorative gaming chips have been exclusively commissioned for Foxwoods and will be in action on select table games. The gaming chips will be available in $5, $25, and $100 denominations.

CHAPTER 5

A Brief History of Gambling in Las Vegas as "Sin City"

The first Las Vegas club, Pair O' Dice Club (1931)

The name *Las Vegas* was given to the city in 1829 by Rafael Rivera, a member of the Spanish explorer Antonio Armijo trading party that was traveling to Los Angeles and stopped for water there on the Old Spanish Trail from New Mexico. At that time, several parts of the valley contained artesian wells surrounded by extensive green areas. *Las Vegas* means "the Meadows" in Spanish. The flows from the wells fed the Las Vegas Wash, which runs to the Colorado River. The settlement of Las Vegas was founded in 1905 after the opening of a railroad that linked Los Angeles and Salt Lake City. Urbanization took off in 1931 when work started on the Boulder Dam (now the Hoover Dam), bringing a huge influx of young male workers for whom theaters and casinos were built largely by the Mafia. Electricity from the dam also enabled the building of many new hotels along the Strip. After Nevada approved legalized casino gaming in March 1931, the city of Las Vegas and Clark County set up licensing procedures for casino games. Most of the gaming applicants came from establishments that had offered legal poker games on Fremont Street downtowns such as the Las Vegas Club, Boulder Club, and Northern Club.

One of the earliest clubs outside of downtown, licensed in April 1931, was the Meadows on Boulder Highway, a couple of miles south of Las Vegas. The Meadows Club was the first resort, hotel, and casino in the Las Vegas area, opening in 1931. The Meadows was located at Fremont Street and East Charleston Boulevard near the Boulder Highway and outside the Las Vegas city limits. Its location was designed to attract workers and tourists from the Hoover Dam. The hotel had thirty to fifty rooms (accounts vary). The hotel-casino operated a nightclub featuring the Meadows Revue and the Meadow Larks band. It also had a landing strip for small airplanes. The first casino to be built in Las Vegas, however, was on Highway 91 called the Pair O' Dice Club in 1931. Local residents Frank Detra and his wife, Angelina, purchased land on Highway 91 (also known then as the Los Angeles Highway) and launched the Pair O' Dice as a private nightclub later that year. As with some other clubs in the Las Vegas area at the time, the Pair O' Dice was a "speakeasy" that offered alcoholic beverages (illegal during the Prohibition) as well as illegal gambling. The Pair O' Dice applied for a casino license; but first, the county issued one to a competing nightclub, the Red Rooster, on April 1, 1931.

The Red Rooster was one of the most famous nightclubs in Las Vegas from the early 1930s to the early 1950s on present-day Las Vegas Boulevard where, as a "speakeasy", it was once raided by federal government agents for selling liquor during the Prohibition. In the 1920s and early 1930s, while the federal Volstead Act outlawing the sale of alcohol was in force, Las Vegas became notorious for tolerating both illegal gambling and the consumption of alcohol in local clubs, mainly on Fremont Street downtown. The Red Rooster was one of a few newer nightclubs, such as the Pair O' Dice, built several miles west of downtown on Highway 91 to get the first crack at the motorists driving to town from California. Owner Alice Wilson Morris opened the Red Rooster in 1931. The one-story Spanish Mission-style building had a stage for a singer and orchestra, a dance floor, and a restaurant. But the place almost immediately became a speakeasy, serving liquor during the Prohibition. In February 1931, the United States Justice Department sent a federal marshal to order the Red Rooster to stop selling alcohol or risk being closed by federal agents as had been done earlier to the Arizona Club in downtown Las Vegas. The club's management complied at least temporarily. After Nevada's state government legalized casino gaming in March 1931, the Red Rooster was one of the first twenty-five businesses to receive a gaming license from Clark County's new license board. On April 1, the club was permitted to operate one blackjack table and three slot machines. But that July, the Red Rooster earned the dubious distinction of being the first new Clark County casino to lose its gaming license after federal agents finally raided the club and charged Morris with illegal liquor sales. In January 1933, the county granted Morris's Red Rooster what it called a dance hall license. After the Prohibition was repealed that year, the county agreed to grant it a license to serve only beer. The club burned to the ground in July 1933, but it reopened on the day before New Year's Eve in 1933. The Red Rooster remained popular throughout the 1930s and World War II. Former movie actress Grace Hayes, who had starred in Hollywood films in the early 1930s, bought the club in 1947 and renamed it the Grace Hayes Lodge. By then, an "auto court" or motel called the Sans Souci had been added. Flamingo operator and organized crime associate Benjamin "Bugsy" Siegel reportedly frequented the club's lounge. Hayes soon changed the club's name back to the Red Rooster, sold the place in 1950, and then purchased it back a year later. Hayes sold the club on the growing boulevard now known as the Las Vegas Strip for good in 1953. New owners renovated and ran it under names such as the Hi-Ho and the Patio Club. In the late 1950s, the former club was transformed into the Sans Souci Hotel, which contained a four-hundred-seat showroom that proved popular with visitors, showcasing mostly middlebrow performers and burlesque dance acts. But the Sans Souci frequently ran into financial trouble. In 1963, a new hotel, the Castaways, was built at the site. It also suffered from a lack of business at first but would survive on the Strip for more than a quarter of a century. Howard Hughes bought the Castaways in 1970. The hotel finally closed in 1987 to make way for the Mirage, which opened in 1989. On May 5, 1931, the county issued the Pair O' Dice's manager, Oscar E. Klawitter, a license to run a roulette table, a craps table, and a blackjack table. Weeks later, the club was opened to the public.

Following the repeal of the Prohibition in 1933, the county permitted the club to serve beer. The Pair O' Dice's facade included Spanish-style archways and a two-story octagonal-shaped entrance with a round ceramic tiled roof. Inside, the decor included art-deco ashtrays and lamps with dice-and-playing-card patterns. Detra himself was said to have woven the linens used by the restaurant.

Las Vegas's original welcome sign in 1931

Detra's club encountered problems with the U.S. government, which threatened to close. The Red Rooster had opened a year after the Pair O' Dice a mile farther south on Highway 91, becoming the first club in the area seen by passing motorists. In 1938, the Detras agreed to sell the Pair O' Dice to a recent arrival from California, Guy McAfee. McAfee had been a vice squad captain for the Los Angeles police department about twenty years earlier. In the 1920s and 1930s, McAfee ran nightclubs in western Los Angeles. Most historians consider McAfee the first person to refer to the highway as "the Strip" after figuring that a line of nightclubs would form there, similar to the clubs he had owned and frequented along the Sunset Strip in Los Angeles. McAfee refurbished the Pair O' Dice with a fancier decor based on the Sunset Strip's Hollywood-style clubs.

The property started as a nightclub called Pair-O-Dice that opened in 1930, then The Ambassador Night Club in 1936 and was renamed the 91 Club in 1939 for its location on US-91. It was subsequently rebuilt and renamed the Hotel Last Frontier in 1942. On April 4, 1955, it was renamed the New Frontier, following a modernization of the resort.

The 91 Club opened in 1931 and The Last Frontier in 1942

When he opened his new place in 1939, he renamed it the 91 Club, intending to attract wealthy Southern Californians with its lavish interior, a house orchestra, and cheap multiple-course steak dinners along with casino gaming. The property was sold in 1941 to the developers of the Last Frontier Hotel who incorporated the octagonal casino building into their new resort Club 21. It remained in use at least through the late 1950s.

The Last Frontier was demolished on April 4, 1955, after it was modernized. It was renamed the New Frontier. In the 1950s and the early 1960s, the New Frontier went through a succession of owners and operators. In 1966 and 1967 (by which time it had been renamed the Frontier) the casino had secret ownership interests by Anthony Joseph Zerilli and Michael Polizzi, "two high-ranking members of the Detroit Mafia family" according to *The Boardwalk Jungle* by Ovid Demaris, along with Emprise Corporation (now called Delaware North Companies). In 1971, a federal trial in Los Angeles found Zerilli, Polizzi, and four other individuals along with Emprise guilty of concealing their interest in the casino. When Elvis Presley made his Las Vegas debut in 1956, the twenty-year-old marvel from Memphis was driving a wedge between the generations with "Heartbreak Hotel." The booking at the New Frontier was an attempt by his manager, Colonel Tom Parker, to break Elvis out of the Southern honkytonk and state-fair circuit and give him national credibility. Elvis was billed in newspaper ads as "the Atomic Powered Singer" and "an extra added attraction" to Freddy Martin and his orchestra and comedian Shecky Greene at the Strip hotel. On September 22, 1967, the resort was purchased for about $14 million by businessman Howard Hughes. Hughes purchased the resort from the previous owners, which had also included Steve Wynn, with a 5 percent interest in one of his early ventures when he first moved to the Las Vegas area. (Wynn indicated that he did not know that the other owners had mob connections.) In 1988, Margaret

Elardi bought the Frontier from the late Howard Hughes company, Summa Corporation. Elardi had previously been the part-owner of the Pioneer Club Las Vegas and the Pioneer Hotel & Gambling Hall in Laughlin. She closed the showroom, which had featured Siegfried and Roy, and downscaled much of the hotel. The New Frontier was imploded Tuesday, November 13, 2007. The sixty-five-year-old casino, the second property built on the famous Las Vegas Strip, was the venue where Elvis Presley made his Las Vegas debut in 1956 but not as the opening act.

The New Frontier Hotel and Casino in 1970 (*left*)
imploded on November 2007 (*right*).

The New Frontier (formerly Last Frontier and the Frontier) was the second resort that opened on the Las Vegas Strip and operated continuously from October 30, 1942, until it closed on July 16, 2007. The resort had the distinction of hosting Elvis Presley's first Vegas appearance in 1956 and the final performance of the Supremes with Diana Ross as lead singer on January 14, 1970.

The El Rancho Hotel opened on April 3, 1941.

The El Rancho Hotel, considered the Strip's first casino resort, debuted in 1941 about a mile closer to downtown than the 91 Club. Although it would not outlast the Red Rooster, the 91 Club would evolve into the second casino resort on the fledgling Las Vegas Strip when it was selected by R. E. Griffith as the future site of his Hotel Last Frontier. Griffith liked that the 91 Club site was further south on Highway 91 so travelers from Southern California would see it before the El Rancho. He bought the 91 Club from McAfee in 1941; and Griffith's Hotel Last Frontier, was built there in 1942. On April 3, 1941, hotel owner Thomas Hull opened the El Rancho Vegas. It was the first resort on what would become the Las Vegas Strip. The hotel gained much of its fame from the gourmet buffet that it offered. Until 1942, it was the largest hotel in Las Vegas with 110 rooms. On June 17, 1960, the El Rancho Vegas's main building, including the casino and restaurants, was destroyed in a fire. Later in the 1960s, the property operated as a nongaming motel known as the El Rancho Vegas Motor Inn. By 1979, the buildings had been demolished or removed. In 1982, the El Rancho Hotel and Casino, formerly known as the Thunderbird and later as the Silverbird, operated from 1948 to 1992.

The Thunderbird Hotel and Casino opened in 1948.

The Thunderbird Hotel and Casino opened on September 2, 1948, with 79 hotel rooms, a casino, and a bar. The cost of construction exceeded $2 million. The Thunderbird was the fourth resort to open on the Las Vegas Strip. The resort was built by developer Marion Hicks and owned by Lieutenant Governor of Nevada Clifford A. Jones. The resort had a Native Amerian theme and featured portraits, a Navajo-based restaurant, the first-ever bowling alley on the Strip, and a showroom. In February 1949, there were plans to add a 78-room hotel for $750,000. In 1953, the Thunderbird opened the adjacent 110-room Algiers Hotel, a sister property to deal with an overflow of guests. In 1955, articles surfaced in the Las Vegas Sun saying that Meyer Lansky and other underworld figures held hidden shares in the hotel. The Thunderbird has the distinction of being the resort where singer Rosemary Garland Clooney made her first appearance in Las Vegas in 1951 and where Judy Garland made her final Las Vegas appearance in 1965. A four-story hotel addition was completed in late 1963 for a total of 750 rooms. In 1964, the casino was purchased by Del Webb for $10 million.

Del Web ran the resort until 1972 when they sold it to Caesars World, owner of Caesars Palace, for $13.6 million. A $150-million two-thousand-room resort called the Mark Anthony was planned for the site, but Caesars was unable to find financing and sold the property four years later to banker E. Parry Thomas at a loss of $5.7 million.

Thomas later sold it to Major Riddle, owner of the Dunes Hotel, who renamed the resort as the Silverbird in 1976. Under Riddle's leadership, the Silverbird quickly became a favorite of locals and tourists alike with Joe's Oyster Bar being "the hangout" to be seen in at the Silverbird. The Silverbird also offered childcare and pet boarding facilities (a novelty at the time) making it a popular choice for families traveling with children and/or pets. The Silverbird opened on January 1, 1977, and by 1980 the resort had 385 hotel rooms. The Silverbird suffered a two-alarm fire on March 3, 1981, when an arsonist set fire to a dressing room under the showroom stage. The hotel was evacuated with no injuries, and only minimal damage was caused. But since the fire was the third in four months at casino resorts, fourteen trucks responded. The Silverbird closed on December 3, 1981, after Major Riddle's estate failed to auction off the lease.

In 1981 Major Riddle sold the Silverbird to Ed Torres, owner of the Aladdin Hotel and Casino. Ed Torres renamed it the El Rancho after the El Rancho Vegas, which burned down in 1960. In 1987 Ed Torres became the first casino owner to appoint a woman, Danou Sears, to the previously male-only position of casino manager. By 1992 declining gaming revenue and competition from new and bigger resort casinos forced Torres to finally close the El Rancho, bringing an end to a legacy that started in 1948 with the opening of the Thunderbird Hotel. The El Rancho opened across the street from the former site of the El Rancho Vegas, creating some confusion. After its closure, the El Rancho sat vacant for eight years while two companies made several attempts to reopen or replace the resort. The El Rancho was eventually demolished in 2000 after a news investigation found the decrepit buildings to violate health and safety regulations. The site later became part of the land used for the Drew Las Vegas, a resort scheduled to open in 2022.

The second El Rancho opened in 1982 (*left*) and
imploded on October 3, 2000 (*right*).

In late 1945, mobster Bugsy Siegel and his partners came to Las Vegas. Vegas reportedly piqued Siegel and his mob's interest because of its legalized gambling and off-track betting. At the time, Siegel held a large interest in *Trans America Wire*, a racing publication. Siegel began by purchasing El Cortez on Fremont Street for $600,000.

His expansion plans were hampered by unfriendly city officials aware of his criminal background, so Siegel began looking for a site outside the city limits.

The El Cortez Hotel and Casino is a relatively small downtown Las Vegas gaming venue a block from the Fremont Street Experience and Las Vegas Boulevard. Slots, table games, and a race and sports book occupy one floor of the main pavilion. It opened on Fremont Street on November 7, 1941, and is one of the oldest casino-hotel properties in Las Vegas along with the nearby Golden Gate Hotel and Casino. Primarily Spanish Colonial Revival in style, it reflects a 1952 remodel when the façade was modernized. On February 22, 2013, the structure was placed on the National Register of Historic Places.

John Kell Houssels partnered with John Grayson from California and Marion Hicks, a Los Angeles architect and developer, to build and operate the El Cortez Hotel and Casino on East Fremont Street. Constructed for $245,000, it was Downtown Las Vegas's first major resort with fifty-nine rooms and designed in a Spanish ranch theme. In 1945 Houssels and his partners sold the El Cortez to a Midwest group that included Gus Greenbaum, Moe

Sedway, and Bugsy Siegel (later investors in the 1946 Flamingo) and Dave Berman on behalf of Meyer Lansky for $600,000. John Kell Houssels reacquired the El Cortez and with Ray Salmon announced a $250,000 expansion in May of 1946, including a barbershop, nightclub, swimming pool, and a four-story wing. The "new" Hotel El Cortez held its grand opening. In 1963 Jackie Gaughan purchases the El Cortez from John Kell Houssels for $4 million and in 2008 El Cortez sold to Ike Gaming Inc. When Bugsy Siegal heard that Wilkerson was seeking extra funding, Siegel and his partners posed as businessmen and directly bought a two-thirds stake in the project. Siegel took over the final phases of construction and convinced more of his underworld associates, such as Meyer Lansky to invest in the project. Siegel reportedly lost patience with the project's rising costs; and he once mentioned to his builder, Del Webb, that he had personally killed sixteen men. Reportedly, when Webb appeared scared upon hearing that, Siegel reassured him, "Don't worry. We only kill each other." Siegel had also built a secret ladder in the "Presidential Suite" to escape if necessary. The ladder led down to an underground garage where a chauffeured limo was always waiting. Siegel finally opened the Flamingo Hotel and Casino on December 26, 1946, at a total cost of $6 million.

Billed as "the West's Greatest Resort Hotel" at the time, the 105-room property and first luxury hotel on the Strip was built just four miles from Downtown Las Vegas.

The Flamingo Hotel and Casino opened in 1946.

During construction, a large sign announced the hotel as "a William R. Wilkerson project." The sign also read, "Del Webb Construction," as the hotel's primary contractor and "Richard R. Stadelman" (who later made renovations to the El Rancho Vegas) as the building architect. Allegedly, Siegel named the resort after his girlfriend, Virginia Hill, who loved to gamble and was nicknamed "Flamingo." It was reported that Siegel called her this because of her long skinny legs. Organized crime king Lucky Luciano wrote in his memoir that Siegel once owned an interest in the Hialeah Park Race Track and viewed the flamingos who populated nearby as a good omen.

The *Flamingo* name was reported to have been given to the project at its inception by Wilkerson. It was opened with sixty-three rooms on April 3, 1941, and was destroyed by a fire in 1960. However, it was New York City gangster Bugsy Siegel who gave Las Vegas its first taste of larger-than-life casinos that would soon dominate the area. His casino, the Flamingo, opened in 1946. A few more resorts were built on and around Fremont Street, but it was the next hotel on the Strip that publicly demonstrated the influence of organized crime on Las Vegas. Although ethnic organized crime figures had been involved in some of the operations at the hotels, the Mafia bosses never owned or controlled the hotels and clubs, which remained monopolized by hard-bitten local Las Vegas families who were unwilling to cede ground to the crime bosses and proved strong enough to push back. This changed in post-war Las Vegas when Jewish gangster Bugsy Siegel, with help from a friend and fellow mob boss Meyer Lansky, poured money through locally-owned banks for a cover of legitimacy and built the Flamingo in 1946. Siegel modeled his enterprises on the long-running gambling empire in Galveston, Texas, which had pioneered the high-class casino concepts that became mainstays on the Strip. The Flamingo initially lost money, and Siegel died in a hail of gunfire in Beverly Hills, California, in the summer of 1947. Additionally, local police and Clark County Sheriff deputies were notorious for their heavy-handed tactics toward mobsters who "grew too big for their pants." However, many mobsters saw the potential that gambling offered in

Las Vegas. After gambling was legalized, the Bank of Las Vegas led by E. Parry Thomas became the first bank to lend money to the casinos, which Thomas regarded as the most important business in Las Vegas. At the same time, Allen Dorfman, a close associate of longtime IBT president Jimmy Hoffa and a known associate of the Chicago Outfit, took over the Teamsters Central States Pension Fund, which began lending money to Las Vegas casino owners and developers. They provided funding to build the Sahara, the Sands, the New Frontier, the Royal Nevada, the Showboat, the Riviera, the Fremont, Binion's Horseshoe (which was the Apache Hotel), and finally the Tropicana.

Even with the general knowledge that some of the owners of these casino resorts had dubious backgrounds, by 1954 over eight million people were visiting Las Vegas yearly, pumping $200 million into casinos. Gambling was no longer the only attraction; the biggest stars of films and music like Frank Sinatra, Dean Martin, Andy Williams, Liberace, Bing Crosby, Carol Channing, and others performed in intimate settings. After coming to see these stars, the tourists would resume gambling and then eat at the gourmet buffets that have become a staple of the casino industry. On November 15, 1950, the United States Senate Special Committee to Investigate Crime in Interstate Commerce met in Las Vegas.

It was the seventh of fourteen hearings held by the commission. Moe Sedway, manager of the Flamingo Hotel and a friend of mobster Bugsy Siegel; Wilbur Clark, representing the Desert Inn; and Nevada lieutenant governor Clifford Jones were all called to testify. The hearings established that Las Vegas interests were required to pay Siegel to get the race wire transmitting the results of horse and dog races, prizefight results, and other sports action into their casinos. The hearing concluded that organized crime money was incontrovertibly tied to the Las Vegas casinos and was becoming the controlling interest in the city, earning the organized crime groups vast amounts of income, strengthening their influence in the country. This led to a proposal by the Senate to institute federal gambling control. Nevada's Senator Pat McCarran was instrumental in defeating the measure in committee along with their connections in Hollywood and New York City. These interests in Las Vegas were able to use publicity provided by these media capitals to steer the rapid growth of tourism into Las Vegas, thereby dooming Galveston, Texas; Hot Springs, Arkansas; and other illegal gaming centers around the nation. Nevada's legal gaming as well as the paradoxically increased scrutiny by local and federal law enforcement in these other locales during the 1950s made their demise inevitable. Organized crime king Lucky Luciano wrote in his memoir that Siegel once owned an interest in the Hialeah Park Race Track and viewed the flamingos who populated nearby as a good omen. The *Flamingo* name was reported to have been given to the project at its inception by Wilkerson. The Flamingo reopened in March despite the hotel not being complete, and this time the results proved different. By May the resort reported a $250,000 profit, allowing Lansky to point out that Siegel was right about Las Vegas after all. But it wasn't quite enough to save Siegel.

On June 20, 1947, relaxing in the Beverly Hills house he shared with Hill, who was away at the time, Siegel was shot to death. A memorial plaque exists on the Flamingo site near the outdoor wedding chapel. Casino management changed the hotel name to the Fabulous Flamingo on March 1, 1947. After Siegel's death, Moe Sedway and Gus Greenbaum, magnates of the nearby El Cortez Hotel, took possession of it. Under their partnership, it became a nonexclusive facility affordable to almost anyone. In 1953, the hotel's management spent $1 million in renovations and remodeling. The original entrance and signage were destroyed. A new entrance with an upswept roof was built, and a pink neon sign was designed by Bill Clark of Ad-Art. A neon-bubbled "Champagne Tower" sign with pink flamingos rimming the top was also installed in front of the hotel. Kirk Kerkorian acquired the property in 1967, making it part of Kerkorian's International Leisure Company. But the Hilton Corporation bought the resort in 1972, renaming it the Flamingo Hilton in 1974. The last of the original Flamingo Hotel structure was torn down on December 14, 1993, and the hotel's garden was built on site. In 1998, Hilton's gaming properties, including the Flamingo, were spun off as Park Place Entertainment (later renamed Caesars Entertainment). The deal included a two-year license to use the Hilton name. Park Place opted not to renew that agreement when it expired in late 2000, and the property was renamed Flamingo Las Vegas. In 2005, Harrah's Entertainment purchased Caesars Entertainment Inc. and the property became part of Harrah's Entertainment. The company changed its name to Caesars Entertainment Corporation in 2010.

It was now 1966, Wayne Newton performed his first show at the Flamingo, and Howard Hughes checked into the penthouse of the Desert Inn and never left, preferring to buy the hotel rather than face eviction.

CHAPTER 6

Howard Hughes's Impact on Las Vegas

In 1966, Howard Hughes arrives in Las Vegas.

In 1963, Las Vegas had a population of 64,405, which represented more than 22 percent of Nevada's total population, even though with just twenty-five square miles it occupied less than 0.02 percent of the state's land. Las Vegas gambling casinos continued to grow in the 1960s, and every time their ownership or name changed. The casino would have to order new gaming chips, cards, and table felts. That was good news for my dad and Paul-Son. It wouldn't matter who the owner was—first, the Mob, then Howard Hughes. Howard Hughes was one of the brightest figures in Las Vegas's gambling history. According to the Las Vegas Sun in 2008, Hughes came to Las Vegas under the cover of darkness during Thanksgiving weekend in 1966. Hughes rode in on a fortune. His father had invented an oil well drill bit that could penetrate hard rock, leaving his son one of the richest people in the world. Howard Robard Hughes Jr., arrived on that dark night for a private holiday, never intending to buy a hotel according to longtime Hughes confidante, "alter ego," and public liaison Robert A. Maheu. But for the next four years, Hughes would wield his fantastic wealth to change and modernize the Las Vegas Strip. The year 1966 brought Las Vegas bad news and good news. The bad news was that mobsters were skimming Las Vegas casinos. The good news came when billionaire Howard Hughes arrived quietly and began buying casinos and real estate. Hughes wanted to change the image of Las Vegas to something more glamorous. He wrote in a memo to an aide, "I like to think of Las Vegas in terms of a well-dressed man in a dinner jacket and a beautifully jeweled and furred female getting out of an expensive car." Hughes bought several local television stations (including KLAS-TV). The eccentric billionaire, it was speculated, was on a mission. He would demob Las Vegas and make the city safe for legitimate business. Mob activity declined during Hughes's four years in Las Vegas, partly because he bought out many of the old-timers but more because the federal government was turning up the heat. Just by showing up, Hughes changed Las Vegas forever. If one of the richest men in the world, one of the nation's largest defense contractors and a genuine national hero, was willing to invest in Las Vegas, it must not be such a sordid, evil place after all.

"He cleaned up the image of Las Vegas," said Robert A. Maheu, who spent thirteen years working for Hughes. "I have had the heads of large corporate entities tell me they would never have thought of coming here before Hughes came." Seven months before his arrival in Las Vegas, Hughes sold his stock in Transworld Airlines and had received more than $546 million. Trans World Airlines (TWA) was a major American airline that existed from 1930 until 2001. It was formed as Transcontinental & Western Air to operate a route from New York City to Los Angeles via St. Louis, Kansas City, and other stops with Ford Trimotors. With Pan Am,

United, and Eastern, it was one of the "Big Four" domestic airlines in the United States formed by the Spoils Conference of 1930. Howard Hughes acquired control of TWA in 1939 and after World War II led the expansion of the airline to serve Europe, the Middle East, and Asia, making TWA a second unofficial flag carrier of the United States after Pan Am. Hughes gave up control in the 1960s, and the new management of TWA acquired Hilton International and Century 21 in an attempt to diversify the company's business. The IRS taxed that money as "passive" income at a higher rate than "active" or "working" income. He would buy hotels in Nevada, $300 million worth, ushering in an era in which mob interests were displaced by corporate conglomerates.

It was the perfect time for Paul Endy to enter the Nevada gaming market. The second wave of growth of gaming in Nevada was in progress. Howard Hughes was buying and building properties on the Strip, and they needed gaming supplies to outfit all the new casino openings. In 1966, the Desert Inn rented Hughes its entire top floor of high-roller suites and the floor below it for ten days only. The checkout time came and went, and Hughes didn't move. Moe Dalitz and Ruby Kolod, co-owners of the Desert Inn, were furious. New Year's, one of Las Vegas' busiest holidays, was looming, and the suites had been promised to high rollers. The squeeze was on Maheu.

"Get the hell out of here, or we'll throw your butt out," growled Kolod.

"It's your problem," Hughes told Maheu.

"You work it out."

Maheu called in a favor from Teamsters Union President Jimmy Hoffa, who phoned the DI boys and asked them to leave "my friends" alone. The reprieve lasted into the new year when Maheu told the boss he had played out his options with the Desert Inn guys. "If you want a place to sleep, you'd damned well better buy the hotel," Maheu told Hughes. To most investors, negotiating a purchase is the means to an end.

To Howard Hughes, it was recreation. After months of arduous logrolling, Hughes and Dalitz agreed on a price of $13.25 million. After the Desert Inn purchase, Hughes discovered the gross receipts of a casino are considered active income. Ecstatic, he called Maheu.

"How many more of these toys are available?" he demanded of Maheu. "Let's buy 'em all," and he almost did.

Howard Hughes checked into the Desert Inn in 1966 and never left.

"He would use every gimmick in the book. He'd pay someone half a million dollars if they could help him avoid paying $10 worth of taxes," said Maheu. "I knew that we'd never make it in the gaming business for the simple reason that he had a standing rule that we could not make a capital investment of $10,000 or more without his approval, and he never gave his approval."

Johnny Rosselli, known as the Mob's "ambassador" to Las Vegas and Hollywood, approached Maheu and told him who was going to be the new casino manager. Maheu told him to go to hell. Not only was he not in bed with the Mob, claimed Maheu, but he also was actually working quietly to ease them out of town. "If you look at what we bought, you'll find that we must have known something," said Maheu. "It was not an accident." That "something," explained Maheu, was a study commissioned by former attorney general Robert Kennedy—a blueprint for exorcising the mob from Las Vegas. "And it said that the best way to clean them up was by purchase. So you put all the elements together, and who is better equipped with the money than Hughes?" To be licensed as the operator of the Desert Inn, Hughes would have to undergo an extensive gaming background check. He also would have to appear before the state gaming commission, which he had no intention of doing. Well-connected Las Vegas attorney Thomas Bell was hired to handle the licensing and would stay on as Hughes's lobbyist in Carson City. The new governor, Paul Laxalt, persuaded the commission to allow Maheu to appear as Hughes's surrogate. "Laxalt saw Hughes as a better option than the mob," said Maheu. "He was an excellent businessman, and he was totally legitimate, the kind of sugar daddy Las Vegas needed." His next purchase was the Sands then a Strip showplace. Dalitz was consulted and allowed that it "would be a good acquisition." Hughes paid $14.6 million for the Sands, which included 183 acres of prime real estate that would become the Howard Hughes Center.

The Sands Hotel, home of the "Rat Pack," imploded on November 26, 1996. It was followed by two smaller places, the Castaways and the Silver Slipper and the Frontier after that.

All three had one thing in common: they came with enormous parcels of empty land. He made a deal to buy the Stardust for $30.5 million but was prevented from closing by the US Securities and Exchange Commission, which was worried about Hughes holding a monopoly on Las Vegas lodging. "If we had been allowed to buy the Stardust, you wouldn't have had…all the terrible publicity from that movie *Casino*," said Maheu. Hughes had visited Las Vegas during World War II, staying at the Desert Inn, El Rancho Vegas, and the Flamingo. In the early 1950s, he acquired about forty square miles near Las Vegas from the BLM, trading seventy-three thousand acres of desert land in five Northern Nevada counties for the federal parcel. It was known as "Husite" before being transformed into today's Summerlin master-planned community. When Hughes finished buying the land, his Nevada holdings were worth an estimated $300 million. His empire included Harold's Club in Reno, nearly every vacant lot on the Las Vegas Strip, an airline, several Nevada ranches, and about two thousand mining claims.

His other on-and-off Strip properties included the Desert Inn Country Club's residential lots, the North Las Vegas Airport, and all the land surrounding McCarran International Airport and several casinos that operated under the umbrella Summa Corporation. Before Hughes bought the Frontier in December 1967, he (or someone claiming to be the billionaire) called Governor Paul Laxalt to assure the state he would continue his good deeds.

Hughes's handwritten offer said he would establish a medical school at UNLV and promised $200,000 to $300,000 a year for twenty years. However, he never funded Nevada's medical school, which was established after the billionaire left Nevada. To most investors, negotiating a purchase is the means to an end. To Howard Hughes, it was recreation. After four years in Las Vegas, Hughes left abruptly. On Thanksgiving Eve 1970, Hughes was reportedly carried out of the Desert Inn on a stretcher driven to Nellis Air Force Base in an unmarked van and flown by private jet to Resorts International's Britannia Beach Hotel in the Bahamas. Hughes's considerable business holdings were overseen by a small panel unofficially dubbed "the Mormon Mafia" because of the many Latter-day Saints on the committee led by Frank William Gay. In addition to supervising day-to-day business operations and Hughes's health, they also went to great pains to satisfy Hughes's every whim. For example, Hughes once became fond of Baskin-Robbins's banana nut ice cream, so his aides sought to secure a bulk shipment for him, only to discover that Baskin-Robbins had discontinued the flavor. They put in a request for the smallest amount the company could provide for special order (350 gallons) and had it shipped from Los Angeles. A few days after the order arrived, Hughes announced he was tired of banana nut and wanted only French vanilla ice cream. The Desert Inn ended up distributing free banana nut ice cream to casino customers for a year. In a 1996 interview, ex-Howard Hughes chief of Nevada operations Robert Maheu said, "There is a rumor that there is still some banana nut ice cream left in the freezer. It is most likely true." The billionaire never returned to Las Vegas, although his legacy continues to feed the city's lore and legend. Hughes, who was born on December 24, 1905, died on April 5, 1976, on a plane flying from Mexico to Houston. A bitter corporate struggle ensued in Las Vegas over Hughes's empire. Hughes's once-trusted aide, Maheu; personal physician, Dr. Robert Buckley; and other top officials were fired after he left the DI's penthouse. Executive Vice President Frank William Gay and Chester Davis, a Wall Street lawyer who defended Hughes in a lengthy and successful battle over alleged antitrust violations involving TWA, ousted Maheu after arriving at the Sands Hotel in December 1970. Laxalt delivered the news to Maheu on December 7. "He told me he had spent over a half-hour talking with Howard and that Hughes had told him that I was fired," Maheu recalled in his autobiography, "next to Hughes."

On Thanksgiving afternoon 1970, I was invited to have lunch with my brother, my father, and some of his "closest" friends at the Las Vegas Country Club. My dad learned to play golf from his partner Curly, but it was much later after we moved to Las Vegas.

My dad believed it was a great way to do business with casino executives and "mingle" (his old-fashioned word for *networking*), which he enjoyed doing on Sundays, the only day he wasn't working. My dad was personally recommended to join the Las Vegas Country Club by Kirk Kerkorian, the chairman of Trans International Airlines and landlord of Caesars Palace. He would eventually build a thirty-story hotel with 1,510 rooms for $50 million. Some believed it was very risky to build such property away from the Strip, but

Kerkorian believed that it would spark the development of a "second Strip" along Paradise Road. Kerkorian's hotel would be named the International Hotel and include the Las Vegas Country Club. Construction began with an elaborate groundbreaking ceremony with Elvis Presley opening the hotel in 1969. It was known for many years as the Las Vegas Hilton then briefly as the LVH Las Vegas Hotel and Casino until taking its current name, the Westgate, in 2014. From 1981 to 1990, it was the largest hotel in the world!

The International first opened in 1969 (*left*),
then the Las Vegas Hilton (*right*).

We saw Elvis Presley perform at both the International and the Las Vegas Hilton.

Then: the LVH Hotel & Casino 1981 (left).
Today: Westgate Las Vegas (right)

The International Hotel changed names three more times and finally the Westgate. Every time the Hotel changed owners or names, they had to purchase new gaming chips, which my father liked. My dad even liked watching Elvis Presley perform at both the International and the Las Vegas Hilton.

In 1964, the movie *Viva Las Vegas* was filmed in and around Las Vegas. Since they needed casino equipment for the filming of the casino scenes, my father accommodated MGM's request and allowed them to film inside Paul-Son Dice & Card Co.'s office. My dad would later tell me that MGM was going to build a hotel and casino in Las Vegas and wanted to do what he could to "help them out."

I never thought my dad could predict the future, but he sure did with MGM because they would build not one but two MGM's, and the largest casino in the world would be an MGM in Reno, Nevada. My mother took us one day to Paul-Son to meet the movie cast, but unfortunately, Elvis Presley was not there that day. However, my dad eventually was able to see and get Elvis and the Jordanaires's autographs for his wife.

ELVIS with the JORDANAIRES

Viva Las Vegas is a 1964 American musical film directed by George Sidney and starring Elvis Presley and Ann-Margret. The film is regarded by fans and film critics as one of Presley's best films, and it is noted for the on-screen chemistry between Presley and Ann-Margret. It also presents a strong set of ten musical song-and-dance scenes choreographed by David Winters and features his dancers. *Viva Las Vegas* was a hit at film theaters, as it was number 14 on the *Variety* year-end box office list of the top-grossing films of 1964.

My dad was invited to Elvis Presley's wedding on May 1, 1967, when he married his girlfriend Priscilla Beaulieu at the Aladdin Hotel. But according to my mother, he wasn't able to attend due to business commitments as usual.

Elvis marries at the Aladdin Hotel in 1967.

CHAPTER 7

Movies and Television Shows Filmed in Las Vegas and at Paul-Son

There have been over one hundred movies and over fifty television shows filmed in Las Vegas. Of the one hundred movies, scenes from three of them have been filmed in and around Paul-Son's office. *Viva Las Vegas* was the second movie I remember being filmed; however, it was *The Only Game in Town* that was the first movie filmed at Paul-Son. *The Only Game in Town* is a 1970 American romantic comedy-drama film, the last directed by George Stevens. It starred Elizabeth Taylor and Warren Beatty. Though set in Las Vegas, this Fox extravaganza was actually filmed at studios in Paris with only a few location shots in the Nevada town. Elizabeth Taylor starred as a showgirl who, for a long time, has been the kept woman of a rich married man from San Francisco. Though Taylor loves him and the many gifts he showers upon her, she is tired of waiting for him to divorce his wife. When handsome compulsive gambler Warren Beatty shows up, she begins a passionate affair. But he, like the businessman, is really only interested in sex, at least at first. In time, the two cannot help but fall in love.

Meanwhile, the businessman finally leaves his wife. Unfortunately, by that time it is too late. Frank Sinatra originally signed to play Joe, but when Taylor became ill and filming was postponed, he had to drop out of the project to fulfill another commitment with Caesars Palace in Las Vegas and was replaced by Beatty. Made with a lavish budget and heavily promoted, *The Only Game in Town* proved to be a major box-office disappointment. Paul-Son was one of the few location shots in Las Vegas because my dad said that Elizabeth Taylor wanted to film the gambling scenes away from Caesars Palace. A fictitious casino was set up in the Paul-Son showroom. Also, since my father was friends with a vice president at 20th Century Fox, he was filmed in the fishing scene on a boat at Lake Mead when Warren Beatty caught a giant fish (that wasn't ever swimming in Lake Mead!) because it was brought to Lake Mead by my dad in his boat.

The second movie filmed at Paul-Son was *Diamonds Are Forever*, a 1971 spy film and the seventh in the James Bond series produced by Eon Productions.

It is the sixth and final film to star Sean Connery, who returned to the role as the fictional M16 agent James Bond, having declined to reprise the role in *On Her Majesty's Secret Service* (1969). My dad met Mort Goldstein, the president of United Artists Movie Studios, when he worked a Las Vegas charity fundraiser for T. R. King.

When *Diamonds are Forever* was going to be filmed in Las Vegas in 1971, Mr. Goldstein called my dad and asked him for a favor. He wanted to film a scene at Paul-Son where a Sean Connery stunt double would meet the opportunistic Plenty O'Toole at a craps table at Paul-Son since Sean Connery was sick that day. The balance of the movie scene was actually filmed at Circus Circus. The film is based on Ian Fleming's 1956 novel of the same name and is the second of four James Bond films directed by Guy Hamilton. The story has Bond impersonating a diamond smuggler to infiltrate a smuggling ring and soon uncovering a plot by his old enemy Ernst Stavro Blofeld to use the diamonds to build a space-based laser weapon. Bond has to battle his enemy for one last time to stop the smuggling and stall Bluefield's plan of destroying Washington, DC, and extorting the world with nuclear supremacy.

The third movie filmed at Paul-Son was *Casino*. *Casino* is a 1995 American epic-crime film directed by Martin Scorsese, produced by Barbara De Fina, and distributed by Universal Pictures. It starred Robert De Niro, Sharon Stone, and Joe Pesci. The film is based on the nonfiction book *Casino: Love and Honor in Las Vegas* by Nicholas Pileggi, who also cowrote the screenplay for the film with Scorsese. The film marks the eighth collaboration between director Scorsese and De Niro. *Casino* follows Sam "Ace" Rothstein (De Niro), a Jewish American gambling expert handicapper who is asked by the Chicago Outfit to oversee the day-to-day casino and hotel operations at the Tangiers Casino in Las Vegas. Supporting characters include Nicholas "Nicky" Santoro (Pesci), a "made man" and friend of Ace, and Ginger McKenna (Stone), a streetwise chip hustler whom Ace marries and has a daughter with. The film details Ace's operation of the casino and the difficulties he confronts in his job. The Mafia's involvement with the casino and the gradual breakdown of his relationships and standing has Las Vegas change over the years. The primary characters are based on real people. Ace is inspired by the life of Frank Rosenthal, also known as "Lefty," who ran the Stardust, Fremont, Marina, and Hacienda casinos in Las Vegas for the Chicago Outfit from the early 1970s until 1981. Nicky and Ginger are based on mob enforcer Anthony Spilotro and former dancer and socialite

Geri McGee, respectively. We were contacted in early 1995 by Tom Foley, Universal Pictures vice president of marketing, to manufacture *Casino* promotional chips and VIP chips for the grand opening. My father was very interested in this movie project because it reminded him of the time he met with the real people in the movie (i.e., Robert Maheu). Even though the casino in the movie was named the Tangiers, it was fictional as were the chips.

Tangiers chips are sixteen grams of solid brass core and are the heaviest chips available in the market. These exact same chips were used in many old Las Vegas casinos, and are still in use at the Hyatt Regency Lake Tahoe. You could have also seen the Tangiers Casino name coming up in the *CSI: Las Vegas* series on CBS. The story of *Casino* is based upon the history of the Stardust Casino, a fact well documented in the Las Vegas history books. Martin Scorsese discreetly documents this fact via the soundtrack in which the song "Stardust" is heard three different times.

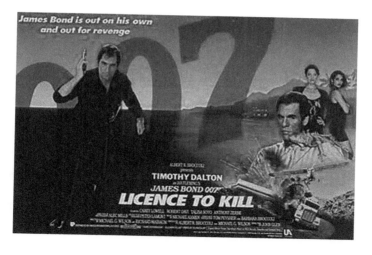

In 1989 we manufactured chips for a second James Bond movie *License to Kill. Licence to Kill* is a 1989 spy film and the sixteenth in the James Bond series produced by Eon Productions and the last to star Timothy Dalton in the role of the fictional MI6 agent James Bond. Its story sees Bond being suspended from MI6 as he pursues drug lord Franz Sanchez, who has ordered an attack against his CIA friend Felix Leiter and the murder of Felix's wife during their honeymoon. Principal photography ran from July 18 to November 18, 1988. The shooting was in Mexico, which mostly doubled for the fictional Republic of Isthmus. Paul-Son was chosen as the manufacture for the fictitious Casino De Isthmus gaming chips used in the movie.

Of the fifty television shows that were filmed in Las Vegas, two of them were filmed at Paul-Son. The first was *Vegas* (stylized as *Vega$*), an American private detective crime drama television series that aired on ABC from April 25, 1978, to June 3, 1981. *Vega$* was produced by Aaron Spelling and created by Michael Mann. The series (except special episodes filmed in Hawaii and San Francisco) was filmed in its entirety in Las Vegas, Nevada. The show stars Robert Urich as private detective Dan Tanna who drove to his assignments around the streets of Las Vegas in a red 1957 Ford Thunderbird convertible.

Working for a wide variety of Las Vegas clients, the detective work included locating missing persons, helping solve crimes, solving casino scams, and making Las Vegas a safer place for residents and tourists alike. Dan Tanna (Robert Urich) is a Las Vegas private detective whose many clients include Phillip Roth (Tony Curtis [aka Slick]), the owner of several hotel-casinos, including the Maxim Hotel Casino and the Desert Inn Hotel and Country Club in Las Vegas. Tanna is often called to help investigate criminal cases, locate missing people, or even in absurd situations such as the case of a nun (played by Cassie Yates) who has a claim deed that says she owns the land on which the Desert Inn Hotel and Casino stands. Tanna lives on the Las Vegas Strip next to Circus Circus Hotel and Casino, in the theatrical showroom props warehouse owned by the Desert Inn Hotel and Country Club. The large props warehouse where he lives has been partially converted into his living quarters. The unique design of Tanna's home allows him to park his red T-bird in his living room. Tanna also uses gadgets considered high-tech for the late 1970s, such as a car phone and an answering machine that physically picks his phone off the hook and into the microphone of a tape recorder. MGM decided to shoot some of the casino close-up scenes at our office. Robert Urich, one time, used our office to "investigate" a chip counterfeit issue that was fictitious. Paul-Son even received a credit in the TV show.

Robert Urich filmed an episode of *Vega$*
at the Paul-Son Las Vegas office.

The second television show that was filmed in Las Vegas and at Paul-Son was called *Las Vegas* in 2003. *Las Vegas* is an American comedy-drama television series created by Gary Scott Thompson that was broadcast by NBC from September 22, 2003, to February 15, 2008. The show focused on a team of people working at the fictional Montecito Resort and Casino dealing with issues that arise within the working environment, ranging from valet parking and restaurant management to casino security. The series originally aired on Monday nights, though NBC later moved the series to Friday nights, first to 9:00 p.m. eastern/8:00 p.m. central and then to 10:00 p.m. eastern/9:00 p.m. central. The show entered syndication in the United States in September 2007. In July 2013, after a long run of weekday back-to-back episodes on TNT, *Las Vegas* reruns were moved to a graveyard slot of 4:00 a.m. then removed totally from TNT's lineup. In May 2020, E! began airing reruns of the show, making a return of the series in syndication for the first time since TNT removed it from its lineup in 2013. The series originally centered on Ed Deline (James Caan), a strict ex-CIA officer who went from being head of security to becoming president of operations of the Montecito, whose job is to run the day-to-day operations of the casino. Following his departure from the series in season five, former marine Danny McCoy (Josh Duhamel), Ed's former protégé, became the Montecito's new president of operations. The series abruptly ended with a cliffhanger because NBC cancelled *Las Vegas* in the off-season following season five. I was contacted by NBC Universal about filming some scenes for their new TV series, *Las Vegas*.

Fictitious Montecito gaming chips used in the show *Las Vegas*.

Since I was told that we would receive free advertising, I allowed them to film some scenes from the first season at Paul-Son. They had first requested to film our security chip vault; however, for security reasons, I refused. In the end, they filmed a few scenes in the showroom, and that was about it. It was always funny to watch the movies and television shows about Las Vegas because the actors/actresses would usually enter one casino and exit from another. I guess I paid more attention to those scenes because I grew up in Las Vegas.

Growing up in Las Vegas definitely had its advantages when it came to seeing superstars perform, especially if you knew the maître d'. My dad was friends with the original maître d' at the Las Vegas Hilton for all of Elvis's performances and a few others as well. My dad and his wife enjoyed watching Elvis, Liberace, and Barbara Streisand perform at both the International Hotel and the Las Vegas Hilton. Since Elvis was also one of my favorite musicians, I also enjoyed going to the shows with them whenever I was invited. My dad always greeted Mr. Muscelli with a loud "Ciao!" and a handshake full of cash that always guaranteed us a great seat. My dad said Muscelli got to know Frank Sinatra and Elvis Presley. Muscelli also partied with billionaire Howard Hughes in the 1950s long before Hughes became a recluse. He also chauffeured Meyer Lansky when the mob boss came to town in the '60s to keep tabs on the Mob's casino operations. Muscelli was an Italian immigrant who worked twenty-seven years as lead maître d' at five major Las Vegas resorts, becoming as popular with some customers as the legendary acts that graced the showroom stages. One of my classmates in high school was Muscelli's son Perry who I often spoke to about how friendly his dad was to us. One of my favorite memories is when my dad surprised me on my eighteenth birthday. He told me we were going out to dinner but didn't tell me where. As we drove down the Las Vegas Strip, my father's valet parked at the Flamingo Hotel and Casino. I immediately recognized the performers for the night, my favorite singing group of all time, the Supremes. As we walked into the showroom, my dad immediately saw and waved to Muscelli, called out, "Ciao!" and told him it was my birthday. Muscelli told my dad that he was also the maître d' for the Supremes show for that night.

The Flamingo Hotel and Casino in 1973

In his usual manner, my dad held out his hand with a wad of cash, and we were seated right in the front row of the theatre. It was a dinner show, which was very popular in Las Vegas in the early days. Typically, casinos would have two superstar shows, an early dinner show, and a late show. Today there aren't any dinner shows in Las Vegas except for the Excalibur Tournament of Kings show and feast.

The Tournament of Kings is a medieval jousting tournament performed with twelve breeds of horses and thirty-two cast members in a 925-seat amphitheater called King Arthur's Arena. The show includes a banquet feast served by a costumed serf or wench and is meant to be eaten without utensils. The Tournament of Kings debuted along with the opening of Excalibur in 1990. Reminiscent of the early medieval times, there aren't any utensils used to eat the feast. Instead, the Cornish game hen meal is eaten with your hands.

I was so excited that I could barely eat anything when the Supremes took the stage at the Flamingo that night. All I remember eating was the strawberry cheesecake for dinner/dessert. Since I had all the Supremes' record albums in my collection, I knew all of their songs and sang along with them during the show; sometimes I was a bit too loud as noted by my father. After the show, Muscelli came over to our table and obviously knew I was mesmerized by the lead singer. He then asked my father and me if we would like to go backstage and meet the group. To say the least, I was shocked as we walked backstage following Muscelli. It didn't take long before the drummer of the group introduced himself and Diana Ross to us. Since I was learning how to play the drums, I was almost as excited to meet their drummer until Diana Ross kissed my right cheek. I didn't wash my cheek for at least a week after that night.

When my father was invited to join the prestigious Las Vegas Country Club, he was told by Kirk Kerkorian that he was honest and fair with him at the International Hotel and Casino, and because of that, he was the only "non-Jew" allowed the privilege of joining the exclusive club at that time. It was a privilege my father would always appreciate and never forget.

The Las Vegas Country Club, my dad's favorite club

The Las Vegas Country Club is a private membership club located in Las Vegas.

It was built on the site of a 1950s horse and automobile race-track named Las Vegas Park and later the Las Vegas Park Speedway. It was developed by businessmen Moe Dalitz, Allard Roen, Irwin Molasky, and Merv Adelson. The 18-hole golf course was completed in the fall of 1967 followed by the completion of a 44,000-square-foot (4,100 square-meter) clubhouse in April 1968. The clubhouse architect was Julian Gabrielle; the golf course designer was Edmond B. Ault. Amenities include two pitching and chipping greens, a 9,500-square-foot (880 square-meter) putting green, indoor and out-door tennis courts, racquetball, swimming pool, and a complete exer-cise facility. The club served as the host for the Las Vegas Invitational Golf Tournament between 1983 and 1991 and also hosted events on a rotational basis from 1992 to 1995. The club also hosted the LPGA Takefuji Classic on the LPGA Tour from 2003 to 2006. My father told me about the time that he and his partner Curly had their first meeting at the Las Vegas Country club where they were intro-duced to Robert Maheu and Burton Cohen, the casino manager at the Desert Inn Hotel. As they had lunch, both Maheu and Cohen informed my father that Hughes was sick and that they were concerned about new management at the resort. Also, they had a gaming chip problem that only my dad could fix. New chips had to be made as soon as possible since some very old DI chips were suddenly being cashed in. It didn't take long for Nevada Gaming to require casinos to retire their old chips and my father was happy to make new chips for the Desert Inn.

Wilber Clark's Desert Inn, 1950 (*left*). Summa's
Howard Hughes's Desert Inn, 1967 (*right*)

From the MGM-D.I.1988 (*left*) to Sheraton Desert
Inn 1993 (*center*). Imploded in 1997 (*right*)

Summa Corporation eventually took control of the Desert Inn and sold the hotel to Kirk Kerkorian and his Tracinda Corporation in 1986, and it became known as the MGM Desert Inn. Kerkorian sold it to ITT Sheraton in 1993, and my dad was happy once again that the Desert Inn had to order new gaming chips. The closure of the Desert Inn in 2000 and subsequent demolition was unpopular with many as it seemed to mark the end of old Las Vegas. Historian Michael Green stated, "To a lot of people outside of Las Vegas, these two places [the Desert Inn and the Sands] really meant Las Vegas.

These were the places that represent the images of Las Vegas in a far greater way than the Dunes, the Aladdin, the Hacienda, and the Landmark." Robert Maheu, Howard Hughes's head of Nevada operations and publicist for many years, remarked that the "Desert Inn was the gem of Las Vegas." The hotel remained popular with locals until the end as the heavily tourism-driven modern Las Vegas emerged in the 1990s. Every time the Desert Inn changed its owner or its name, it was required by Nevada Gaming to order new logo chips and other gaming supplies. My dad liked the fact that the casinos had to order new supplies with every name change.

Finally, April 28, 2005, the Wynn Las Vegas

The Wynn Las Vegas, often simply referred to as Wynn, is a luxury resort and casino located on the Las Vegas Strip in Paradise, Nevada, United States, on the site of the old Desert Inn Hotel. The $2.7-billion resort is named after casino developer Steve Wynn and is the flagship property of Wynn Resorts. The Wynn resort covers 215 acres. It is located at the northeast corner of Las Vegas Boulevard and Sands Avenue directly across the Strip from the Fashion Show Mall. Wynn would be a driving force in changing the Las Vegas skyline from family designed resorts to luxury accommodations. I personally preferred Las Vegas when it originally built themed resorts. The newer resorts built here recently are no longer designed by theme but by the luxury amenities they offer. For the first time in Las Vegas gaming history, casino revenue would generate less money than food, beverage, and entertainment.

Paul-Son Dice & Card Co. would be my dad's entrance into the legalized gaming industry in 1963. He would transform the company with its trademarked mission statement "growing larger by serving better" into a worldwide casino supply business. We would continue to expand and improve Paul-Son's product offering that was demanded by the changing casino business in Las Vegas.

The Las Vegas Strip in 1963

CHAPTER 8

Paul-Son Dice arrives
in Las Vegas

In 1963, Paul-Son Dice & Card Co. opened in Las Vegas.

My dad sent our family back to California and launched his new business in 1963, which was called Paul-Son Dice & Card Co. The name would pay tribute to his father as Paul Endy's son. My father worked all day initially manufacturing gaming dice and table furniture and all night selling what he could to the growing Las Vegas gambling industry. A short time later, he bought a building on Industrial Road and moved his company there. In the early years, the business struggled with Dad living in a sixteen-foot trailer behind what he called "lucky" 2121 Industrial Road, an address reflecting not one but two winning blackjack hands, where he showered daily with a garden hose.

My dad's "lucky" 2121 Industrial Road

Years later, Dad would tell *Forbes Magazine*, "If we got an order for five hundred dice, we'd say, 'Wow, what a week.'" As the business grew, my father realized he couldn't operate, manufacture, and deliver what he had produced by himself and also wanted to go after T. R. King's business in California. Also, the Nevada Gaming Commission, which regulates gaming establishments and suppliers, began to pressure my father by requiring him and certain products he manufactured, in particular chips, to be licensed. My dad missed his family and moved us along with my maternal grandparents to Las Vegas where we would reside in their double-wide trailer on Boulder Highway for months.

Grandpa Johnny and Granny Pat's mobile home

One of the best memories I have, when we lived with my grand-parents, is that they both loved to bowl. I would often go with my grandmother on Saturdays to Showboat Hotel and Bowling Alley to watch her and "root her on." The one quirk they had was playing nickel slot machines in the casino after they finished bowling. Since I was under twenty-one at the time and couldn't go into the casino, I would hang out in the video game arcade or practice my poor bowling skills, to say the least. Unfortunately, I never got better at bowling. My grandfather Johnny was a meat cutter by trade; however, he would also end up working at Paul-Son for a few years.

The Showboat opened in 1954, and the Castaways was imploded in 2005.

The Showboat was built by William J. Moore of the Last Frontier and J. Kell Houssels of the Las Vegas Club for $2 million. The first resort within Las Vegas city limits, it had one hundred rooms on two floors. While Moore and Houssels ran the hotel, the casino was leased by a group of managers from the Desert Inn, including Moe Dalitz. The Showboat opened on September 3, 1954.

After several unsuccessful years, Joe Kelley took over management and began successfully targeting local customers with forty-nine-cent breakfast specials and other promotions. Kelley added a bowling alley in 1959, which soon became the Showboat's signature attraction. The Showboat hosted nationally televised PBA tournaments.

Showboat bowling leagues were organized in Los Angeles and Phoenix, offering winners free trips to Las Vegas for championship events. By 1979, the bowling alley grew to 106 lanes, making it the nation's third-largest. A nineteen-story hotel tower was built in two phases with the first nine floors opening by 1973 and the remainder in 1976, bringing the property to a total of five hundred rooms. In the early 1980s, a large unused space on the second floor was converted into the Showboat Sports Pavilion, which hosted American Wrestling Association events and Los Angeles Thunderbirds Roller Derby matches and competed with Caesars Palace to book high-profile boxing matches. The Pavilion was later converted into a bingo hall. The hotel was successful until the 1990s when it suffered the same fate as the downtown casinos, which were losing business to the new megaresorts on the Las Vegas Strip. Many visitors also believed that this casino was located on the Strip since the exterior of Harrah's Las Vegas resembled a showboat. In 1998, Harrah's Entertainment bought Showboat Inc. and sold the Showboat in 2000 for $23.5 million to VSS Enterprises, a group owned by Dan Shaw, Mike Villamor, and Greg Schatzman. Harrah's refused to sell the Showboat name, not wanting the Las Vegas property to be confused with Showboat Atlantic City, so VSS renamed it as the Castaways. The new owners never did well and according to the Associated Press, the facility was crippled by a downturn in tourism that occurred in the wake of the September 11, 2001, attacks. Discussions were held in 2002 to rebrand the property as a Holiday Inn and start a $57 million renovation and expansion, but these plans did not come to fruition. Foreclosure proceedings in June 2003 prompted the Castaways to file for Chapter 11 bankruptcy protection, listing $50 to $100 million in debt, shutting it down. Vestin agreed to sell the property for $21.6 million to MGI Group, owners of the Bighorn and Longhorn Casinos, who planned to rebrand it as La Joya del Sol and market it to Latino customers. Before MGI's license application could be approved; however, Station Casinos stepped in and paid MGI $12.1 million to take their place in the deal, paying the full $21.6 million. Station was primarily interested in the site's grandfathered gaming license, soon determining that the existing structures were not usable and had construction quality problems. Demolition began in July 2005, and the hotel tower was imploded on January 11, 2006. The company made plans for a $90 million casino and restaurant with a Spanish motif named Castaways Station. By 2009, however, no progress had been made; and Station itself, on the verge of bank-ruptcy, put the lot up for sale for $39.5 million. Station had made the original request in late 2007 with the portable casino's most recent appearance in late 2013. As of 2014, however, Station still owns the property. To keep its development options open, it has been allowing a portable casino to operate on the site. This is because of a loophole in the law that allows a gaming license to be renewed so long as a casino is on the property and open to the public for at least eight hours every two years.

CHAPTER 9

Living in Las Vegas Next Door to Famous Neighbors

Our first Las Vegas house at 5391 S. Evaline St.

I remember when my brothers and I were told by my dad that we were moving to Las Vegas. We were very sad about it. We would miss our friends and the great Los Angeles weather. Las Vegas, on the other hand, was a hot desert climate with little to do if you were under twenty-one years old. When we were told that at school, instead of running outside for physical education classes, all Las Vegas schools had swimming pools to swim laps, we were a little happier. Also, my dad told us that we would buy a house with a swimming pool because of the hot, dry summers. When my dad told us that, we were relieved and ready to move to Vegas. We eventually moved out my grandparent's trailer into our Las Vegas house, which did have a swimming pool.

The first year we moved to Las Vegas, I didn't need to think about swimming because it actually snowed in February around Las Vegas and the "Welcome to Fabulous Las Vegas" sign. Multiple snow days in February aren't common in Las Vegas.

Since 1937, February has seen more than three snowfall days only twice. The last time in 1963 just happened to snow when we moved there. The last time Las Vegas had any measurable snow was just over a decade ago when 3.6 inches fell on December 17, 2008. However, In Las Vegas, the summers are sweltering, the winters are cold, and it is dry and mostly clear year-round. Over the year, the temperature typically varies from *38°Fahrenheit* to *105°Fahrenheit* and is rarely below *30°Fahrenheit* or above *111°Fahrenheit*. We were still happy to have a swimming pool in the summer. The "Welcome to Fabulous Las Vegas" sign is a Las Vegas landmark funded in May 1959 and erected soon after by Western Neon. The sign was designed by Betty Willis at the request of Ted Rogich, a local salesman, who sold it to Clark County, Nevada. Willis considered the sign her gift to the city, so the sign was never copyrighted, hence why you find it on so many souvenirs in Vegas.

The sign cost a mere $4,000 to build, and Young Electric Company currently owns it while leasing it to Clark County. The sign stands at twenty-five feet tall, which is smaller than most Las Vegas signs, like the famous Vegas Vic sign, which reaches forty feet.

Vegas Vic is a neon sign portraying a cowboy that was erected on the exterior of the Pioneer Club in Las Vegas, Nevada, USA, in 1951.

The sign was a departure in graphic design from typeface-based neon signs to the friendly and welcoming human form of a cowboy. The sign's humanlike abilities of talking and waving its arm received an immediate acceptance as the unofficial welcoming sign, reproduced thousands of times over the years and all over the world. The sign can still be found at 25 East Fremont Street where it has been since 1951 on the exterior of what used to be the Pioneer Club but is currently a souvenir shop. The trademark is currently owned by Pioneer Hotel Inc., which owns and operates the Pioneer Hotel and Gambling Hall on the Colorado River in Laughlin, Nevada. Laughlin has a twin of the Vegas Vic image on another large sign referred to as River Rick. In 2008, the decision was made to design a parking lot by the "Welcome to Fabulous Las Vegas" sign. Before doing so, taking pictures of the sign posed as risky because tourists would stand in the middle of the road to get their photo opportunities. The parking lot allows for access to view the sign as well as a paved walkway going from the parking lot to an official viewing area. The sign has gained so much popularity that there have been two replica signs built in Las Vegas, one on Las Vegas Boulevard that read, "Welcome to Fabulous Downtown Las Vegas" and one on Boulder Highway. Unfortunately, the replica sign in downtown Vegas was destroyed by a car crash in 2016. For anyone who wants a piece of the actual sign, you are in luck! When the lights on the sign are replaced, they are sold as souvenirs, and a portion of the proceeds is donated to local charities. In 2013, the Consumer Electronics Association made a $50,000 donation to Green Chips, which planned to use the donated funds to help make the sign solar. Although the Pioneer Club no longer operates as a casino, the forty-foot (twelve-meter) neon cowboy that was its mascot still exists. In 1947, the Las Vegas Chamber of Commerce hired a West Marquis firm to draw visitors to Las Vegas. The company then created the first image of Vegas Vic and his friendly "Howdy Podner!" greeting. Due to the popularity of the cowboy, Young Electric Sign Company was commissioned to build a neon-sign version by the owners of the Pioneer Club. They then commissioned Pat Denner, who modeled it after the image in use by the Las Vegas Chamber of Commerce. The neon version was complete with a waving arm, a moving cigarette, and a recording of "Howdy Podner!" every fifteen minutes. Vegas Vic was then erected on the exterior of the Pioneer Club in 1951 on the southwest corner of First Street and Fremont Street, replacing the sign that simply said, "Pioneer Club," with an image of a horse-drawn covered wagon. One of the coolest things about moving to Las Vegas was our neighborhood. Across the street and next door to my friend Kevin Hutchinson's house was Sal and Marlene Constantino. Sal performed at the Stardust Hotel and Casino and was the lead vocalist in the Happy Jesters group. You might remember the Happy Jesters one-hit-wonder, "Heart of my Heart."

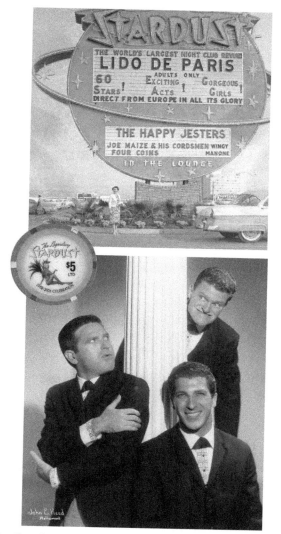

The Stardust Hotel and Casino with the Happy Jesters

Almost every other day, I would walk across the street to Sal's house and feed their pet piranha. Peter the Piranha loved to eat raw hamburger, and I enjoyed feeding it to him.

As I held the raw meat above the fish tank, Peter would jump up at least three feet to eat the hamburger meat out of my hand. One day, when I was at their house feeding Peter, I met their famous friend Jim Nabors, who was one of my father's favorite actors and singers. Jim Nabors was born and raised in Sylacauga, Alabama, but later moved to Southern California because of an asthmatic condition. He was discovered by Andy Griffith while working at a Santa Monica nightclub, and he later joined *The Andy Griffith Show* as Gomer Pyle. The character proved popular, and Nabors was given his own spin-off show *Gomer Pyle, U.S.M.C.* He was best known for his portrayal of Gomer Pyle, but he also became a popular guest on variety shows that showcased his rich baritone singing voice in the 1960s and 1970s, including frequent appearances on *The Carol Burnett Show* and two specials of his own in 1969 and 1974. Jim Nabors signed a recording contract with Columbia Records in 1965 and subsequently recorded numerous albums and singles, most of them containing romantic ballads. He recorded for Ranwood Records during late 1970. When I was first introduced to Jim Nabors, I was lucky to find my father, who was rarely at home on a Sunday. I immediately told my dad that his favorite actor/singer was across the street. At first, he didn't believe me and asked me who it was. He was thrilled to meet Jim Nabors, and we went to see him perform with Carol Burnett at Caesars Palace at least twice.

Jay, Marilyn Nemeth, and Jay Junior (who was called JJ at the time) were another of our neighbors whose backyard just happened to face ours. Jay Nemeth was a famous ventriloquist who performed on some of the biggest stages in Las Vegas, including the Hacienda Hotel and Casino and the Holiday Hotel and Casino, and he appeared on *The Ed Sullivan Show*. *The Ed Sullivan Show* was an American television variety show that ran on CBS from June 20, 1948, to June 6, 1971, and was hosted by New York entertainment columnist Ed Sullivan. It was replaced in September 1971 by the *CBS Sunday Night Movie*. In 2002 *The Ed Sullivan Show* was ranked number 15 on TV Guide's 50 Greatest TV Shows of All Time. In 2013, the series finished number 31 in *TV Guide Magazine*'s 60 Best Series of All Time. Jay Nemeth was originally from Hungary and was well known for "throwing his voice" to his beloved dog Nikki and their famous song, "How Much Is That Doggy in the Window."

Jay Nemeth and Nikki

Jay even volunteered to help me on a high school geography project that I picked about Hungary. My classmates thoroughly enjoyed my presentation, but most importantly my teacher Mr. Spielberg gave me an A. My mother was also good friends with his wife, Marilyn, and I am still friends with Jay's son, Jay Junior. Jay was so talented that we went to see Jay Nemeth perform on numerous occasions in Las Vegas at the Hacienda Hotel and Casino and the Holiday Hotel and Casino.

Another one of our famous neighbors lived right next door to Jay Nemeth. John Elroy Sanford (December 9, 1922–October 11, 1991), better known by his stage name Redd Foxx, was an American stand-up comedian and actor best known for his portrayal of Fred G. Sanford on the hit television show *Sanford and Son*. Foxx gained success with his raunchy nightclub acts during the 1950s and 1960s. Known as "the King of the Party Records," he performed on *The Red Foxx Show* and *The Royal Family*.

His film projects included *All the Fine Young Cannibals* (1960), *Cotton Comes to Harlem* (1970), *Norman... Is That You?* (1976), and *Harlem Nights* (1989). In 2004 Foxx ranked 24th in Comedy Central Presents: 100 Greatest Stand-ups of All Time. Red Foxx influenced many comedians and was often portrayed in popular culture as well, mainly as a result of his catchphrases, body language, and facial expressions. Red Foxx appeared on the television show *Sanford and Son*. During the show's five-year run, Foxx won a Golden Globe Award and received an additional three nominations along with three Primetime Emmy Award nominations. Foxx was posthumously given a star on the St. Louis Walk of Fame in 1992. Red Foxx performed at the Hacienda Hotel on the Strip for many years until he passed away in 1991, and the city even named a street after him. The Hacienda Resort Hotel and Casino was a hotel and casino on the Las Vegas Strip in Paradise, Nevada, that operated from 1956 to 1996. Located by itself on the far south end of the Las Vegas Strip, it was the first resort seen by tourists driving up from California. Since it was so far from the other resorts at the time, many people who stayed at the Hacienda would not go elsewhere. The Hacienda was also located close to McCarran International Airport; and at one point they had their own airline, Hacienda Airlines, to fly in gamblers from all over the US. The Hacienda was known for their inexpensive all-inclusive junkets marketed to American Midwestern retirees.

I never saw Red Foxx perform in Las Vegas because his show was an all adult X-rated revue. But I remember my dad saying that he enjoyed seeing him and that he was funny. In 1995, the Hacienda was purchased by Circus Circus Enterprises from Lowden's Archon Corporation. By this time, it was dwarfed by the many new megaresorts that were being built, in particular the Luxor, which had just been recently completed. On December 10, 1996, the Hacienda was closed to the public after forty years. The implosion was on December 31, 1996, and in March 1999, it was replaced by the Mandalay Bay.

Since I was a Michael Jackson fan from when he first started singing, we saw a teenage Michael Jackson and his brothers perform on the Strip with the Jackson 5 in April 1975. I saw also got to see him perform in 1984 at Dodger Stadium in Los Angeles during the Jackson 5's 84 World Tour. In 2013, I took my family to see the Cirque du Soleil show *Michael Jackson: One* in 2013 at Mandalay Bay, featuring Michael Jackson songs. He even appeared as a hologram singing in the show, which was special.

Me; my wife, Cathy; and children, Celine, Nevin, and Daren

The second year we moved to Las Vegas, we even saw the Beatles concert at the Las Vegas Convention Center on August 20, 1964, which was the only venue large enough at the time to hold this concert where they performed two shows that day. I liked the Beatles but preferred Diana Ross and the Supremes. Since I was only ten years old at the time, I remember my mother went with me and my brothers to see the Beatles. However, my dad didn't go because he didn't like them and called them "mopheads." He was, of course, referring to their Beatle-style haircut. For the most part, *mophead* was used derogatorily. "I'll just pick you up by your feet and mop the floor with your hair if that's how you want to look!" On the flip side, though, with interest in the Beatles so overwhelming to be called a mophead eventually became a form of flattery, at least in more liberal social settings. I didn't think that it would be an enjoyable concert if my mom went, but I was surprised to see her singing along with almost every Beatles song they played. So I started singing along with her, and finally my brothers started singing with us. Before you knew it, the entire audience was singing so loud that we couldn't hear the Beatles any longer. My mother especially liked Paul McCartney and said, "He is cute." This was the only time the Beatles' performed in Vegas. In the 1960s, Vegas was no stranger to performers with devoted fans. At the Sands Hotel and Casino, Frank Sinatra's and Dean Martin's (Rat Pack) fans were willing to sleep in their cars and hotel lobbies on busy weekends just for a chance to see the crooners. But nothing had prepared the city for Beatlemania during that time. When booking agents first approached Las Vegas hotels on behalf of the Beatles, they were turned down. Stan Irwin, director of entertainment at the Sahara, had the foresight to realize what a Beatles' concert would mean to both the Sahara and Las Vegas. In a 1989 interview with newspaper columnist Mike Weatherford, Irwin said, "I'm the only one who seemed to have known about the Beatles, so I bought them." Weatherford, in his book *Cult Vegas: The Weirdest! The Wildest! The Swingiest Town on Earth*, reasons that it was more likely that the hotels considered the Beatles an act appealing only to teenagers. Casino owners had seen the indifference Las Vegas audiences had toward an earlier teen idol. In 1956 Elvis Presley failed to capture the interest of audiences and critics when he performed at the New Frontier Hotel and Casino. Whether it was foresight or luck, Irwin and the Sahara managed to secure the hottest ticket in Las Vegas when they booked the Beatles. "I'd been thinking of putting them in our main showroom, the Congo Room, but it held just six hundred. And there was no way to get any more seats in the place," Irwin told John Romero in his book *Las Vegas, the Untold Stories.* "I said, 'Hold it, these guys belong in the convention center.' And I rushed over there to check the seating. They told me they could put 7,000 a show in the rotunda. I said that it was still too small and asked for the balcony too. They agreed, and that pushed the total seating for each show to 8,408." Tickets ranged from $2.20 for the cheapest balcony seats to $5.50 for the best seats. Following a common Las Vegas practice, Irwin had set aside blocks of tickets (casino comps) for not only his own casino's high rollers but also for neighboring hotels.

"I put aside a block of tickets for every major casino in town, but up to the day the Beatles arrived, there were hardly any takers," he told Romero. "Even our own casino bosses didn't seem to catch on until about a week before the concert when our big players started calling for tickets. And at the last minute, every casino on the Strip called us and pleaded, 'Do you still have my Beatles tickets.'"

While high rollers and casino hosts may have been slow on the uptake, Las Vegas teenagers were not. More than 1,400 teens stood in line on June 29, 1964, to get tickets to the two shows. Hotel and local officials were no doubt congratulating themselves when the Beatles' chartered plane arrived at McCarran International Airport at 1:45 a.m. on August 20, 1964. The landing was hours before the Fab Four's scheduled arrival and managed to avoid the chaotic scenes that had greeted them at other appearances. A *Las Vegas Sun* newspaper photographer managed to get past security, snap a few photos of the group arriving, and instruct Ringo on how to operate the "telly" before being thrown out of the group's suite. After that, the Beatles were self-imposed hostages. Having booked their Las Vegas gig so they could see the famous Sin City, the group was stuck in their hotel room except when they were taken to the Las Vegas Convention Center to perform. The Sahara brought up a few slot machines for the Fab Four to enjoy and created a photo op seen around the world. Less than twelve hours later, the Beatles would perform their only two Las Vegas shows. Crowd estimates ranged from 11,000 to 16,800 total for the two shows, a record in Las Vegas at the time. Today, Celine Dion performs to an audience of 4,100 at the Colosseum at Caesars Palace; and only high capacity venues like the MGM Grand Garden Arena, Mandalay Bay Events Center, and Thomas & Mack Center can boast capacity of 14,000 or more. "When I walked on stage at the convention center to introduce the first show, only four words left my mouth, 'Ladies and gentlemen, the—" And all hell broke loose," Irwin told Romero. "Like the rest of us from the Sahara who were there, I never heard a note. The screaming drowned out everything." The *Las Vegas Sun* reported that the stage was surrounded by police officers and guards, some from as far away as Phoenix. The show was almost inaudible. A poor sound system and screaming fans drowned out the group as they performed their hits and songs of fellow artists, including "She Loves You," "Do You Want to Know a Secret, "I Want to Hold Your Hand," "All My Loving," "Twist and Shout," and more. Thirty minutes after taking the stage, the Fab Four were done, leaving the screaming fans in their wake. A few hours later, the Beatles left Las Vegas, never to perform as a group in the city again. August 20, 1964, marked a turning point in Las Vegas entertainment. Beatlemania introduced the Las Vegas Strip to a new concept, the arena show. It would eventually lead to major venues like The Joint, The Colosseum, MGM Grand Garden, Mandalay Events Center, Thomas & Mack Center, and the 20,000-seat arena scheduled for development behind the Park MGM and New York-New York hotel and Casino. It also proved to casino operators that rock 'n' roll was not only here to stay but that there was a growing audience who wanted to see it in Las Vegas. Today the city welcomes resident shows from Cher, Bruno Mars, Santana, Celine Dion, and Lady Gaga. While the Beatles never performed as a group again in the city, their legacy lives on in *Love* by Cirque du Soleil. Here, acrobatics, fantastical dance numbers, and colorful characters combine with the Beatles' music in an enormously popular Las Vegas show. We enjoyed watching the *Love* show, especially when the Beatles songs came to life.

One of the best presents I ever received from my dad was a real surprise! When I came home from school one day, when I went outside to our back yard, my dad and Sheriff Ralph Lamb were unloading a wild burro that had been rescued in the desert.

They had already built a coral for the burro and when my dad saw me, he said, "Happy birthday, son." One of Sheriff Lamb's incentives was to help burros that were trapped in the desert and rescue them. We became the new home rescue for our pet burro, Jenny. After many days and hours taming our pet burro Jenny, my mother decided to ride her.

It didn't take very long for Jenny to buck her off to the ground. Thankfully, she was fine; however, Jenny had been gaining too much weight and seemed uncomfortable. My dad called Sheriff Lamb and asked for his advice. Since the sheriff was also educated as a veterinarian, he came immediately over to our house and inspected Jenny. I asked Sheriff Lamb, "Was I feeding Jenny too much hay every day?" I had followed his instructions on what to feed her, so I was confused as were my parents.

Jenny, Tammy, and me

It didn't take the sheriff long to tell us that Jenny was pregnant. Three weeks later, Jenny welcomed a baby burro that we affectionately named Tammy after my mother's favorite song. Jenny and Tammy were a welcome addition to our dog, Duffy, and Polly, our talking parrot. Polly used to be Gramps's parrot, but when "Big Grandma" passed away Gramps gave Polly to us to take care of. One of the most amazing things about Polly is that she liked to eat ice cream from a spoon and play ball. So we would often take her out of her cage, place her on the floor, and roll the ball to her. She would grab the ball with her beak and roll it back to us, which could last for hours.

We would rarely see my father, who was at work, and work hard at Paul-Son he did. When we did, on occasion, go see my dad at work, we were usually awarded a special treat from an old Las Vegas classic, Luv-It Frozen Custard, near Downtown Las Vegas. Frozen custard is a cold dessert similar to ice cream but made with eggs in addition to cream and sugar. It is usually kept at a warmer temperature compared to ice cream and typically has a denser consistency. It's the best-tasting frozen dessert ever!

Luv-It Frozen Custard of Las Vegas, Nevada, specializes in sundaes. They have been serving the Las Vegas community since 1973, selling shakes, cones, malts, and hard packs to go. My dad's favorite custard flavor was rocky road, and he would often buy gallons of it and bring it back to the office for all the employees to enjoy.

Also, every summer. in August, my dad would rent a trailer, load it up with twenty to thirty tubs of Baskin-Robbins ice cream (including rocky road), and have an ice cream social at Mount Charleston where the weather was so much cooler in the summer.

My father found John "Curley" Ashworth who operated an early Ford dealership in Las Vegas when he needed a small loan to buy a used Ford pickup and a silver-paneled van. He got the loan from Valley Bank and took on Curley as his equal partner, a decision he would later regret. Curley handled day-to-day operations while Dad was the salesman who also packed up a van with gaming merchandise and drove to California ten days a month selling to his father's old customers and eventually stealing them away from T. R. King & Co. My brothers, Tom and Patrick, both joined Dad after they graduated from college to help him grow the business just as my dad had joined his father's gaming business. Tom was a natural salesman at Paul-Son and had a great personal relationship with many casino operators, including Richard Englestad, the brother and partner of the Imperial Palace owner, Ralph Englestad. They would often go hunting together on weekends in Utah. I would later take over the account after Tom's untimely passing.

The Imperial Palace Hotel and Casino 1979 (*left*)
and the LINQ/High Roller today (*right*)

My brother Patrick was more interested in operations and became Paul-Son's general manager in 1975. At that time, I was in high school working weekends at Paul-Son, cleaning the bathrooms and learning what I could at the time about the business.

I decided early on that I didn't want to work at Paul-Son. I wanted to be a doctor instead. However, I would keep my eye on the business just in case things didn't work out for me in my future endeavors. On a hot summer night in 1975, my dad's sense of humor almost went a bit too far. According to my mother, my dad invited his closest casino friends and associates to go to a midnight movie on Paradise Road in Las Vegas. Since there were about fifty of them, my dad rented a school bus to drive them to the local X-rated movie theater on Paradise Road. My mother said she was so embarrassed when they arrived at the movie theatre that she could hardly speak to their friends.

However, when the movie started, it was a classic John Wayne movie from the 1950s. No one ever forgot who Paul Endy was after that night. In the 1960's more resort casino properties began construction in Las Vegas. Caesars Palace with a luxury Roman theme was built on the strip in 1966.

It was closely followed by Circus Circus with a giant circus-tent-shaped main structure, which opened on October 18, 1968, by Jay Sarno and Stanley Mallin. At its opening, the $15 million Circus Circus resort only included a casino. Don't let the big top fool you.

Designed by Rissman & Rissman Associates and opened in 1968, Circus Circus was intended for grown-ups. At its opening, the $15 million Circus Circus resort only included a casino.

Circus Circus originally opened on October 18, 1968.

An article in the *Las Vegas Review-Journal* stated that "the huge casino would have numerous circus acts performing around the cavernous room, trapeze and high-wire acts performing over the heads of gamblers and bevies of showgirls dancing and singing throughout." The Circus Circus casino had cocktail waitresses dressed in sexy majorette outfits, blackjack dealers in polka-dot shirts, and even had a slide for tipsy gamblers to ride from the midway to the gaming floor. In 1972 the Circus Circus opened its first hotel tower with a loan that led to mob entanglements. In fact, notorious mob enforcer Tony Spaltro (aka Nicky Santoro in the movie *Casino*) eventually owned a gift shop in the lobby of the casino. Two years later, Jay Sarno sold Circus Circus to William Bennett, who got rid of some of the bawdier shows and continued the hotel expansion adding circus games that were popular with families with children.

The Excalibur Hotel and Casino opened on June 19, 1980.

Circus Circus became a public company in 1980 as Circus Circus Enterprises, opening Excalibur and Luxor family destinations. Circus Circus was one of the first casino properties to court families, and it remains their modus operandi. Chief among the draws for those with little ones is the Adventuredome, an indoor amusement park that opened in 1993 and was expanded since then with dozens of rides and roller coasters. Circus Circus was a great addition to Las Vegas as it was the city's only real amusement park until Excalibur and Luxor both opened in 1980. Wet'n'Wild was built in 1985, and the MGM Grand Adventures opened in 1993. Excalibur, named for the mythical sword of King Arthur, uses the medieval theme in several ways. Its facade is a stylized image of a castle. Until 2007, a wizard-like figure representing Merlin looked out from a high turret (since replaced by a figure advertising Dick's

Last Resort). The Excalibur is situated at the Tropicana-Las Vegas Boulevard intersection. The hotel is linked by overhead pedestrian bridges to neighboring casinos to the north (New York-New York, across Tropicana Avenue) and the east (Tropicana, across the Strip). A free tram connects Excalibur to its sister MGM Resorts International properties to the south, Luxor, and Mandalay Bay. The fun dungeon is an arcade from which you can access the Tournament of Kings arena and includes a laser tag arena.

Caesars Palace Grand Prix 1982

The Caesars Palace Grand Prix was a car race held in Las Vegas between 1981 and 1984. For the first two years, the race was part of the Formula One World Championship before becoming a round of the CART series in 1983. Nissan/Datsun was a presenting sponsor of both races, and the track was set up in the parking lot of the Caesars Palace Hotel. It was surprisingly well set up for a temporary circuit. It was wide enough for passing, provided ample run-off areas filled with sand, and had a surface that was as smooth as glass. Its counterclockwise direction put a tremendous strain on the drivers' necks. The 1982 race, held in intense hea—another unpleasant feature of this race—was won by Michele Alboreto in a Tyrrell, but that was the end of Formula One racing in Las Vegas since the races had drawn only tiny crowds and the 1981 race turned out to be a huge loss for the hotel. We went to see the Caesars Palace Grand Prix in 1983 with my dad and Al Facinto Sr., the director of casino operations at the time. We were treated to great elevated seats and all the food and drinks we wanted. What my dad didn't drink was alcohol, he was adamant about refraining from any alcoholic drinks or drugs except smoking cigarettes was okay with him. After the closure of the Caesars Palace Grand Prix, there was for a brief time the Stardust International Raceway. The raceway was an auto racing track from 1965 to 1971 that featured a flat 3-mile (4.8-kilometer) thirteen-turn road course and a 0.25-mile drag strip. Stardust International Raceway was developed in 1965 by the Stardust Racing Association, a Nevada corporation headed by the primary owner of the Desert Inn and Stardust Hotel and Casino. The track was developed ostensibly to attract high rollers to the Stardust Hotel. The Stardust Racing Association also owned the property and functioned as an event promoter.

The drag strip hosted the NHRA Stardust National Open in 1967, 1968, 1969, and 1971. The Stardust Racing Association was dissolved on April 1, 1968, one day after the USAC Stardust 150. The hotel and raceway were sold in January 1969 to the Parvin-Dohrmann Corporation, and the new owners closed the track shortly thereafter. Larry Horton, the track's manager, reopened the drag strip in August 1970 and ran drag racing events until October 1971. Real estate developers Pardee Homes acquired the Stardust International Raceway property and related adjacent properties in August 1970 and built the Spring Valley Community. A subsequent racing facility, the Las Vegas Speedrome opened in 1972 across from Nellis Air Force Base. The Speedrome property was later redeveloped into the current Las Vegas Motor Speedway in 1996. The $200-million state-of-the-art facility is a 1,600-acre complex that has complete accommodations for virtually every form of motorsports activity along with any type of function. In March 1999, the Speedway broke a Nevada attendance record when more than 250,000 fans attended Pennzoil World of Outlaws, Orleans 150 NASCAR Winston West Sam's Town 300, and Las Vegas 400 NASCAR Winston Cup race events.

The Luxor Hotel and Casino opened on October 15, 1993.

The Luxor Las Vegas is a thirty-story hotel and casino situated on the southern end of the Las Vegas Strip. The hotel is owned and operated by MGM Resorts International and has a 120,000-square-foot (11,000 square-meter) casino with over two thousand slot machines and eighty-seven table games. The casino opened in 1993 and was renovated and expanded several times. The 1998 renovation work modernized the sign of the property and raised the hotel's capacity to 4,407 rooms, including 442 suites. The hotel's rooms line the interior walls of the main tower, which has a pyramid shape, and other recent twenty-two-story twin ziggurat towers. The hotel is named for the city of Luxor (ancient Thebes) in Egypt.

Wet'n'Wild opened at the Las Vegas Strip in 1985.

Wet'n'Wild was located originally on the Las Vegas Strip, between the Sahara and El Rancho hotels and casinos across the street from Circus Circus. Wet'n'Wild opened on May 18, 1985, after $14 million was spent on its construction. When Wet'n'Wild opened, we especially enjoyed going to the water park during the hot Las Vegas summer days and birthday parties. However, Circus Circus was my favorite theme park while we were growing up. It was always fun playing midway games and watching circus acts. We would often have our birthday parties and after Christmas festivities playing games and winning prizes at Circus Circus with cousins (Greg, Tim, Kelly, and Jacqueline Evans) or (Kevin and Annie Chang) always without my father. My mother would usually take us to Paul-Son after Circus Circus so we could visit our dad, where he was always hard at work. Even though he worked hard, my dad always supported our activities and financially supported us, which was how he showed his love.

During the end of my junior year in 1975 at Valley High School, my music director, Jim Garoufes (aka Mr. G) resigned due to the "harassment" he received from the school principal Marshall Darnell. Mr. G was the nicest teacher at Valley/Western High Schools who I respect and affectionately care about even to this day. When I first tried out for TIME (Todays Individual Mind Expression), the award-winning performing pop-choir group in my sophomore year at Valley High School, I was selected as an alternate in case someone got sick or just dropped out of the group.

TIME (Todays Individual Mind Expression) in the classroom

At first, I was disappointed. I don't know if it was fate or good luck, but I became a regular TIME singer when one student had to move out of the state. In many ways, Mr. G was a lot like my father—kind but a hardworking get-results kind of guy. With encouragement from my mom and Mr. G, I worked even harder at improving my vocals. Mr. G cared about his students and his music, often having rehearsals before a performance later in the day. Mr. G was our musical director; and his lovely wife, Marget, was our choreography director, teaching us "cool" dance moves while we sang around microphones. Mr. G graduated from Ithaca College with a master's degree in education, a major in music, and a minor in psychology. They were married in 1963 after they met in college and moved to Las Vegas in 1965. Mr. G and his wife were professionals and demanded it from us as performers to get the best results from our audience. We were enormously successful because of them and that's what worried the principal at Valley High School. I recall once during the final minutes of class when Principal Darnell confronted Mr. G about the trash piling up in the rubbish can in his classroom. I was as shocked as Mr. G was about the confrontation. We both believed that Darnell must be "jealous" of him and our immensely successful singing group TIME as we continually brought donations in from local conventions even more than the sports programs, which upset Darnel. We performed at various venues in Las Vegas, including the Sahara Hotel Space Center, various schools, and Disneyland in California.

When Mr. G resigned from Valley High, he had already been offered a new teaching position at Western High School and was going to start a new pop group called Jubilation. I decided that I wanted to transfer to Western High School due to my disgust with the administration at Valley and the treatment of Mr. G. When Principal Darnell of Valley High School found out that I was transferring, he called me to his office and refused to grant the transfer and not allow me to go to Western High School on the grounds of "prostalation." At first, I didn't know what he or what the word even meant, but it didn't sound good! I looked the word up in the dictionary at the time. Even today, I still can't find its meaning even on Google:

Mr. Jim Garoufes

Prostalation…did you mean *prostalator*?

No dictionary or Google definition!

That night, when my father arrived home late for dinner, I told him about the meeting I had with Darnell, and he was furious. I told him that the principal insisted that Mr. G somehow was "prostalating me to go to Western High School, whatever that meant." I told him, "It's my own decision, not Mr. G's."

My dad then asked me, "Do you really want to go to Western?"

I replied, "Absolutely yes. More than ever now."

It would be a decision I wouldn't regret. My dad told me to set up a meeting with Darnell for the next day and that he would meet me at Valley High School. The meeting was set for one in the afternoon; and when I got to the principal's office, my dad was already there, anxiously pacing up and down the hallway like he was waiting for a new baby. Upon entering Darnell's office, my dad loudly said, "So you are accusing my son's music teacher of 'prostalating' my son and not allowing him to transfer to Western?"

"That's right, Paul, and there isn't anything you can do about it," sputtered Darnell.

My father then grabbed Darnell by his neck and, while squeezing tightly, demanded, "You will allow my son to go to Western, or you will be gone."

After Darnell could barely say, "Let me go right now!" my father squeezed harder on his neck and said, "Only if you let him transfer to Western and put it in writing right now!"

As his face turned red, Darnell said, "Okay, you win this time, Paul." He barked out to his personal assistant to approve my transfer to Western. What I didn't realize until just recently was Mr. G told me that it was that Mr. Bruce Miller, the principal of Western High School, who told Mr. G when he hired him that Principal Darnell also accused him of "prostalating" Mr. G. I never regretted my decision to transfer to Western High School in my senior year even though I didn't have any friends at Western High School.

Western High School's first Jubilation, 1973

But I had Mr. and Mrs. G. Our pop-choir group, Jubilation, was so successful at Western High School that not only did we record an album but the group also won first place in the prestigious Reno International Jazz three years in a row. As a result of my singing experience in high school, I was awarded a music scholarship to the University of Utah.

In 1973 during my senior year of high school, I was working in the radiology department at Sunrise Hospital when I received a disturbing telephone call from my brother Pat. Patrick said my dad was on his way to Sunrise Hospital in an ambulance and that he thought my dad had a minor stroke. When I found out that he was in the hospital, I immediately went to the emergency room, and he was there and not a bit happy about it. My dad loved to eat and was overweight, had high blood pressure, and smoked like a horse; so I wasn't surprised he was there. My brothers and I all tried to talk him into improving his poor health, but he didn't really seem to care and just said that he would "die with his boots on," which is about what he did. Even one of his friends who owned an insurance business couldn't get him life insurance. Once they took my dad to the operating room to perform an artery cleaning procedure, I went back to the radiology department. When I arrived at his hospital room a few hours later, my dad was sitting up in bed and ready to leave! He was connected to tubes, wires, and hoses everywhere; and he was mad. "Eric, we have to leave", he said.

"Dad, what are talking about? You just had surgery!"

"I don't care," he said. "I have an appointment with the new owner of the Tropicana, and I'm not going to miss it. It's a big deal for us."

My dad's new Tropicana chips in 1973

As he started to rip off the wires and rip out the IV tubes, I pleaded with him not to and called a nurse. By the time Nurse

Diggins came into the room, sirens were going off, and blood was shooting all over the place. She panicked and said that when my dad ripped out his IV line, he left a piece of plastic in his arm. Nurse Diggins was nervous that the piece of plastic would get stuck in his vein or worse, an artery, and travel to his heart.

She immediately paged Dad's doctor about the situation to come and look at his arm stat. Unfortunately, Dr. Williams was in surgery and couldn't be reached. My dad also had a drain in his neck that he pulled out, and a brown fluid was leaking all over his hospital gown. My dad then instructed me to get his clothes out of the closet, or he would go back to Paul-Son in his hospital gown. I begged him one more time not to leave, but it fell on deaf ears. Gown on, he grabbed his clothes, called a taxi, and went back to the Paul-Son. As an employee of the hospital, I regrettably asked them to let him leave and said that I would take responsibility for him. I immediately called our family doctor and told him what had happened. By the time Dr. Hoffman and I reached Paul-Son, my dad was sitting behind his desk and asked, "What can I do for you?" Dr. Hoffman rushed to his side as blood was still gushing down his arm. He told him that he really shouldn't have left the hospital as he just had a serious medical procedure. He grabbed a pair of needle-nose pliers from his black bag and removed the small piece of plastic tubing that was now turning blue in dad's arm. Dr. Hoffman then grabbed what looked like a stapler and started stitching both of my dad's bleeding arms and neck. Dr. Hoffman prescribed my dad antibiotics and told him to call if anything went wrong. Fortunately, on that day nothing else did go wrong, but unfortunately it would be a major stroke years later that would befall my father.

The second half of the twentieth century in Las Vegas was marked by growth in Las Vegas's population, the number of resorts in the city, and the size of the resorts themselves. Familiar names such as Howard Hughes and the Rat Pack helped shift Las Vegas's image from an outlaw Wild West city to the one we know today. New casino resort properties were being built and opening rapidly up and down the Strip and in downtown Las Vegas as well. Each new casino required layouts and tables and an initial supply of chips, playing cards, and dice; but the real volumes came in replacement sales. Cards had to be replaced every few hours, felt was worn down after just two months, and even chips lasted only about five years. And dice were replaced almost every hour. They were changed because if the player was winning, the casino wanted to change its outcome of the dice; and if the casino was winning, the gambler wanted to change his outcome of the dice since it was all about who was winning. But it didn't matter to Paul-Son who was winning. As long as the casinos kept buying its products, it was a winner too. According to *Forbes Magazine*, Paul-Son held a major advantage in entering the gaming market, "a known record in a business equipment is imperative." Endy said, "In this business they [casino operators] want to know who they're doing business with," and with Paul Endy they knew they were protected, particularly with their chips. When we were interviewed by *Forbes Magazine* in 1994, my dad said, "During a gold rush, it's not the miners who get rich, it's those who sell the pans. In Las Vegas Paul-Son Gaming sells dice, cards, and chips. So let the big guy [new megaresorts] come." Would one of these new megaresorts manufacture their own gaming chips? My dad said, "Don't bet on it."

Forbes Magazine interview, December 5, 1994

My dad had a great reputation in the gaming industry; so did Paul-Son's gaming products. I remember working in the Paul-Son factory, manufacturing dice at an early age. Manufacturing dice is a "labor of love" as my dad would call it. Not only were dice very labor-intensive but they were also manufactured to rigorously measured tolerances—to be exact, within one-hundredth of an inch, the thickness of a piece of paper. The majority of casinos use more than one manufacturer of dice as there is still a lot of superstition in craps. Paul-Son dice are the best in the industry even though they were made in Mexico from very early on. I remember when one of our competitors told the casino manager at the Imperial Palace Hotel that our dice were inferior because they were made in Mexico. My dad's repetitive reply to everyone including me was "Not much is made in the United States anymore." As a result, my dad successfully continued to move different phases of manufacturing to Mexico, starting with the dice shop.

CHAPTER 10

A Brief History of Paul-Son Casino Dice

The word *dice* comes from the Old French *déh* and from the Latin *datum*, meaning "something which is given or played." Dice (singular die or dice) are small throwable objects with marked sides that can rest in multiple positions. Legend has it that Roman soldiers invented the game of craps using the knucklebones of a pig as dice and their armor shields as a table. Others believe craps originated from an Arabic dice game called Al Dar, which means "dice" in Arabic, and that merchants brought the game over to Europe in the twelfth century. The most commonly accepted version of the game's creation is that it was invented by Sir William of Tyre in 1125 during the Crusades and named after a castle named "Assert" or "Hazarth," later called "Hazard." Fast forward a bit, this English game "hazard" became extremely popular in French taverns during the seventeenth century. It is believed around this time that the name *craps* was invented as a spin-off of the French word *cramped*, meaning "toad," in reference to the original style of play by people crouched over a floor or sidewalk. What later became the American version was brought to New Orleans by Bernard Xavier Philippe de Marini de Mandeville, a wealthy gambler and politician descended from colonial Louisiana landowners. A flaw in the game allowed players to exploit the casino until American dice maker John H. Winn, also known as the father of the modern game, corrected this issue during the nineteenth century by introducing the "don't pass" betting option. It was his version that continued to flourish, spreading throughout the French Louisiana colony of Arcadia and later along the Mississippi River in gambling boats. In 1931, the explosion of Las Vegas gambling lent even more popularity to the game. Dice are also used for generating random numbers, commonly as part of tabletop games, including dice games, board games, role-playing games, and games of chance. The traditional die is a cube with each of its six faces marked with a different number of dots (pips) from one to six. When thrown or rolled, the die comes to rest showing a random integer from one to six on its upper surface with each value being equally likely. Dice may also have polyhedral or irregular shapes and may have faces marked with numerals or symbols instead of pips. Loaded dice are designed to favor some results over others for cheating or entertainment. Paul-Son's precise casino dice may have a polished or sand finish, making them transparent or translucent, respectively. Casino dice have their pips drilled then filled flush with a paint of the same density as the material used for the dice, such that the center of gravity of the dice is as close to the geometric center as possible. This mitigates concerns that the pips will cause a small bias. All such dice are stamped with a serial number to prevent potential cheaters from substituting a die. If you're not familiar with the game of craps, it is essentially a game played with dice in which the players make wagers on the outcome of the roll or a series of rolls of a pair of dice. Players may wager money against each other (street craps) or a bank (casino craps or table craps). Because it requires little equipment, street craps can be played in informal settings.

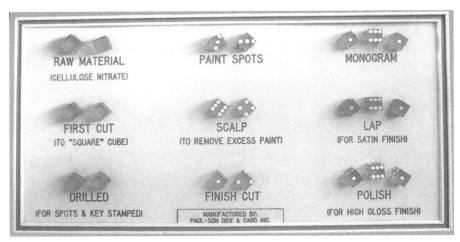

My Paul-Son dice-manufacturing model

When I worked in the factory, dice had to be manufactured within 1/10,000th of an inch (the thickness of a piece of paper) of the ordered size, which was usually 3/4 inch for a 12-foot craps table. Each die is drilled and cut by hand eventually being measured with a micrometer for correctness. I also developed a dice-manufacturing model/chart so the various gaming commissions and casino customers were better informed about manufacturing precision dice.

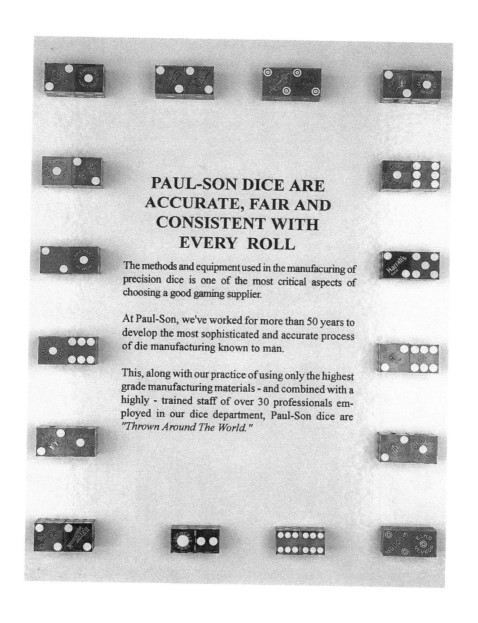

PAUL-SON DICE ARE ACCURATE, FAIR AND CONSISTENT WITH EVERY ROLL

The methods and equipment used in the manufacuring of precision dice is one of the most critical aspects of choosing a good gaming supplier.

At Paul-Son, we've worked for more than 50 years to develop the most sophisticated and accurate process of die manufacturing known to man.

This, along with our practice of using only the highest grade manufacturing materials - and combined with a highly - trained staff of over 30 professionals employed in our dice department, Paul-Son dice are *"Thrown Around The World."*

Paul-Son dice are machined from cellulose acetate material which is specially formulated to give the ultimate in clarity, hardness and demensional stability to micro precision tolerances of 1/10,000th of an inch (1/20th the thickness of a hair). There are three spot designs available: Flush, Birds Eye and Ring Spot. The spots are inserted in the body of the dice and machined flat to the surface with high precision. Your personal logo can then be added and serialized. If required, the dice can be marked with a secret "key". All our dice are micro - polished or sand finished.

My father brought legitimacy to the gaming supply industry that had its own history of questionable creditability in the early days. On April 3, 1941, hotel owner Thomas Hull opened the El Rancho Vegas, which was the first resort on what would become the Las Vegas Strip. The hotel gained much of its fame from the gourmet buffet that it offered. On October 30, 1942, Texas cinema magnate R. E. Griffith rebuilt on the site of a nightclub called Pair O' Dice that first opened in 1930 and renamed it Hotel Last Frontier. A few more resorts were built on and around Fremont Street, but it was the next hotel on the Strip that publicly demonstrated the influence of organized crime on Las Vegas. This changed in post-war Las Vegas when Jewish gangster Bugsy Siegel, with help from a friend and fellow mob boss Meyer Lansky, poured money through a Mormon-owned bank for the cover of legitimacy and built the Flamingo in 1946. Money from organized crime combined with funds from more respectable investors, Wall Street banks, union pension funds, the Mormon Church, and the Princeton University endowment. A hearing concluded that organized crime money was incontrovertibly tied to the Las Vegas casinos and was becoming the controlling interest in the city, thereby earning for the groups vast amounts of income, which was strengthening their influence in the country. This led to a proposal by the Senate to institute federal gambling control. Only through the power and influence of Nevada's Senator Pat McCarran did the proposal die in committee. Along with their connections in Hollywood and New York City, these interests in Las Vegas were able to use publicity provided by these media capitals to steer the rapid growth of tourism into Las Vegas, thereby dooming Galveston, Texas; Hot Springs, Arkansas; and other illegal gaming centers around the nation.

Nevada's legal gaming as well as the paradoxically increased scrutiny by local and federal law enforcement in these other locales during the 1950s made their demise inevitable. Paul-Son produced quality products that were becoming increasingly more sophisticated as gamblers attempted counterfeiting more often. Paul-Son was the first to embed a small piece of encoded microfilm in chips to help prevent counterfeiting. This patented process, developed by my father, was a major improvement in anticounterfeiting and paved the way for additional chip protection. In the early 1990s Paul-Son developed a proprietary molding system that made it possible to produce full-color graphics on a chip. While previous chips featured an inlay (decal) of the casino's logo less than an inch in diameter, Paul-Son molded chips had an inlay that measured 1 inch—almost the entire surface of the 1.54-inch chip. This allowed for more detailed graphics, which Paul-Son was able to do in-house with computers. While many of the new chips simply featured a larger version of the casino's logo, the new technology led to the idea of special-event chips, including those that commemorated the Super bowl, championship boxing events, and even the wedding of Donald Trump to Marla Maples.

The Dunes Hotel and Casino in 1972

I remember when some questionable Paul-Son gaming chips were passed at a famous strip casino in 1972. My dad received a call from his customer, an angry casino manager at the Dunes Hotel and Casino, and later from the Nevada Gaming Board demanding my father "fix" his chip problem. My dad suspected that the counterfeit chip must have been made in China since they were experts at copying anything. I remember when the Imperial Palace Casino reordered a logo T-shirt for a blackjack tournament. When they received the order from China, the shirt was made exactly like the sample, including a cigarette burn hole above the right pocket. My dad immediately called his friend Jerry West, an FBI agent in Los Angeles, and had the counterfeiter arrested at his toy company in China. Jerry would later tell us that the toy company claimed it didn't know that making copies of casino chips was illegal and would take orders from anyone who provided a sample. Even if the sample was a "live" casino chip. The toy company was shut down the next day.

Paul Endy would never forget Jerry West and would later appoint him as an independent board member when Paul-Son went public in 1994 and he served until he passed away in 2006. One of Jerry West's claim to fame was the arrest of John DeLorean charged with conspiracy to obtain and distribute cocaine in Los Angeles on October 19, 1982.

Jerry West arrests John DeLorean in 1982 (*top left*),
my wife, Cathy (*top right*), with my DeLorean

As an interesting side note, I owned a DeLorean automobile in 1981 and rented my DeLorean for what I thought was a new blockbuster Hollywood movie sequel to *Back to the Future*.

Backside to the Future on VHS

However, when I drove my car to the Sahara Hotel Space Center for the movie convention, I was told that my car would be in an X-rated movie, *Backside to the Future*. I wasn't entirely comfortable with my car in an X-rated movie but decided to rent it anyway.

When I arrived at the Sahara Hotel, I had to drain the gas tank and unplug the battery cables to the car. At the end of the convention, when I went to pick up my car, I was shocked that there were scantily covered girls lying all over the hood.

Since the DeLorean is a stainless-steel car, it easily shows fingerprints and, in this case, had body marks all over my car. I drove as fast as I could to take my DeLorean to the closest car wash! I rented out my DeLorean two more times—once in 1985 and once in 1986—to a venue I was more familiar with.

In 1985 I rented my DeLorean to the UNLV men's basketball head coach Billy Bana for the cover of "Center Court". In 1996, I rented my DeLorean to the UNLV Women's Basketball team who were attempting to make it once again to the playoffs.

UNLV Men's Basketball program, 1985 (*left*), and UNLV Women's Basketball program, 1986 (*right*).

After the UNLV Women won the Mountain West Basketball Tournament, I auctioned off my DeLorean because it became less practical to drive because of the unavailability of parts and its very small front window. However, it was still a super cool car to drive with its gull-wing doors. At least I made some money from renting it out before I sold it.

In the same year, my father thought the name Paul-Son Dice & Card Co. seemed to be too restrictive for the company and wanted to change the name.

He believed that the company needed a new name that was more representative of the company now that Paul-Son was manufacturing, distributing, and selling a wide range of gaming supplies including manufacturing table games. The new name would include a retail store in Las Vegas for the public as well. The new name would be Paul-Son Gaming Supplies, a name that better represented the expanding gaming industry.

CUSTOM GAMING FURNITURE
NO JOB IS TOO LARGE - OR TOO SMALL

Paul-Son manufactures and distributes the most complete line of custom gaming furniture available to the industry. Each piece is hand-crafted with meticulous care and fine workmanship. The result is individualized "State of the Art' gaming furniture that even the most elegant resort properties are proud to place in their casinos.

Our furniture cabinet making capabilities range from Blackjack Tables, Poker Tables and Crap Tables to Slot Stands, Change Booths and Roulette Wheels. We will work directly with your architect in developing casino layout and floor plans, to make certain all our furnishings are properly coordinated with your basic decor.

Our custom power coated metal bases for riverboats are availabe in a variety of colors and designs. Let us fabricate one for you today.!

CHAPTER 11

Same Company, New Name

Paul-Son Gaming Supplies would be the new name of the company to better inform its customers of its complete gaming product line. Paul-Son was now manufacturing tables, gaming felts, and roulette wheels and distributing a brand of playing cards. As Las Vegas continued to grow, the first MGM Grand Hotel opened on the site of the old Bonanza Hotel and Casino in 1973 and cost a whopping $106 million, the equivalent of $560 million today. MGM sold that property in 1985 (it's now Bally's) and moved to the current site at what was once the Marina Hotel. When the new MGM opened in 1993, it was the largest single hotel in the United States with 6,852 rooms.

It is also the third-largest hotel complex in the world by the number of rooms and the second-largest hotel resort complex in the United States behind the combined the Venetian and the Palazzo.

The property was originally the site of the Golf Club Motel during the 1960s and became the Marina Hotel. The seven-hundred-dred-room Marina, located at 3805 South Las Vegas Boulevard, was built by Wiesner Investment Company and was opened in 1975.

In 1989, Wiesner and his partners sold the Marina to Kirk Kerkorian, who also bought the Tropicana Country Club, located behind the Marina and across Tropicana Avenue from the Tropicana and San Remo Hotels to obtain the site that would become the home of the MGM Grand. Kerkorian saw the Marina as a stable and solidly built resort and decided not to destroy the hotel, but to build around it. During that time, the Marina was known as the MGM-Marina Hotel.

The Marina Hotel and Casino becomes part of the
MGM Grand Hotel and Casino in 1975.

The Marina closed on November 30, 1990, and ground was broken for the new casino-hotel complex on October 7, 1991. When the latest MGM Grand opened on December 18, 1994, it was owned by MGM Grand Inc. At that time it had an extensive *The Wizard of Oz* theme, including the green "Emerald City" color of the building and the decorative use of *The Wizard of Oz* memorabilia. After entering the casino's main entrance, one would find themselves in the Oz Casino facing Emerald City. Dorothy, the Scarecrow, the Tin Man, and the Cowardly Lion were seen in front of the city. The Emerald City attraction featured an elaborate yellow-brick road walk-through, complete with the cornfield, apple orchard, and haunted forest as well as audio-animatronic figures of Dorothy, the Scarecrow, the Tin Man, the Cowardly Lion, and the Wicked Witch of the West. It would end at the door of the city, leading inside for a performance of "The Wizard's Secrets." When MGM Grand began its extensive refurbishment in 1996, the Oz Casino was the first to go. The Emerald City was demolished, and the Emerald City Gift Shop was moved to a new shopping section of the casino. The store remained open until early 2003. When the MGM Grand opened, the intention was to create a destination hotel in the Las Vegas area by including the MGM Grand Adventures Theme Park behind the casino. The plan was to make the Las Vegas Strip more family-friendly by providing activities for those too young to linger inside the casino. The theme park performed poorly and did not reopen for the 2001 season. The site was redeveloped as a luxury condominium and hotel complex called the Signature at MGM Grand opened in 2006. The resort's original entrance consisted of a giant lion head made of fiberglass and blocky in appearance with visitors entering through the lion's mouth.

The lion was a cartoonlike version of MGM's logo, Leo the Lion. The MGM Grand performed unusually poorly with Asian gamblers in its first years of existence. A study by the management found that many Chinese patrons found it bad luck to walk through the jaws of a lion and avoided the hotel as a result—part of why the entrance was renovated to remove this feature. I personally liked the original Lion entrance and the Wizard of Oz theme.

The MGM Grand Las Vegas in 1993 (*left*) and today (*right*)

My family and I enjoyed going to the MGM Grand Adventures Theme Park when we were young as it was one of the only attractions in Las Vegas for those under the age of twenty-one. The original plan for the theme park was to make it family-oriented by providing activities for children. When MGM Grand Adventures first opened, it was never really busy and lacked the quality of major theme park attractions except for one water ride and roller coaster. In 2001, the theme park was renamed as the Park at MGM Grand and served as a rental facility for corporate functions before being closed permanently in 2002. Since 2006, the property has been occupied by the Signature at MGM Grand, a luxury resort hotel addition.

Paul-Son opens an office in Reno, Nevada, in 1974.

In 1974 Paul-Son opened an office in Reno, Nevada, to serve the casinos in that city. Throughout the '70s, Reno began to visually see the industry grow as big hotels and casinos took form. Reno is the other major gambling city in Nevada. It's the perfect place for those who like to gamble in the casino but like the feel of a simpler setting. Reno isn't as big and flashy as Las Vegas, but that doesn't mean it's any less a part of gambling history in the United States. Reno is known as "the Biggest Little City in the World" and is full of casinos where you can go and find all of your favorite games. In 1931, Governor Fred Balzar signed Assembly Bill 98. This bill allowed wide-open gambling so illegal betting in the back of casinos could now be legalized and brought to the main floor and conducted with regulations. This legislation allowed gambling to boom in Reno and was the base for the gambling that's enjoyed in Reno today. Already existing card rooms, small casinos, and bingo parlors were the first to be licensed and many new gambling operators began flocking to the area to open their gambling establishments. In 1937 William Fisk Harrah opened his first bingo parlor in Reno, eventually calling it the 1938 Heart Tango. The Heart Tango location was between Virginia and Center Streets, in the heart of the Reno Casino. Over time, Harrah slowly acquired neighboring casinos adjacent to his Virginia Street casino. William Harrah slowly built his downtown operation into Harrah's Reno. Nevada Club Casino and Harrah's Club, later known as Harrah's Hotel and Casino, both opened in Reno in 1946 and have subsequently closed this year.

With such a rich history in the gambling world, it's kind of surprising that Reno hasn't become more similar to Las Vegas or Atlantic City.

It hasn't tried to change the way the city was built; instead, it has embraced its small size and used it to bring in gamblers who love the games but not the craziness of the bigger cities. During the 1970s, Reno saw a huge growth in the number of casinos opening starting with the Sands Regency. The trend continued with the Peppermill, which was designed with a Tuscany theme. It had 1,621 rooms, a spa, a health club, and an indoor pool. The Atlantis Casino Resort Spa was opened in 1972. This resort covers sixty-four thousand square feet and has a total of 824 rooms with a thirty-thousand-square-foot spa.

The next year, the Eldorado opened and had seventy-eight thousand square feet of the resort set aside for gaming space, plus a 580-seat theater.

In the same year Eddies Fabulous 50's Casino, the Onslow Hotel and Casino, the Money Tree Casino, and the Riverboat Casino were opened. Reno was busy, and my dad wanted to be part of the action.

New 1970s Reno casino chips

By 1975 the state's gambling revenue had topped the one-billion mark and was covering most of the cost of the state's budget. Also, during '75, the legislature lowered the sports betting tax that allowed for sports betting to become a part of the casino gaming floor. Reno also saw the opening of another hotel, the Sundowner Hotel and Casino.

This trend continued throughout the 1970s with other hotels like the Fitzgerald Hotel and Casino in 1976. Both casinos are now closed. Also, during this time frame, the IRS decided to jump in on the booming industry and started to require all hotels and casinos to report the winnings of players to them to allow them to track who wasn't filing accurate tax forms. Up to 1975, Reno/Sparks resorts lacked any major casino theming, However, that was about to change when MGM came to town. Three years prior in the summer of 1975, officials from the Metro-Goldwyn-Mayer Company began to scout out Reno locations for their proposed high-rise hotel-casino that they wanted to model after their very high-profile Las Vegas casino, the MGM Grand. Following a deal with and approval from the city council, MGM purchased land between Mill and 2nd Streets, at that time a gravel pit. The summer of 1976 saw construction begin on the twenty-six-story 1,015-room property with a casino two football fields long, which would then be the largest in the world! After two years of fast-tracked construction, the building opened with fanfare, fashion, and media attention on May 3, 1978.

In the summer of 1981, MGM opened an expansion of the hotel with a twenty-six-story wing plus an additional 900 rooms, making a total of 2,001 rooms and suites.

The world's largest casino opens in Reno—MGM in 1978, Bally's in 1986, becoming the Reno Hilton in 1992, and is currently the Grand Sierra Resort.

Three years later, in November of 1984, MGM revealed plans to expand the Reno Hotel further with a $60-million twenty-six-story wing with another 954 rooms, which never materialized. After fights and issues with the city council, the expansion was later approved on September 23, 1985, amid rumors the MGM would be sold. Less than five months later, on November 16, 1985, those rumors proved to be true with Bally Manufacturing announcing that it would acquire the MGM Reno and Las Vegas for $440 million, further questioning the newly approved expansion for Reno. When the MGM Grand Las Vegas ordered their casino supplies from Paul-Son, it would be our largest order ever received from a casino customer, just short of three million dollars. But it came with catch—a short delivery time. I remember my brother complaining that the factory had to work twenty-four hours just to complete the chip order.

However, my dad didn't mind as long as we got the order and not our "one friendly competitor, Bud Jones Co.," he said fictitiously. The Bud Jones Co. was a Las Vegas gaming supply company founded by Bernard "Bud" Jones in 1965 and operated until 2001. The Bud Jones Co. made an even different kind of chip than T. R. King or Paul-Son. It is manufactured with a plastic injection manufacturing process that produces chips that are more durable and virtually indestructible. The plastic is injected around a metal slug, which gives the chip its weight. Those chips were one of the only ones at the time that would work in the roulette chipper champ used on many casinos' roulette games. The chipper champ is used to automatically sort the mixed-up roulette chips and deliver them back to the dealer. Bud Jones would market their chips at a lower price than Paul-Son's; however, due to quality and slipperiness issues, the vast majority of casinos preferred Paul-Son chips.

When my dad found out through his Las Vegas connections at the Las Vegas Country Club that MGM in Reno was considering ordering their chips from Bud Jones, he was furious. His company had successfully delivered chips, casino supplies, and furniture to MGM Las Vegas five years prior after working overtime 24-7 for many months, and he thought he deserved it. After calling and asking his friend Sid Wyman, a VP at MGM Studios in Burbank, for a favor, my dad asked for a meeting at the Las Vegas Country Club in August 1977. My dad had worked with Mr. Irving years earlier at a Charity Las Vegas night at MGM Studios. Within a couple of days, after the meeting was held in Las Vegas, my dad had the chip order in hand for the MGM Reno. I will never forget that my dad told me never to ask a casino boss for a favor. "He'll want one back," he said, so I never did.

The year 1978 brought the opening of Circus Circus Reno, which was based on the successful hotel and resort that originated in Las Vegas. The resort has a total of 1,620 rooms, sixty-six thousand square feet of gaming space, thirty-three carnival games, and circus acts throughout the day for free.

Circus Circus Reno opened with Paul-Son Gaming Supplies on July 1, 1978.

As the gambling and casino industry continued to grow throughout the '70s, the dawn of the '80s shed some concern for both Reno and Las Vegas.

Atlantic City had officially legalized gaming as the '70s were wrapping up, and that meant that the legal monopoly Nevada had formed and held for forty-five years was coming to a halt.

Looking at the casino industry as a whole, this was major progress. But now this meant that gamblers didn't have to travel out west to enjoy a legal game of cards.

For Reno, the 1980s was not as successful as the years before, mostly because it was a smaller town and the newly legalized gambling laws in Atlantic City took away some of the visitors from the east coast that no longer needed to travel to Nevada to legally gamble. The state had undergone huge growth in population and revenue in the prior years, but Reno didn't have any new hotels being constructed or scheduled to open and was worried about not being able to draw in more visitors.

When my brother Patrick moved to Reno in 1974 to manage the Paul-Son office, I would see and help him quite often while I attended the University of Nevada in Reno. We would often have the pan roast at John Ascuaga's Nugget when it was cold and snowing in Reno. Patrick would live in Reno until that fateful day on May 13, 1993, when our brother Tommy passed away. It would be my father's second-worst day of his life. My brother Pat would move back to Las Vegas, and I would officially join Paul-Son at my father's request. At about the same time in 1993, my dad decided that he didn't want to keep going out to eat for lunch and wanted a more convenient location. That location would be Toby's Deli and would be right next door to Paul-Son at 2121 Industrial Road. My father met Toby, a former chef, when he was introduced to him by Geno Munari, who was the casino manager at the Astro Hotel at the time. Geno Munari was both a friend of my brother Tom and my father. He was involved in all facets of the gambling and hospitality business and obtained a nonrestricted gaming license in the 1970s for Cowboy Gene's Casino. Also, he worked at the Dunes Hotel for eight years. He also helped develop the San Remo, Bourbon Street, and the Astro Hotel. During the same year, Geno, my wife, and I opened Paul-Son School of Gaming right next door to Paul-Son and the restaurant.

I liked the convenience of going right next door for lunch, and we could also invite casino customers as well. However, when my father decided to expand the lunch deli into a dinner restaurant, I wasn't too happy. He told my brother and me that we would open Pablo's Mexican Restaurant at night with an all-you-can-eat taco bar and that we would work at the restaurant when we were done for the day at Paul-Son. The taco bar would be inside a Paul-Son craps table. Now not only did I give up audiology for Paul-Son but now I also would have to work at a restaurant at night! We eventually had to put a limit on the all-you-can-eat taco bar when a repeat customer made twenty trips to the taco bar in one night. However, we continually lacked customers at night because of where the restaurant was located on Industrial Road, which was dark and secluded in the "Naked City" area. Naked City is a neighborhood located in Las Vegas, Nevada, north of the Strip and near the intersection of Las Vegas Boulevard and Sahara Avenue. We eventually closed Pablo's at night and changed the name to Ernie's Deli, another friend of a friend of my dad's.

The MGM Grand Las Vegas fire on November 21, 1980

One of Las Vegas's biggest tragedy was when the MGM Grand fire occurred on Friday, November 21, 1980, at 7:07 a.m. at the MGM Grand Hotel and Casino in Las Vega, Nevada. The fire killed 85 people mostly through smoke inhalation. The tragedy remains the deadliest disaster in Nevada history and the third-deadliest hotel fire in modern US history after the 1946 Winecoff Hotel fire in Atlanta that killed 119 people and the San Juan (Puerto Rico) Dupont Plaza Hotel fire on December 31, 1986, in which 97 perished. At the time of the fire, about 5,000 people were in the hotel and casino, a twenty-six-story luxury resort with more than two thousand hotel rooms. At approximately 7:07 a.m. on Friday, November 21, 1980, a fire began in a restaurant known as the Deli. The fire was caused by an electrical ground fault inside a wall socket. The fire was confined to the casino and restaurant areas.

The hotel (originally built in 1973) was repaired and improved, including the addition of fire sprinklers and an automatic fire alarm system throughout the property.

When I received a call from my dad at 7:30 a.m. on November 21, 1980, to meet him at the MGM Grand, I knew there was something wrong—dead wrong. I just heard on the news that there was a fire at the hotel and that my dad wanted to meet him there of all places. He insisted that the casino manager needed his order of dice and "couldn't wait. He's out." My dad told me to park across the street at the Barbary Coast, saying, "Michael Gaughan, the owner of the Coast, will let us park there."

The Barbary Coast Hotel and Casino was the site of Empey's Desert Villa from 1952, and in 1979 it became Barbary Coast. The casino was built by Michael Gaughan and opened on March 2, 1979, for $11.5 million. Over time, this property, along with others owned by Gaughan, would become Coast Casinos Inc Gaughan shared partnership in the Barbary Coast with Kenny Epstein, Tito Tiberti, Frank Toti, and Jerry Herbst. In July 2005, Boyd Gaming purchased the Barbary Coast Hotel. In September 2005, Boyd purchased the 4.3 acres (1.7 hectares) of land the hotel occupied for $16 million. The hotel had previously been leasing the land. In 2007, Boyd gave the Barbary Coast to Harrah's Entertainment in exchange for the 11-acre (4.5-hectare) site of the demolished Westward Ho! to be used for the Echelon Place project. The Barbary Coast closed at 2:00 a.m. on February 27 and reopened on March 1 as the newly rebranded Bill's Gamblin' Hall and Saloon in honor of company founder, Bill Harrah.

After nearly six years of continuous operations, Bill's closed on February 4, 2013, for complete renovation into a luxury boutique hotel. Plans called for a complete renovation of the entire property, the guest rooms and casino floor, a new restaurant, and the construction of a sixty-five-thousand-square-foot rooftop pool and day club/nightclub. Caesars announced in March 2013 that the hotel would be renovated for $185 million and converted to an outpost of the New York-based Gansevoort Hotels chain of boutique luxury hotels with 188 rooms, a forty-thousand-square-foot casino, and a sixty-five-thousand-square-foot indoor/outdoor beach club/nightclub overseen by Victor Drai. In October 2013, however, Caesars terminated its agreement with Gansevoort and said that it would continue the redevelopment of Bill's without the Gansevoort name. The move came after Massachusetts gambling regulators recommended denying Caesars a license for a proposed casino at the Suffolk Downs racetrack due to alleged connections between one of the Gansevoort's investors and the Russian Mafia. Plans announced in late 2013 indicated that Giada De Laurentiis would open her first restaurant in the new hotel and that Caesars would run the hotel. Caesars confirmed on January 31, 2014, that the hotel would be named the Cromwell. It marked its soft opening to guests on April 21, 2014. The hotel rooms were available starting May 21, 2014.

When we arrived at the MGM Grand, I couldn't believe that I was the one cautioning my dad that it was dangerous since "the Grand is on fire, and we really shouldn't go!" But my father insisted and said, "If you don't want to go, it's okay. But I'm going. He's a great customer." I knew my dad wanted me to go with him, so I begrudgingly went. After parking at the Barbary Coast and locating my father at the valet, we ran across the street with the Grand's 500 pair-dice order.

We were immediately stopped at the hotel's front door by Las Vegas Metro Police and security. "I don't think dice are Mr. Jaeger's main concern right now if you can't tell this joint is on fire," angrily replied the security guard. "I can take the dice, but I can't let you in."

Dad quickly responded, "Can you get Jaeger on your walkie-talkie? I want to make sure he knows I was here."

"I can try, but I can't guarantee it," the guard replied as his walkie talkie blurted out, "Customers are now jumping off the hotel tower. OMG."

The security guard signed the delivery slip for the dice, and we quickly scurried back across the street to the Coast. My dad's final comment before we got in our cars was, "I sure hope Jaeger gets his dice." In the end, it wasn't about the danger, the fire, or the jumping that my father was most concerned about; it was about his customer. He was dedicated to a fault in taking care of his clients no matter what even if it meant delivering dice during a fire! It wouldn't be his only time facing a firestorm.

In the early 1970s, Bob Stupak purchased 1.5 acres of land at 2000 South Las Vegas Boulevard, located north of the Sahara Hotel and Casino and the Las Vegas Strip, in a seedy part of the city. The land was occupied by the Todkill/Bill Hayden Lincoln Mercury Dealership and was purchased by Stupak for $218,000 with money he raised himself and from his father's friends. On March 31, 1974, he opened a small casino called Bob Stupak's World Famous Million-Dollar Historic Gambling Museum and Casino. Stupak said, "The name was about ten feet longer than the casino." The casino featured fifteen slot machines, including a quarter slot that offered a $250,000 jackpot and a nickel slot that advertised a $50,000 payout. The casino also featured various memorabilia, including antique slot machines, a gambling chip collection, and photographs of former gambling figures such as Bugsy Siegel. The casino's floors and walls were papered with $1 bills that were covered by plastic. The casino also featured a $100,000 bill. Shortly before 8:00 p.m. on May 21, 1974, a fire broke out at the casino. Nine fire units responded. Thirty-five firefighters battled the fire for several hours, during which a section of South Las Vegas Boulevard had to be closed. The fire was visible for several miles throughout the Las Vegas Valley. The casino was destroyed, although firefighters successfully saved most of the money attached to the casino's walls. The fire was believed to have been caused by an air conditioner. Stupak's insurance company, the San Francisco-based Fireman's Fund American Insurance Company, suspected Stupak of arson and filed a suit against him in June 1975, alleging that he burned down his casino to collect insurance money of $300,000. The insurance company eventually settled the claim.

After the fire, Stupak managed to persuade Valley Bank to lend him more than $1 million to complete what would be known as Vegas World. Groundbreaking was scheduled to begin on June 22, 1978, on the same property occupied by Stupak's previous casino. Stupak opened the space-themed Vegas World on July 13, 1979, with ninety hotel rooms in an eight-story tower and a 15,000-square-foot (1,400-square-meter) casino. Construction cost $7 million.

Bob Stupak's Vegas World opened in 1978
(*left*) and closed in 1995 (*right*).

Vegas World debuted with the slogan "The Sky's the Limit."
At first, Vegas World suffered, only making $7 million in revenue
its first year. However, at its peak, Vegas World made $100 million a
year in gambling revenues. This time, however, it wouldn't be a fire
that would upset my father; but it would be Bob Stupak's bill. One
day before the Vegas World's grand opening, I was nervous because
their chips were ready to be delivered but Bob Stupak wasn't returning my calls. As I waited impatiently, I finally received a call from
him saying that he was ready to receive the chips. I told to him that
my father said I would need to be paid in cash when I delivered his
chips. Before he hung up the phone in a rush, he said I could deliver
the chips and that he would be at the hotel the rest of the day to
receive them.

My father told me, "Load his chips into your truck, take them
to the casino cage, and don't forget to get the balance in cash first
before you count them in and deliver them. Do you understand me,
son? I don't trust Stupak. I don't think he has the money to make it.
He's in way over his head financed by Valley Bank."

I told my dad, "Okay," and that I would call him if I had any
problems.

When I arrived at Vegas World, I was greeted by a security
guard at the front entrance who notified the casino cage that I was
there and needed to pick up the balance for the chips in cash. The
cage manager told security he didn't have it and would have to get

ahold of Mr. Stupak. After waiting for about an hour, a seemingly embarrassed Bob Stupak greeted me at the front door. "Hey, kid, do you have my gaming chips? You know, I open my casino tomorrow."

"Yes, Mr. Stupak," I replied. "But my father said I need to collect cash for the balance, $5,450.50."

"Oh, I think he's mistaken, son. I have good credit. Open account and I will send a check later," he insisted.

I stepped aside and called my dad, who told me to either get the cash or bring the chips back to Paul-Son, no exceptions. I told Mr. Stupak, "I can't count the chips in without the money first, per my dad."

"Oh yeah? Are you sure he said that about me? I'm going to go see him right now," replied Stupak. Stupak followed me back to Paul-Son, only a couple blocks away from his hotel, in his brand-new silver Rolls-Royce. When we entered the office, my dad was sitting at his desk waiting for us, and Sheriff Ralph Lamb was sitting right next to him.

"Good day, Sheriff," said Bob Stupak and I almost simultaneously.

"Have a seat, Mr. Stupak," Dad said, always courteous to even his worst customers.

Stupak began to pound his fist on my father's desk, complaining about having to pay cash for his chips. Every time he pounded on my dad's desk, Dad's face became redder and redder. Stupak told my dad that he had good credit, that he shouldn't have to pay cash and he threw his car keys on my father's desk. "If you don't trust me, Paul, you can have the keys to my car."

My father jumped out of his chair, walked to the front of his desk and, nose to nose with Stupak, said, "I don't want your car, anyway. I know it's leased from Valley Bank anyway."

Sheriff Lamb added, "Bob, just pay for your chips, and everything will be good."

"Okay, you win. I'll pay cash this time. Have your son follow me back to the hotel, and I'll pay him," Stupak blurted out.

This time, my father had the sheriff accompany me just in case I had any problems with Stupak. When we arrived back at Vegas World, Sheriff Lamb and I followed Stupak to his casino vault, where he prudently began counting hundred-dollar bills in front of me until only fifty cents were left.

"Well, I guess that's for Uncle Sam, right?" he said. "It's all there, kid. A total of $5,450.50, right, Sheriff?"

As we walked toward the exit of the property still under some construction, Sheriff Lamb told me, "Be careful with the cash, and say hi to your dad."

I knew the Sheriff had better things to do than protect me, so I thanked him for his help and voted for him in the next election and, of course, so did my dad, in addition to a donation to his reelection fund. Paul-Son would continue to have a relationship with the sheriff because in the same year Patrick hired his brother, Larry Lamb, to work in our dice department. Vegas World closed on February 1, 1995, to be remodeled and integrated into Stupak's new project, the Stratosphere.

Stratosphere opened in 1996 and became the Strat in 2020.

The Strat Hotel, Casino and SkyPod (formerly the Stratosphere) is a hotel, casino, and tower located on Las Vegas Boulevard just north of the Las Vegas Strip in Las Vegas, Nevada, United States. The Stratosphere opened on April 30, 1996. In March 2018, Golden

Entertainment announced plans for a $140-million renovation of the Stratosphere that will be unveiled in three phases. The Strat is owned and operated by Golden Entertainment, which acquired the resort and three other properties from American Casino & Entertainment Properties for $850 million in 2017. The property's signature attraction is the 1,149-feet (350.2-meter) Stratosphere Tower, the tallest freestanding observation tower in the United States and the second-tallest in the Western Hemisphere, surpassed only by the CNN Tower in Toronto, Ontario. It is the tallest tower west of the Mississippi River and also the tallest structure in Las Vegas and the state of Nevada.

CHAPTER 12

Paul-Son arrives in Atlantic City

In 1979, he was a casino owner in Atlantic City. In
2016, he became our forty-fifth US president.

Paul-Son received a major boost later during the decade when New
Jersey legalized casino gaming in Atlantic City in 1978. According to
Forbes, Paul-Son held a major advantage entering this market, "a known
record in the business where huge amounts of cash change hands and
tamper-proof equipment are imperative," said Endy. "In this business,
they [casino operators] want to know who they're doing business with."
However, getting to Atlantic City, to either open an office or to see a
customer would prove to be a major challenge for my father due to his
fear of flying. In 1974, Nevada was the only state with legal casino gambling and New Jersey voters voted against legalizing casino gambling
statewide. However, two years later approved in an effort at revitaliz-
ing the city, New Jersey voters in 1976 passed a referendum approving
casino gambling for Atlantic City. This came after a 1974 referendum
on legalized gambling failed to pass. Immediately after the legislation
passed, the owners of the Chalfonte-Haddon Hall Hotel began con-

verting it into the Resorts International. It was the first legal casino in the Eastern United States when it opened on May 26, 1978.

Other casinos were soon constructed along the Boardwalk and later in the marina district for a total of eleven today. The introduction of gambling did not, however, quickly eliminate many of the urban problems that plagued Atlantic City. Many people have suggested that it only served to exacerbate those problems as attested to by the stark contrast between tourism intensive areas and the adjacent impoverished working-class neighborhoods. Also, Atlantic City has been less popular than Las Vegas as a gambling city in the United States. Donald Trump helped bring big-name boxing bouts to the city to attract customers to his casinos. The boxer Mike Tyson had most of his fights in Atlantic City in the 1980s, which helped Atlantic City achieve nationwide attention as a gambling resort. Numerous high-rise condominiums were built for use as permanent residences or second homes. By end of the decade, it was one of the most popular tourist destinations in the United States.

In the Roaring Twenties, Atlantic City was the place to be. With the Prohibition largely unenforced, the city's famous boardwalk was teeming with hedonists on a weekend away, ordinary Joes, politicians, and the Mafia all hitting the casinos and brothels together. Atlantic City is a resort city in Atlantic County, New Jersey, the United States, known for its casinos, boardwalk, and beaches. In 2010, the city had a population of 39,558. It was incorporated on May 1, 1854, from portions of Egg Harbor Township and Gallow Township. It borders Absecon, Brigantine, Pleasantville, Ventnor City, Egg Harbor Township, and the Atlantic Ocean. Atlantic City inspired the US version of the board game *Monopoly*, especially the street names. Since 1921, Atlantic City has been the home of the Miss America pageant. In 1976, New Jersey voters legalized casino gambling in Atlantic City. The first casino opened two years later.

In 1978, Resorts Atlantic City, which still operates from the same Boardwalk location to this day, became the first legalized Atlantic City casino to open to the public.

By the close of the 1970s, Caesars Boardwalk Regency, which would later become Caesars Atlantic City; and Bally's Park Place, which would later become Bally's Grand Atlantic City, had opened their doors as well.

In the summer of 1978, after graduating from the University of Nevada, I stayed in Reno, working part-time at Circus Circus valet parking cars or working at Paul-Son's branch office in downtown Reno. I received a surprising call from my father in Las Vegas telling me that he was going to Atlantic City to open an office and visit an unhappy customer and wanted to know if I wanted to go. The coup de grâce was that he would be driving to Atlantic City from Las Vegas. Even though I was happy that he asked me to go with him, I was concerned because my dad was a heavy cigarette smoker. He was a heavy smoker as in a chain, especially when he was driving. I reluctantly decided to go with him but would regret my decision later. On a hot August Monday morning in 1978, my dad and I loaded a one-way moving van with everything we could to open an office in Atlantic City.

Paul-Son opens an office in Atlantic City in 1978.

I remember that all I could think of was how long it would take us to get there, smoking and all. I didn't smoke and just the smell of tobacco made me cough. It was 2,532 miles from Las Vegas to Atlantic City, or thirty-seven hours driving time. Even if we drove eight hours a day it would still take us over four days to get there. Thankfully my father had invited another driver, employee Henry, to go with us and help drive, but that meant I had to sit in the middle, closer to the smoke, since at some point, they both smoked at the same time. I made it a total of 1,222 miles or a total of seventeen hours when I decided to leave the truck and fly to Atlantic City from Dallas, Texas. I thought my dad would be mad at me for leaving him, but surprisingly he wasn't; as a matter of fact, he liked that I would get to Atlantic City before him. He instructed me to call Merv Griffin at Resorts International when I arrived and set up a meeting with him in three days.

"Two days? You won't be there in two days," I told my dad.

He immediately barked back at me, "You want to bet?"

I wouldn't take the bet because I knew they would drive straight through, and I just was glad that I wasn't coughing as I exited the truck. Resorts Casino Hotel, the first casino hotel in Atlantic City, also became the first legal casino outside of Nevada in the United States when it opened on May 26, 1978. The resort completed an expansion in 2004, adding the twenty-seven-story Rendezvous Tower, and underwent renovations in 2011, converting the resort to a Roaring-Twenties theme. Resorts International, which was formed in March 1968, first became interested in developing a resort in Atlantic City after the company learned of a planned fourth attempt to bring casino gambling to New Jersey by limiting it to Atlantic City. The company heavily contributed to the November 1976 gaming referendum which successfully passed that year. While campaigning for the gaming initiative, Resorts International also began planning for a future Atlantic City casino by securing an option for fifty-five acres of land on the Atlantic City Boardwalk from the city's Housing and Redevelopment Authority as well as acquiring Leeds & Lippincott Company, which owned the property before Resorts. Resorts purchased 67 percent of Leeds & Lippincott Company in August 1976 and completed the acquisition the following month, paying a total of $2.489 million before again being renamed Resorts International Hotel on July 1, 1977. Resorts International's new casino opened its doors at 10:00 a.m. on May 26, 1978. Initial gaming laws in New Jersey only allowed casinos to operate for eighteen hours during the week and twenty hours during the weekends. People waited for hours for a chance to play the eighty-four table games and 893 slots within the 33,735 square feet of casino space. The Resorts casino floor was open from 10:00 a.m. to 4:00 a.m. The one exception was on Saturdays, Sundays, and federal holidays when it remained open until 6:00 a.m. The developers spent $45.2 million to refurbish the old Chalfonte-Haddon Hotel with total expenditures of $77 million. The debt was totally repaid eleven months later! Resorts had first-year gross revenues of $224.6 million and a win of $62.8 million. That first year, the state of New Jersey collected $18 million in taxes.

The first acts in the hotel's 1,700-seat Super Star Theater were Steve Lawrence and Edie Gorme with Lawrence throwing out the first dice roll at one of the casino's craps tables.

Resorts International would have a monopoly in Atlantic City as the only casino allowed to open for one full year. Following a takeover target by Donald Trump, Merv Griffin, the popular game show celebrity, through his Griffin Gaming & Entertainment Inc., made a bid and purchased all of the stock in Resorts International. The casino later became the location for filming Merv Griffin's variety game show *Ruckus*. When I arrived in Atlantic City, I took a cab to Resorts International and headed to the registration desk. There were lines everywhere, but the line leading into the casino must have been a mile long stretching down the boardwalk! There were two security guards at the casino entrance checking IDs and allowing casino patrons in one at a time. I overheard one of them tell a casino customer, "If you leave the casino, you can't come back in without waiting in line."

"Wow, what a business," I thought as I made my way finally to my room after it took more than an hour to check in.

Resorts International opened to large crowds in 1978.

After getting settled in my room per my dad's instructions, I called Merv Griffin's office and set up an appointment in three days at 2:00 p.m., giving my father a little more time on the road just in case he needed it. He didn't need it as he called me the next day to find out what time I set up the appointment. I immediately called Griffin's office back and changed the appointment to the next day, which his secretary Betty did without objection. When my father arrived at Resorts, I met him in the executive offices promptly at 2:00 p.m. When we met Merv Griffin, I was somewhat intimidated by his presence. I mean who in America hadn't seen him as a game show host or ever watched his television shows *Jeopardy* or *Wheel of Fortune* while growing up? However, he now was a casino owner/operator, and he wasn't happy. Griffin reached his hand out to shake ours and introduced us to his casino manager Irv Rogers. "Mr. Paul-Son, we have a serious problem here, and it's on you," said Mr. Griffin. "We ordered all of our casino equipment from your company, and now it's all falling apart."

My father was shocked, to say the least, and told Griffin his last name was Endy and questioned him as to what equipment was falling apart.

Mr. Griffin said all of the seating around the tables was "break-ing down". After Mr. Griffin introduced us to his casino manager Mr. Irv Rogers, my dad asked "Is there a blackjack stool up here in your office we can look at?" Merv Griffin replied that there wasn't and that we would have to go down to the casino floor, which is what we did. The casino was packed that night as usual with casino patrons not only sitting at the tables but also standing behind them, placing as many bets as possible. I had never seen so many people gamble in my lifetime, even after living in Las Vegas. We weren't able to get to an unseated stool but noticed a strange smell as we got closer to the table. My dad immediately recognized the odor and reached his hand out to touch an unoccupied seat that became available for just a moment, and it was somewhat wet. As if a lightbulb had just gone off, my dad said he knew what it was but needed the lab to verify his hunch. When George Gasser arrived around 8:00 p.m., we went to dinner at the hotel to discuss our findings and what our next plan would be for Griffin. When the lab results arrived the next day, they verified what my dad had suspected. It was urine, and it was the casino's fault, not Paul-Son's. We met with Griffin and Rogers the next morning to reveal the lab results. The casino had a fire marshall requirement that only a certain number of casino patrons were allowed in the casino and the casino had a further restriction as well. Unlike in Las Vegas, if a casino patron had to leave a gaming table to "use the bathroom," they would lose their place at the table. As a result, Resorts' customers were instead urinating on the stools at the table rather than losing their gaming position, which just didn't seem right.

Also, all the gaming stools were originally ordered with a fabric seat cover instead of a typical leather cover that Las Vegas casinos ordered. This allowed the urine to further penetrate the chair and destroy the material. Griffin didn't initially believe my father's findings, but once he saw the lab results and felt the "wet" fabric, he was finally convinced, and he was embarrassed. He apologized for "their problem" and asked my dad and Mr. Gasser for their recommendations. Gasser said they would work with Resorts and prebuild new seat covers for the casino seating and exchange them for a small fee. Griffin and Irv both appreciated their efforts and agreed to the plan going forward. Also, my dad said the new cushions should be leather or leatherette like all the other casinos and not fabric that was previously ordered. Griffin firmly agreed and said, "That was our first mistake."

Trump Entertainment Resorts Inc. is a gambling and hospitality company that currently does not own or operate any properties in Atlantic City, New Jersey, owned by Donald J. Trump. The company previously owned and operated the now-renamed and the shuttered Trump Taj Mahal, Trump Plaza, the demolished Trump World's Fair, the renamed Trump Marina, Trump Lake Michigan, and the renamed Trump 29. The company filed for bankruptcy in 2004, 2009, and 2014. Trump Entertainment Resorts currently owns one property, Trump Plaza Hotel and Casino, which is currently shuttered and vacant. Trump Entertainment Resorts and its predecessors have filed for Chapter 11 bankruptcy protection four times in 1991 (following the construction of the $1-billion Trump Taj Mahal) and 2004, 2009, and 2014. In 2004, Trump Hotels & Casino Resorts explored various options for restructuring its debt, amid speculation that it might file for bankruptcy. A possible arrangement with Credit Suisse First Boston was not completed because the bondholders rejected it. In February 2013, the company agreed to sell the Trump Plaza for $20 million to the Meruelo Group, a California-based company whose holdings include the Grand Sierra Resort in Reno, Nevada. The proceeds would be used to pay down the company's debt to a level of $270 million. CEO Robert Griffin said that TER would consider also selling the Trump Taj Mahal for the right price. However, Carl Icahn, who held the mortgage on the Trump casinos, would reject the sale of the Trump Plaza. In early August 2014, Donald Trump filed a lawsuit demanding the removal of his name from the company's two casinos because they had allegedly been allowed to fall into disrepair in breach of the licensing agreement for Trump's name. In September 2014, Trump Entertainment Resorts filed again for bankruptcy and closed the Trump Plaza. When Donald Trump opened the towering Trump Taj Mahal Casino in Atlantic City in March 1990, he declared it as "the eighth wonder of the world" and joined in the celebrations at a launch ceremony filled with portly actors dressed as genies brandishing tacky golden lamps even though it was purchased with almost $700 million worth of junk bonds, which meant the Taj had to come up with $94 million a year just to pay off its debts and $1 million a day to be profitable. Trump insisted the casino would make Atlantic City great again, returning the area to its Prohibition-era glory days. I find it more than coincidental that Donald Trump used the same motto, "Make Atlantic City Great Again," just as he used it in his presidential campaign to "Make America Great Again." At one point, Trump had three casinos in Atlantic City, employing eight thousand people and accounting for nearly a third of the area's gambling revenues. But they eventually became unsustainable thanks to a mixture of enormous debts, rival venues, weak local demand, and negative press, which suggested Trump's businesses were facilitating money laundering, something that was later given credence when the Taj was fined $10 million for failing to report suspicious transactions.

Two, the Trump Castle and the Taj now have new owners; but the famous Trump Plaza, which once hosted WrestleMania and Mike Tyson fights, stands derelict and is set to be demolished. Donald Trump took "incredible" amounts of money out of Atlantic City, borrowing cash from third parties so his own wealth wasn't affected by his various businesses going under. According to Rose, his legacy is best reflected by Atlantic City's 7.4 percent unemployment rate nearly double the national average. "When Trump failed with his casinos," said Brian Rose of *The Guardian*, "he turned Atlantic City into a ghost town. His legacy still haunts the boardwalk. Tourists go to Atlantic City, go straight into their hotel and the casino, and then they don't leave, which means the town outside is very isolated and dangerous with the casinos cannibalizing all the local businesses. Drug use and crime are so high, and this is something we see in other American cities too like Baltimore and Cleveland, where a commercial center dwarfs the rest of the society." It would be unfair, however, to put the blame solely on the forty-fifth president of the United States. One of the reasons Atlantic City's gambling industry started to fail was because the New Jersey town was no longer the only major draw on the eastern seaboard with Pennsylvania and Connecticut offering attractive alternatives. As an interesting note, Caesars in

Atlantic City is acknowledged as the first casino to introduce a commemorative chip to the Boardwalk.

Donald Trump's first three casinos in Atlantic City. All three casinos owned by Trump are now demolished or under new ownership.

The fact that the coast is freezing cold for at least two-thirds of the year also makes it a gray and isolated place. Nor were Trump's the only casinos to close. The Revel was another expensive failure, and there will undoubtedly be more in the future.

CHAPTER 13

The History of Paul-Son Playing Cards

Playing cards were invented by the Chinese before AD 1000 during the Tang dynasty around the AD ninth century as a result of the usage of woodblock printing technology. The first possible reference to card games comes from a ninth-century text known as the *Collection of Miscellanea at Duyang* written by Tang dynasty writer Su Zhe. It describes Princess Tongchang, daughter of Emperor Yizong of Tang, playing the "leaf game" in 868 with members of the Wei clan, the family of the princess's husband. The first known book on the leaf game was called the *Yezi Gexi* and allegedly written by a Tang woman. It received commentary by writers of subsequent dynasties. The Song dynasty (960–1279) scholar Ouyang Xiu (1007–1072) asserts that the leaf game existed at least since the mid-Tang dynasty and associated its invention with the development of printed sheets as a writing medium.

However, Ouyang also claimed that the "leaves" were pages of a book used in a board game played with dice and that the rules of the game were lost by 1067.

They reached Europe around 1360 not directly from China but the Mameluke Empire of Egypt. The history of suit marks demonstrates a fascinating interplay between words, shapes, and concepts. A playing card is a piece of specially prepared card stock, heavy paper, thin cardboard, plastic-coated paper, cotton-paper blend, or thin plastic that is marked with distinguishing motifs. Often the front (face) and back of each card have a finish to make handling easier. They are most commonly used for playing card games, and are also used in magic tricks, cardistry, card throwing, and card houses. Cards may also be collected. Some types of cards such as tarot cards are also used for divination. Other games revolving around alcoholic drinking involved using playing cards of a sort from the Tang dynasty onward. However, these cards did not contain suits or numbers. Instead, they were printed with instructions or forfeits for whoever drew them. The Cloisters set of fifty-two playing cards is currently accepted as the oldest complete deck of playing cards in the world, estimated to be made between 1470 and 1480.

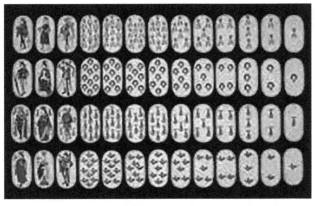

The Cloisters set of fifty-two playing cards (1470–1480), the oldest deck of playing cards

The earliest dated instance of a game involving playing cards occurred on July 17, 1294, when "Yan Sengzhu and Zheng Pig-Dog were caught playing cards [zhi pai] and that wood blocks for printing them had been impounded, together with nine of the actual cards." William Henry Wilkinson suggests that the first cards may have been actual paper currency which doubled as both the tools of gaming and the stakes being played for similar to trading card games. Using paper money was inconvenient and risky so they were substituted by play money known as "money cards." One of the earliest games in which we know the rules is madiao, a trick-taking game, which dates to the Ming Dynasty (1368–1644). Fifteenth-century scholar Lu described it is as being played with thirty-eight "money cards" divided into four suits. Rong described it is as being played with thirty-eight "money cards" divided into four suits, nine in coins, nine in strings of coins. They may have been misinterpreted as sticks from crude drawings, nine in myriads (of coins or strings), and eleven in tens of myriads (a myriad is one thousand). The two latter suits had *Water Margin* characters instead of pips on them with Chinese to mark their rank and suit. The suit of coins is in reverse order with nine of coins being the lowest going up to one of coins as the high card. Playing cards are typically palm-sized for convenient handling and are usually sold together in a set as a deck of cards or pack of cards. Unless you grew up under a rock, almost everyone has played a game of cards however casino cards are somewhat different. Since the outcome of a black-jack or baccarat game is determined by the player's hand, playing cards must be manufactured with the highest quality and security. In 1980 my dad structured a distributorship business deal with George Mattison, whose name represented Gemaco, a licensed fast-growing playing card company in Independence, Missouri. Gemaco would settle for being second in playing card sales behind the industry giant US Playing Card Company and their well-accepted casino "Bee" brand.

Gemaco brand casino playing cards.

Paul-Son would help improve the quality of the Gemaco playing cards and sell them exclusively to the growing gambling industry in Nevada and New Jersey except for existing casinos that were already buying from Gemaco. George Mattison became infuriated that casino customers, especially in Atlantic City, were taking sometimes up to sixty days to pay Paul-Son for their cards and then pay Gemaco for his product. When George Mattison blamed Paul-Son for "holding hostage" his money, my father immediately terminated the distributorship and began looking for another playing card company. This time it would be a Paul-Son brand playing card. Two years after terminating his "deal" with Gemaco, my dad purchased a struggling playing card company, VII, in Las Vegas. To accommodate the massive playing card printing presses and inventory, Paul Endy had to sell his lucky 2121 address, and he didn't like it. To consolidate the additional playing card manufacturing, my dad only had to look further north on Industrial Road. Fortunately, Las Vegas Color Graphics, a printing company at 1700 Industrial Road, was moving to Henderson and needed to sell their oversize building as soon as possible. My dad was able to strike a deal, get a line of credit, and move into the building over the weekend. He had to move as quickly as possible to service his customers.

Paul-Son manufactured paper playing cards and distributed plastic playing cards from KEM Plastic Playing Card Company in Poughkeepsie, Ohio. KEM Company began producing playing cards during the first half of the 1930s. The company's proprietary manufacturing methods gave KEM cards the enviable title of the first mass-produced plastic playing card. Made of cellulose acetate, KEM cards were bendable, washable, and retained their shape long after paper-based cards had withered and died.

KEM's unique polymer gave the cards their distinctive texture, snap, and handle. Unlike other cards, KEM cards were able to withstand the occasional spilled beer, making them an instant hit with seasoned poker players. KEM cards gained substantial popularity during the Second World War as troops gathered in barracks across Europe to play stud, draw, and other poker games. The cards could withstand the humidity of jungle weather and were less affected by desert sand and grit. KEM cards set the standard for poker card design. In fact, KEM'S red and blue arrow design is arguably the most well-known card design in the world and has become an icon for poker players across the globe. This design was featured in the 1998 movie *Rounders* in which Matt Damon battled John Malkovich in an underground card room in New York City. For seventy years, KEM cards ruled the plastic playing card industry. The company experienced great success through the 1950s and 1960s. Then in 2004, after many years of success, KEM cards sold their plants and copyrighted artwork to the US Playing Card Company. This historic corporate purchase left the industry with a shortage of plastic playing cards. Finally, after almost two years of silence, the presses once again began churning and the US Playing Card Company began rereleasing KEM's vintage Arrow and Paisley designs. In 2007, KEM was selected as the official playing card of the World Series of Poker. This signified that the KEM Brand was once again the top runner when it came to card games. Since then, KEM has been happy to remain the official playing card of the greatest poker tournament ever. My dad started selling KEM plastic playing cards when he first worked for his father at T. R. King & Co. Paul-Son would eventually make their own brand of plastic playing cards in the future.

PAUL-SON PLAYING CARDS, INC.
MADE IN NEVADA, "PLAYED THE WORLD OVER

Established in 1988 Paul-Son Playing Cards, Inc. Has become the largest manufacturer of casino playing cards in the West, and the fourth largest in the United States. Adhering to a high standard of service, reliability, and quality control we have gained acceptance in casinos throughout North America, the Far East, Europe and the Caribbean.

Paul-Son's first deck of paper playing cards was the Park Casino.

The Park Hotel and Casino in Downtown Las Vegas was formerly the Holiday International (1977–1987) and was then remodeled again to become the Main Street Station (1991–present).

In 1984 my dad decided to move the playing card factory to Mexico. The large printing presses and coating machines needed more space and more employees to operate and inspect the playing cards for defects. Also, since manufacturing playing cards was extremely labor-intensive, the Mexico factory provided an abundance of employees at $3 per hour, including all benefits. As a result, the playing card manufacturing was moved to San Luis, Mexico, and is still there today manufactured in building number 2.

The 1980s and 1990s saw the rise of the big resorts that make up much of Vegas today, such as the MGM Grand, the Bellagio, and Treasure Island. In 1982, much of our manufacturing was moved to San Luis, Mexico, close to the Arizona border, to save labor and cut costs. The "Mafia/Rat Pack" Las Vegas of the mid-twentieth century came to a gradual end in the 1980s with the aging out of the World War II generation, the decline of organized crime elements, and the rise of baby-boom entrepreneurs who began a new chapter in the city's history, the so-called megaresort era. Las Vegas began to become a more commercialized, family-oriented place with large corporations coming to own the hotels, casinos, and nightclubs in place of Mafia bosses. The megaresort era kicked off in 1989 with the construction of the Mirage. Built by developer Steve Wynn, it was the first resort built with money from Wall Street, selling $630 million in junk bonds.

The Mirage opened November 22, 1989.

The Mirage's 3,044 rooms, each with gold-tinted windows, set a new standard for Vegas luxury and attracted tourists in droves, leading to additional financing and rapid growth on the Las Vegas Strip. More landmark hotels and other structures were razed to make way for ever-larger and more opulent resorts. With the growth of casinos in Las Vegas and the many employee benefits they offered, my dad found it more and more difficult to hire workers. Fortunately, Nellis Air Force base provided the bulk of its spouses as part-time employees, which is just what Paul-Son needed during this rapid casino growth period, but it wasn't enough. Also, my dad saw that major manufacturers in the US, such as automakers, were setting up plants off-shore; so he decided to evaluate transferring manufacturing operations to Mexico. Since most Paul-Son products at the time were produced by hand in particular chips, it made sense to manufacture them outside the United States. My dad always said that "any product that requires more than 50 percent labor should be manufactured in Mexico." When my father returned from a fishing trip, he stopped in San Luis Mexico and, upon meeting his future general manager Francisco Moreno, decided to move his manufacturing there. Eventually, in 1982, most of the manufacturing was moved to San Luis, Mexico, close to the Arizona border to cut costs. Only playing cards and felt table layouts continued to be produced in Las Vegas. As a result, Paul-Son was able to lower prices and gain a competitive edge. Aside from the price, the company also produced high-quality products, which were becoming increasingly more popular and more sophisticated. The type of playing cards that Paul-Son produced was paper used exclusively in blackjack and baccarat. However, Paul-Son also distributed Kem plastic playing cards for poker that were expensive and were also having quality problems at the time. My dad's search for a new plastic playing card would lead me to Mr. Yamamoto at Ace Playing Card Company in Kyoto, Japan, in 1983. Yamamoto had been referred to my dad by a customer in Aruba who had successfully used Ace playing cards in his casino. When I arrived in Kyoto, Japan, after a long seventeen-hour trip with two stops, I was exhausted. When I arrived at the airport, I was met by Yamamoto and his secretary, Kyoto, who took me out for dinner and taught me how to play pachinko machines most of the night. Pachinko (パチンコ) is a type of mechanical game originating in Japan and is used as both a form of recreational arcade game and as a gambling device much more frequently, filling a Japanese gambling niche comparable to that of the slot machine in Western gaming. I never played Pachinko again after leaving Kyoto, Japan. I also didn't tell my dad that I played as he was opposed to any gambling. As a matter of fact, because we were licensed in almost every gaming jurisdiction, we were unable to gamble in US casinos. I found out later that Pachinko didn't count because we didn't win money; we only won prizes.

Ace Playing Card Company, Kyoto, Japan

A relatively new company with about ten employees, Ace Playing Card had a good plastic playing card in the retail market but was untested in the Nevada casino environment. After returning from Kyoto, I gave the playing cards to Wendell Olk, the casino manager at the Imperial Palace, for a field test. In the end, my dad would formulate his own plastic and eventually print our own brand of Paul-Son plastic playing cards. Since I was armed with a successful card field test, we attempted to place our first major order with Ace for plastic playing cards. Unfortunately, we were informed that Mr. Yamamoto had stolen all the money, and the company was filing bankruptcy. It would eventually be Angel, a Japanese playing card company, that years later would own Paul-Son's product line.

My dad's second-worst day of his life would be on Friday, the thirteenth of May. When I received his call on Saturday morning, May 14, 1983, I was completing an internship in audiology at Camp Pendleton, California. I had received my master's degree from California State Los Angeles and thought that the beaches of Oceanside would be my new playground, but it was not to be. I recall the summer of 1983 in Las Vegas was especially hot but not as hot as my dad when he called me. He told me, "Well, Eric, your brother Tommy passed away last night. And we need your help."

I was shocked as I asked, "What happened?"

"We don't know yet. Heart attack, I think."

"But, Dad," I said, "he's only thirty years old and fit. How's that even possible?"

My dad was much angrier than he was sad. I couldn't even understand what it must feel like for a parent to lose their child before they go. When he asked once again for a favor, which he didn't very often, he said, "Can you move back to Vegas and work at Paul-Son? You can fill in for your brother Tommy. Patrick's moving back from Reno to become general manager and maybe you can help out up there as well. I know you like Reno."

I thought about it for a second, but what was there really to think about? Yes, I was giving up my college medical profession, but how could I say no to my father who just lost his middle son? I told my father I would move back and work part-time at Paul-Son but also work part-time in audiology as I had just accepted a job offer as an audiologist with Dr. Mead Hemmeter. My father agreed to me initially working part-time; however, due to the excessive travel and abundance of work at Paul-Son, I resigned from Dr. Hemmeter's audiology clinic after giving them my two weeks' notice.

CHAPTER 14

Native American and Riverboat Gaming History

In 1988, Congress passed the Indian Gaming Regulatory Act, granting Native American tribes "the exclusive right to regulate gaming on Indian lands if the gaming activity is not specifically prohibited by federal law and is conducted within a State which does not, as a matter of criminal law and public policy, prohibit such gaming activity."

As a result, new casinos began opening across the country on tribal lands, resulting in increased business for Paul-Son. The idea behind tribal gaming was to encourage economic development and promote tribal self-sufficiency. Soon states turned to gaming to fund their own programs, establishing and promote tribal self-sufficiency. Soon states turned to gaming to fund their own programs, establishing legalized casinos on riverboats, in particular, in such places as Gulfport and Greenville, Mississippi. Native American gaming comprises casinos, bingo halls, and other gambling operations on Indian reservations or other tribal lands in the United States. Because these areas have tribal sovereignty, states have limited ability to forbid gambling there, as codified by the Indian Gaming Regulatory Act of 1988.

As of 2011, there were 460 gambling operations run by 240 tribes, with a total annual revenue of $27 billion. Currently, all attempts to challenge the Indian Gaming Regulatory Act on constitutional grounds have failed. In the early 1960s, the Cabazon Band of Mission Indians near Indio, California, were extremely poor and did not have much land because of neglected treaties in the 1850s by state senators. As Stuart Banner states, the Cabazon Band and the neighboring Morongo Reservation had "some HUD buildings and a few trailers, but that was about it. There was nothing really there. The people simply didn't have a lot." The Cabazon Band turned to casino operations, opening bingo and poker halls in 1980. In 1988, Congress passed the Indian Gaming Regulatory Act (IGRA) (signed by President Ronald Reagan), which kept tribal sovereignty to create casino-like halls in states. Natives must be in tribal-state compacts, and the federal government has the power to regulate the gaming. The Native American gaming industry has been described as "recession-resistant." Tribal casinos in the eastern US generated roughly $3.8 billion in FY02. Those in the Central US recorded gross revenues of approximately $5.9 billion while those in the Western US generated nearly $4.8 billion. Most of the revenues generated in Native gaming are from casinos located in or near large metropolitan areas. Currently, 12 percent of Native gaming establishments generate 65 percent of Native gaming revenues. Native gaming operations located in the populous areas of the West Coast (primarily California) represent the fastest-growing sector of the Native gaming industry. As suggested by the above figures, the vast majority of tribal casinos are much less financially successful, particularly those in the Midwest and Great Plains. Many tribes see this limited financial success as being tempered by decreases in reservation unemployment and poverty rates, although socioeconomic deficits remain. The first Indian casino was built in Florida by the Seminole Tribe, which opened a successful high-stakes bingo parlor in 1979 and was supplied by Paul-Son. Other indigenous nations quickly followed suit, and by 2000 more than 150 tribes in twenty-four states had opened casino or bingo operations on their reservations.

The first Seminole Tribe's Hard Rock-themed casino in Florida today

The first years of the twenty-first century saw precipitous growth. By 2005, annual revenues had reached more than $22 billion, and Indian gaming accounted for about 25 percent of all legal gambling receipts in the United States. This was about the same amount generated by the country's aggregate state lotteries albeit somewhat less than the 40 percent share generated by commercial casinos in Nevada, Florida, and New Jersey. Notably—and unlike gambling operations run by non-Indians—tribal casinos are required by law to contribute a percentage of their annual revenue to state-controlled trust funds.

These funds are then distributed to local communities to offset costs related to the subsidiary effects of tribal gaming operations such as the expansion or maintenance of transportation, electrical, or sewage systems and other forms of infrastructure; the need for increased traffic patrols; and treatment for gambling addiction. Some of these funds are also distributed as assistance to tribes that do not have gaming operations.

As Native American casinos began opening one after another around the country, Riverboat gaming was also starting to take off literally. The prosperity of Indian gaming operations depends to a great extent on location; those near or in major urban areas can be very successful while those in remote areas (where many reservations are located) tend to generate much less revenue. Although tribes with successful operations have been able to use gaming income to improve the general health, education, and cultural well-being of their members, many Indian casinos have not made significant profits. Thus, the success of some operations on some reservations cannot be generalized to all casinos or all reservations. On the contrary, US census data consistently indicate that the legalization of Indian gaming has not affected the indigenous population in aggregate. Native Americans remain the most impoverished and Darian-Smith. As native American casinos began opening one after another around the country, Riverboat gaming was also starting to take off, literally. A riverboat casino is a type of casino on a riverboat found in several states in the United States with frontage on the Mississippi River and its tributaries or along the Gulf Coast. Several states authorized this type of casino to enable gambling but limit the areas where casinos could be constructed. It was a type of legal fiction as the riverboats were seldom if ever taken away from the dock. Paddlewheel riverboats had long been used on the Mississippi River and its tributaries to transport passengers and freight. After railroads largely superseded them, in the twentieth century, they were more frequently used for entertainment excursions, sometimes for several hours, than for passage among riverfront towns. They were often a way for people to escape the heat of the town as well as to enjoy live music and dancing. Gambling was also common on the riverboats, in card games, and via slot machines. When riverboat casinos were first approved in the late twentieth century by the states, which generally prohibited gaming on land, these casinos were required to be located on ships that could sail away from the dock. In some areas, gambling was allowed only when the ship was sailing as in the traditional excursions. In 1989, the state of Iowa was the first state to enact legislation to allow the Racing and Gaming Commission to issue licenses to qualifying organizations who wished to have gambling on boats. The legislation was enacted on July 1, and it included a $5 betting limit and a $200-per-cruise gambler loss limit. In December of the same year, Illinois legalized riverboat gaming. The law stated that fifteen percent of gaming revenue would go to the state and five percent to the local community. According to the commission, licenses were requested in eight counties, and only one (Clayton County) failed to receive approval. Four riverboat casinos began operation in 1991. Additional casinos opened in the following years. As of 2010, there were a total of seventeen in operation. They were approved in states with frontage along the Mississippi and its tributaries, including Illinois, Indiana, Louisiana, Mississippi, and Missouri (Sloca 1998). In Missouri, voters approved amending the state constitution to allow "games of chance" on the Mississippi and Missouri rivers. By 1998, "according to the state Gaming Commission, just three of the sixteen operations comprising Missouri's $652-million riverboat gambling industry were clearly on the main river channel." The state supreme court had ruled that boats had to be "solely over and in contact with the surface" of the rivers.

In 1992, Mississippi saw five riverboats begin operation. The boats were required to float but did not have to sail or cruise. Riverboats were not required to have engines nor crews. Also, in 1992 a Casino Magic opened in Bay St. Louis, Mississippi, in September. Several casinos had been located on riverboats located in a moat or an area with water adjacent to a navigable waterway, leading them to be referred to as "boats in moats."

Casino Magic Bay St. Louis gaming chip

The state legislatures were unwilling to give up the revenues generated by gambling. Over time, they allowed gaming casinos to be built on stilts, but they still had to be over navigable water.

Following Hurricane Katrina in 2005, which destroyed most riverboat casinos and their associated facilities of hotels, restaurants, etc., in states along the Gulf Coast, several states changed their enabling legislation or amended constitutions.

They permitted such casinos to be built on land within certain geographic limits from a navigable waterway. Most of Mississippi's Gulf Coast riverboat casinos have been rebuilt since the hurricane. In 1989 South Dakota and Colorado legalized casinos.

In the same year, the Riverboat Gaming Act was passed during the regular legislative session. The act provided for five licenses to be granted by January 1, 1991, with an additional five licenses to be granted by March 1, 1992. In 1991 the first riverboat casino in Illinois was opened and Missouri legalized riverboat gaming. The state allowed for seven riverboats and one continuously docked boat. Only "games of skill" such as blackjack were allowed, thus no slot machines. Also in 1991, Louisiana legalized riverboat gambling and Foxwoods Casino opened in February in Ledyard Connecticut. It is owned by the Mashantucket Pequot Tribe and had an initial construction cost of $70 million. It was financed by Kien Haut Realty of Malaysia because US lenders would not underwrite it. It had operating margins of 45 percent, double that of Atlantic City casinos. The state of Connecticut received more than $100 million a year in donations in place of taxes so long as there is no other casino gaming in the state. The casino was estimated to cost $670 million, including a $165-million cash payment to the city of New Orleans. In the United States by 1994, Native American revenues from gaming on reservations reached $4.5 billion, thirty-five state lotteries were in operation, thirty-eight states offered offtrack betting a 111 percent increase from 1993, forty-four states had legal horse racing and thirteen states had legalized casinos, and more were proposed in other states. In 1993, the first riverboat casino, the Casino Star, was opened in November in Louisiana on Lake Pontchartrain; and riverboat gaming was legalized in Indiana.

The original Casino Star in Louisiana

During the same year, the governor of New York signed a casino gaming compact with the Oneida Tribe, creating the first high-stakes gambling casino in the state in more than a century, located just outside Syracuse. Later that year, a compact was signed with St. Regis Tribe to open a casino near Montreal. Finally, Missouri legalized casino gaming in 1994. It was initially brought about by a Supreme Court Decision that allowed games of skill such as blackjack, craps, and poker. The electorate subsequently voted to expand legal gaming to include games of chance such as slot machines.

The Casino Star was eventually purchased by Harrah's Corporation (now Caesars). But twenty-five years ago, when Harrah's opened the first casino in Shreveport-Bossier City, there was much fanfare. Gamblers lined up to enter the docked riverboat, which served as a casino. And yes, there was an actual line to get into the casino. Dignitaries minus then-Shreveport mayor Hazel Beard were there. There was much hope and excitement that April night. Besides gambling, the casinos were bringing entertainment, buffets, fine dining, and hotels to town. Some were excited about the tax dollars. Others were hoping for sponsorship opportunities. "We knew so little back then about how gaming would affect this area. There was concern about crime. It was hard to operate in a positive light, and it caused people to step back," said Anthony Sanfilippo, general manager when Harrah's opened its Shreveport casino after gaming had been in the market for ten years. Twenty-five years after the casinos arrived, there isn't a line to get into a casino. Going to such an establishment is not all that unusual for a generation of Shreveport-Bossier City residents who have grown up with casinos. After Harrah's opened on April 18, 1994, the Isle of Capri opened the following month on May 20. Horseshoe opened the next month on June 9.

CHAPTER 15

New Business Meant
New Sales Offices

Paul-Son was growing and to maintain customer sales and service my dad would drive, opening offices one by one along the Mississippi River. He also thought it made sense at the time to open retail stores and called them "Jacks or Better." They would prove to be a compliance nightmare for the company going forward. We would eventually close the retail stores in Las Vegas and the outside sales offices. To take advantage of the explosion in the number of new casinos being built and further to grow the business, in the short time between 1991 and 1994, Paul-Son had opened sales offices in Gulfport, Mississippi; New Orleans, Louisiana; Oregon; Canada; Florida; and had an international distributor in South America and was looking to expand into Europe. However, expanding outside of North America proved to be a challenge for Paul-Son.

Paul-Son standard roulette wheel

The international gaming supply market at the time was dominated by the English firm, John Huxley Company, which distributed the Bud Jones chips. The CEO of John Huxley was Jeff Lyndsey who had a major grip on London in Europe and Bourgogne et Grasset founded in 1923, pretty much had the rest. Since London Casino Supplies wasn't able to get a Nevada gaming license for making roulette wheels, it was good and bad news. The good news was that we assumed full control of London's manufacturing in Nevada. The bad news was that London wasn't selling any notable quantity of Paul-Son chips. The owners eventually claimed that since roulette was the most popular game in Europe, the plastic injection molded chip was preferred since it was more durable, and our chip broke apart in the "chipper machines" on the roulette table. We eventually terminated our relationship with London Casino Supplies and looked for other international opportunities. However, at the same time, Paul-Son decided to manufacture its own roulette wheel after receiving a call from CEO Mr. Steve Wynn, who eventually built Wynn Resorts. My dad and I met Steve Wynn at the Golden Nugget Casino. In 1971, Wynn bought a controlling interest in the Golden Nugget Las Vegas, one of the oldest casinos in the city. His company stake increased so in 1973, he became the majority shareholder and the youngest casino owner in Las Vegas. In 1977 he opened the Golden Nugget's first hotel tower followed by several others. Frank Sinatra was a periodic headliner at the Golden Nugget, and Wynn has since maintained a relationship with the Sinatra family, even naming a restaurant at Encore *Sinatra*. In 1980, Wynn began construction on the Golden Nugget Atlantic City in Atlantic City, New Jersey. It was Atlantic City's first and only "locals casino" and the city's sixth casino after the city legalized gambling in 1976. Though at its opening, it was the second smallest casino in the city, by 1983 it was the city's top-earning casino. Wynn's first major casino on the Las Vegas Strip was the Mirage, which opened on November 22, 1989. It was the first time Wynn was involved with the design and construction of a casino, and he financed the $630 million project largely with high-yield bonds issued by Michael Milken. Its construction is also considered noteworthy in that the Mirage was the first casino to use security cameras full-time on all table games. The hotel became the main venue for the *Siegfried & Roy* show in 1990. Wynn's next project, Treasure Island Hotel and Casino, opened in the Mirage's old parking lot on October 27, 1993, at an overall cost of $450 million. The establishment was the home of the first permanent Cirque du Soleil show in Las Vegas. In 1995, Wynn's company proposed to build the Le Jardin Hotel & Casino in the marina area if the state of New Jersey built a road that connected to the hotel-casino.

The company had also agreed to allow Circus Circus Enterprises and Boyd Gaming to build casinos on the site but later reneged on the agreement. While the road, called the Atlantic City—Brigantine Connector, was eventually built, Le Jardin was canceled after the company was acquired in 2000 by MGM Grand Inc., which later built the Borgata in a joint venture with Boyd Gaming on the site.

On October 15, 1998, Wynn opened the even more opulent Bellagio, a $1.6 billion resort considered among the world's most spectacular hotels. Wynn brought Mirage Resorts' style to Biloxi, Mississippi in 1999, where he oversaw the development of the 1,835-room Beau Rivage. Mirage Resorts was sold to MGM Grand Inc. for $4.4 billion in June 2000 to form MGM Mirage. Five weeks before the deal was closed (April 27, 2000), Wynn purchased the Desert Inn for $270 million. He sold the Desert Inn later that year. On April 28, 2005, he opened his most expensive resort at the time, the Wynn Las

Vegas, on the site of the former Desert Inn. Built for $2.7 billion, it was the largest privately funded construction project in the nation as of 2005. Wynn successfully bid for one of three gaming concessions opened for tender in Macau. This property, known as Wynn Macau, opened on September 5, 2006. In 2016, Wynn opened the Wynn Palace in the Cotai Strip in the People's Republic of China. It was previously approved by the Macau government in 2012. In September 2014, Wynn was awarded the license to build the Wynn Boston Harbor casino in the eastern Massachusetts city of Everett, near downtown Boston.

PAUL-SON ROULETTE WHEELS:
THE ROULETTE WHEEL OF THE "NEXT CENTURY"

Who said you can't reinvent the wheel? The roulette wheel has been virtually unchanged for two centuries. Paul-Son has now introduced new compounds and technologies that will set roulette standards for the next two centuries.

A one piece bowl and ball track tooled from a solid "block" of ebonite, the same material used in bowling balls.

A solid brass fret ring, instead of little pieces glued or riveted to the wheel, this one piece brass fret ring is movable, creating as close to an unbiased wheel as can be made.

A solid brass plate made from aircraft quality aluminum which will literally last two centuries.

A one piece number and pocket laminate no cracks, no dirt, no loose or "hollow" spots.

The Paul-Son wheel has been manufactured to give years of trouble free operation and designed to practically eliminate any bias in the wheel.

But....That's not all. While all the major components of the wheel have been redesigned, not one sacrifice has been made in the wheel's beauty!

All Paul-Son roulette wheels are designed and engineered with the utmost care and precision with the casino operators confidence in mind. We can offer custom wheels to match your casino decor. From our elegantly simple stock wheel, to the most ornate custom wheel, Paul-Son guarantees your total satisfaction.

And...Please remember....Paul-Son has been supplying gaming equipment for over 1/2 century. Our reputation for service, reliability and standing behing what we sell is without peer in the gaming industry. The Paul-Son roulette wheel is already in many of the major casino properties. Please call and we will tell you where you can view the roulette wheel of the "next century" today!

When we met with Steve Wynn at the Golden Nugget Hotel/Casino in downtown Las Vegas, he suggested we make a major change in the way roulette wheels are manufactured. He was concerned that the wheel could have a natural "bias" in the fret ring. The fret ring is the metal divider that separates the numbers. He suggested that if there was a "dead" spot in the fret ring that the roulette ball would naturally stop on the number near the "dead" spot in the ring. He believed that if we made the fret ring movable, it would eliminate any potential bias in the roulette wheel.

Roulette Wheel Components

Movable fret ring.

We appreciated and incorporated Steve Wynn's suggestion, made a roulette wheel with a movable fret ring, and sold twelve of them to the Golden Nugget and every casino Wynn opened. Also, at one time the New Jersey Gaming Commission in Atlantic City recommended all roulette wheels to have a movable fret ring that Paul-Son invented. We eventually received a patent for the roulette wheel with a movable fret ring.

The 1989 gaming show with our customers at my wedding

On October 5 to 7, 1989, Paul-Son once again displayed its product offerings at the World Gaming Exposition at the Las Vegas Convention Center, just as it had done for the past ten years, but this year would be very different. I met my wonderful Chinese wife, Hsiaochin (also known as Cathy), in 1987 when I was a casino salesman for Paul-Son.

We were introduced on a blind date by a matchmaker who was a customer of mine at the Imperial Palace Hotel and Casino. However, I knew what Cathy looked like before she knew me. I was told by our matchmaker that she was a shoe model, had a print ad in the *Las Vegas Magazine*, and a television commercial for the Paddlewheel Hotel and Casino.

The Paddlewheel was a riverboat-themed hotel and casino built in 1983. The hotel was known as being family-friendly, including some amusement rides and multiple arcade games similar to Circus Circus and Excalibur. The hotel was also known for all-you-can-eat crab legs and baby back ribs. The Paddlewheel originally opened in 1970 as a Royal Inn, was a Debbie Reynolds Hotel and Casino from 1993 to 1999, and was sold in 1999 to the WWF (World Wrestling Federation) and then sold and remodeled as the Greek Isles. It was a Clarion Hotel, the only Clarion with a casino from 2009 until it was imploded in 2014. When I found this out on my way home from work, I immediately went to the closest 7-Eleven to my house and purchased a glossy new magazine. After arriving home and preparing my dinner, I turned on the TV to watch my favorite show, *The Love Connection*, and there she was during the commercial; and she was beautiful. The television commercial was an advertisement for the Paddlewheel's famous baby back ribs, which Cathy was promoting in Chinese. My only hope was that one day I could meet her, and two weeks later my dream came true! My wife and I married one year later with over four hundred families, friends, and our best customers on October 7, 1989, at the Desert Inn Country Club. My dad liked my wife and not only thought she was pretty but also very smart in every sense of the word.

One night, when we were at his house for dinner, my dad brought out a metal horseshoe contraption he had for over two years from his bedroom and gave it to us. He said the object was to remove the metal ring and that most people couldn't remove it. I struggled with the device for a while and was unable to remove the ring. However, when I gave it to my wife, she removed the ring within one minute! My father was more than surprised by how quickly she was able to do it. What he didn't fully realize at the time was that she had a successful business in downtown Las Vegas and a college degree in business that could help Paul-Son. When Cathy looked at the cost and selling price of most Paul-Son products, she notified us that the margins had been eroding over time and recommended raising prices. A historical financial review of Paul-Son's selling prices showed some prices hadn't been raised in years. In the early days, my father's partner would oversee banking relationships and Paul-Son pricing. As a result, we raised prices and continued to do so every year thanks to her. As my wedding day approached, my father had Paul-Son on his mind more than ever. He was concerned that the company would continue in the Endy family name and questioned my wife's family's intentions regarding Paul-Son. As a matter of fact, when my wife and I first married, I had recently graduated from college, and I had little or no disposable income. When we decided to build a house in Las Vegas, my wife had to purchase the land with her own money since I didn't have it. We eventually built a custom waterfront home that Cathy designed and supervised on Lake Jacqueline at Desert Shores. Cathy not only assisted with the financial growth at Paul-Son but also by purchasing the land that we eventually built a house on proved to me that she had no intention of taking advantage of the Paul Endy's estate. It was my dad's idea to invite the casino industry to my wedding after my marriage plans were announced to him. "What a great party we'll have, and maybe we can keep our customers away from our competition during that gaming show!" he exclaimed. He enjoyed himself at my wedding, mingling with the presidents from Carnival Cruise Lines and the Tropicana Hotel. When he offered a toast to my wife and me, he also thanked his customers for attending our wedding even though they were primarily here for the gaming show. Most of them said they had a better time at

our wedding than they had at "just another gaming show." We had two ministers at our wedding—Rev. Wes MacPherson, who spoke English, and another female minister who spoke Chinese so my mother-in-law could understand the wedding ceremony. When the Jim Garris (Garoufes) band played our favorite waltz, "Could I Have This Dance," I asked my wife for the first dance. After I danced with my wife, I asked my mother for a dance, and then we took photographs on the Desert Inn golf course.

My mother-in-law, Yu Chin; Celine; Cathy; Daren; Nevin; and me

My wife and I gave my mother and father three grandchildren—Daren, Nevin, and Celine. Although Paul-Son did some international business selling direct to casinos in Monte Carlo, the Caribbean, England, and South Africa, 90 percent of its sales came from the domestic market. During the first five years of the 1990s, the number of table games at US casinos grew from 6,200 to 10,000. As a result, the company's revenues grew from $7.4 million at the start of the decade to $22.8 million in 1994, and net income improved from breakeven to $1.4 million.

On January 26, 1993, the Dunes closed its doors after being sold to Steve Wynn, and the famed casino was imploded on October 27, 1993.

The Dunes Hotel and Casino imploded, and
the Bellagio opened Oct 15,1998.

The Bellagio is a resort, luxury hotel, and casino on the Las Vegas Strip in Paradise, Nevada. It is owned by the Blackstone Group and operated by MGM Resorts International and was built on the site of the demolished Dunes hotel and casino. Inspired by the Lake Como town of Bellagio in Italy, Bellagio is famed for its elegance. One of its most notable features is an 8-acre (3.2-hectare) lake between the building and the Strip, which houses the Fountains of Bellagio, a large dancing water fountain synchronized to music. Bellagio was conceived by Steve Wynn; and Atlandia Design (a Mirage Resorts Inc.—wholly owned subsidiary) managed the design, construction, and furnishing of the facility following the purchase and demolition of the legendary Dunes Hotel and Casino on October 27, 1993, after the grand opening of Treasure Island Las Vegas. Bellagio's design architect was DeRuyter Butler, and Peter Smith was the project executive. Construction on the Bellagio began in May 1996. Bellagio had an original design and construction cost of $1.6 billion.

MGM Resorts International owned the Bellagio until 2019 when it sold the resort to the Blackstone Group for $4.25 billion. MGM continues to operate the property under a lease arrangement. Later that year, the Luxor casino opened, and Kirk Kerkorian's MGM Grand Hotel and Theme Parks opened at the world's largest hotel for $1 billion.

In the same year, there was trouble brewing at Paul-Son between my dad and Patrick. Frustrated with some of my father's business decisions and the company's negative cash flow, Patrick decided to leave the company and open his own gaming supply company called Gamblers General Store. Unfortunately, at about the same time, Patrick was diagnosed with multiple sclerosis and had to stop working.

Patrick and Gamblers General Store later filed bankruptcy protection and my dad reconciled with my brother in 1998, a year before he died. My dad asked me to promise "to take care of my brother for just as long as he lives," and I did. Patrick C. Endy, fifty-seven, passed away on September 24, 2008. He was born on January 26, 1951, in Alhambra, California, and was a resident of Nevada for forty-four years. I will never forget Patrick for his love and compassion for his family and the gaming industry. In 1993 Paul-Son began taking steps to become a public company. In March 1994, the company made an initial public offering of stock.

CHAPTER 16

Paul-Son Goes Public in 1994

My dad knew he needed to expand his manufacturing business in Mexico to meet the growing demand for its product offering. To do so he would have to raise more money, which is what he started to do in 1992. All Paul-Son Gaming Corporation shares in the initial public stock offering sold out in just over an hour at $10 a share without Paul Endy ever leaving his office in Las Vegas. As a result of my dad's fear of flying, I was the one who represented the company in my new position as a chief operating officer on the "road show" as I flew from Las Vegas to Boston, New York, and eventually Los Angeles.

I appeared on the Neil Cavetto show *Fox Business* in New York in 1994.

After my appearance with Neil Cavuto on *Fox Business* in New York City, I was convinced the public offering would be a success and it was. I made the analogy on television that Paul-Son was like the replacement razor-blade business, which my father approved of. I explained on Cavuto's show that "the gaming table was the table or the razor and all the replacement items like the chips, dice, and table felts were like razor blades with a limited life span before they wore out." The audience was impressed with our business strategy, and shareholders bought all the available stock. Paul-Son sold 44 percent of the company, netting $11 million, which was earmarked to pay down debt and for expansion. As a result, Paul Endy still held more than 50 percent (56 percent to be precise) of the stock in his company, and many "old-time" shareholders would hold onto their shares. This combination ended up being a major disadvantage to the share price in the future since there were so few shares being traded in the market at any one time. The share price wouldn't provide my dad any liquidity for his stock, and it would be up to me to improve the stock price in the future.

Unfortunately, Paul-Son produced mixed results after going public. Craps games were rapidly losing popularity because it was deemed too complicated by younger gamblers, thus cutting into the sale of Paul-Son dice.

Early in 1995, after receiving the public generated funds, my dad was spending the majority of his time at our factory in Mexico. He opened a new forty-five-thousand-square-foot manufacturing facility in San Luis, Mexico, to help meet the increasing demand for replacement products. He also installed a new state-of-the-art playing card cartooning machine capable of packaging two thousand decks of playing cards per hour, a 50 percent increase over the speed of the previous equipment. The system would also be able to wrap a bridge—(smaller for poker) and blackjack-size cards simultaneously and assessed optics able to detect a deck's color and automatically assemble the appropriate box.

The growth of riverboats and Native American casinos would further propel Paul-Son Gaming into the twentieth century, and for the first time Paul Endy Jr. wasn't sure he made the right decision to go public. The added costs for all the lawyers, the accountants, and a board of directors he had to deal with just didn't sit right with him. Even though the public funds would help Paul-Son further expand its manufacturing and sales force, it would end up costing the company over a million dollars a year for just licensing and public expenses. He liked the idea that the company was flush with cash but was losing control of "his baby" even though he individually controlled the majority of the public shares. Well, he thought so, and that's all that really mattered.

In 1997, we tried to expand Paul-Son's product offering outside the gaming industry by entering the growing collectible sports and memorabilia market.

As a result, we entered a joint venture with DeBartolo Entertainment to form Brand One Marketing to market collectible and commemorative chips and playing cards.

In Paul Endy's words, "We were already producing great-looking full-graphic chips that are taken by casino customers. Why not the general public? They will love them." And while it lasted, most of them did! We bought out DeBartolo's share in Brand One a year later. We formed the company Authentic Products to market Paul-Son products outside the gaming industry.

Authentic Products Inc. was a subsidiary of Paul-Son which manufactured forty-three- and fifty-millimeter collectible commemorative discs and promotional playing cards customized for any special event, promotional giveaway, anniversary, or company incentive. Two successful limited-edition commemorative discs launched by Authentic Products were the 1997 inductees to the Rock & Roll Hall of Fame in Cleveland and the fiftieth anniversary of the NFL's San Francisco 49ers. A commemorative disc was distributed at the 1998 home opener and other home games during the inaugural season of Major League Baseball's Arizona Diamondbacks. We also designed and produced playing cards commemorating the Grateful Dead, Porsche Automobile Company, the Pillsbury Doughboy, and Pall Mall Cigarettes.

By the close of 1998, Authentic Products had signed an exclusive distribution agreement with HA-LO Industries Inc. under which HA-LO agreed to market, sell, and distribute Authentic Products nongaming specialty advertising products in the US and Canada. HA-LO was the nation's leading distributor of promotional products (Las Vegas Millennium edition, Pioneer Publications).

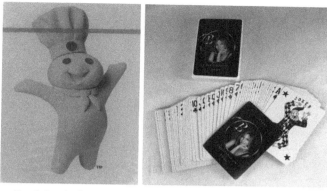

Paul-Son's first decks of collectible playing cards were
the Pillsbury Doughboy and Barbara Streisand.

We also received an order to produce memorabilia including
playing cards and collectible chips for the new James Bond Movie
featuring Roger Moore in *The World Is Not Enough*. It was a successful movie and project that sold over ten thousand sets of cards and
chips.

The World Is Not Enough premiered on November 19, 1999,
in the United States and on November 26, 1999, in the United
Kingdom. Its world premiere was November 8, 1999, at the Fox

Bruin Theater, Los Angeles, USA. My father believed that the retail gaming market was an important revenue source just as it had been at T. R. King & Co. So when sales offices were opened in Mississippi and Louisiana, retail showrooms were also included just like the one Paul-Son had in Las Vegas. Since gambling was still illegal in many states and Paul-Son was shipping to retail customers from any one of them, Nevada Gaming officials clamped down on the company and put strict gaming compliance requirements on Paul-Son. When I was appointed the company's compliance officer, our new compliance plan made it imperative that we only ship to licensed casino companies. As a result, we eventually closed the retail department but had some success with Brand One. Despite these steps, Paul-Son failed to realize its growth potential in the eyes of investors, especially in light of the consolidation that was taking place in the gaming supply industry. In October 1997, Paul-Son hired Ladenburg Thalmann & Co. as a financial advisor to review strategic alternatives, including the sale of the company. *Mergers & Restructuring* quoted one analyst as saying, "I don't know why someone would buy them." He added that the company should have transformed itself into a fully integrated gaming manufacturer instead of devoting so much of its resources to manufacturing dice (which was labor-intensive) and playing cards (which almost anyone could make). My dad said, "He was wrong, dead wrong," and that he didn't know what he was talking about. "It takes a certain formula and skill to make casino-quality dice and playing cards."

In 1997, most of a casino's revenues were now coming from slot machines and video poker, not just table games. To grow the business internally, Paul-Son formed a new games division to develop and lease new casino gaming products. The first offering was "Paul-Son's Draw Poker," a five-person game played on a blackjack-size table. Players did not play against the dealer or other players. Instead, they chose among draw poker, Joker's Wild, and Deuces Wild and were permitted to draw up to five new cards. Hands are then compared to a paytable to determine winnings. Unfortunately, Paul-Son draw poker had little success for Paul-Son. The successful new games of the future would be electronic and computer-driven and would feature a "bonus players" round. Paul-Son did not have the expertise nor technology to drive the electronic table game business.

Instead, Paul-Son would focus on expanding internationally except for one novelty "talking-poker machine," which we would distribute from Intermark Gaming in Phoenix, Arizona.

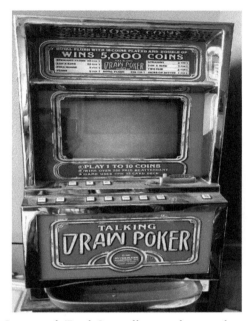

Intermark/Paul-Son talking poker machine

CHAPTER 17

A Short History of Video Poker Machines

The first poker machine, 1901 (*left*) and Pokermatic, 1970 (*right*)

The ancestors of the first-draw poker machines were poker slot machines that were based purely on luck with no option to hold or draw any of the dealt cards. They included five reels that were spinning just like a slot machine, and when they stopped, the random cards formed a poker hand. The first poker machine was created when the draw feature was introduced. Suddenly it was not purely a matter of luck. Players could affect the outcome of the game to some degree. The first poker machine was called "Skill Draw." It included the draw feature and was created by Charles Fey in 1901. The initial spin of the five-reel machine created a poker hand, then the player could hold some of the cards and spin the remaining reels again to complete the poker hand. The first poker machines included only fifty cards; in most cases, the jack of hearts and ten of spades were excluded. That meant that players could hit the royal flush in two suits only, halving the probability of hitting a royal flush. According to Casino Guru, slot machines are currently the most popular games in a casino. The basic rules of this game haven't changed since 1899 when Charles Fay assembled the first slot machine.

A player bets and spins a set of reels with symbols. Each of these spinning reels stops at a random position. The player wins if the reels stop in a way that they make a line of the same symbols. The rarer the winning symbols, the higher the amount of the win. The size of the win for each winning combination is defined in the paytable. Nowadays the randomness of mechanically stopped reels has been replaced by random numbers generated by a computer, but the principles remain the same. These principles of randomness are honored by every licensed game provider. The randomness of slots has several very interesting consequences, and every smart slot player must understand them. The first video poker machine called Pokermatic was introduced in 1970 by Dale Electronics Corporation as soon as it was able to combine a television monitor with a central processing unit. Its screen was similar to television screens back then. Video poker first became commercially viable when it became economical to combine a television-like monitor with a solid-state central processing unit. The earliest models appeared at the same time as the first personal computers were produced, in the mid-1970s, although they were primitive by today's standards. Even though the machine was installed across all the casinos in Las Vegas, it didn't become popular. People back in the '70s just didn't trust electronic gambling machines without being able to see the reels spinning. Later, in the mid-1970s, the father of video poker, William "Si" Redd (1911–2003), whose Bally Distributing Company was acting as a game distributor for Bally Gaming, presented the company executives with a new invention—a game called video poker.

However, they did not want to move away from slot machines and let him keep the patents. Redd quickly struck a deal with

Reno-based Fortune Coin Company to form Sircoma (Si Redd's Coin Machines), which started the mass production of video poker machines. And by 1979, a new video poker machine called draw poker was distributed across US casinos. In 1980, the company went public and changed its name to now-worldwide-renowned International Game Technology (IGT). Later on, with the addition of touch-screen and more video poker games like Deuces Wild and Double Bonus being created, the popularity of video poker grew even more significantly. Now you can find them everywhere in Las Vegas as one of the most popular games in land-based casinos. Also, casinos have invested in licensed TV shows, movies, superstars, and superheroes for new and exciting video gaming machines.

New 007 casino video slot machines

Video poker is a casino game based on five-card draw poker. It is played on a computerized console similar in size to a slot machine.

A few people who are skilled in calculating odds have made money playing video poker. In the United States, slot machines and other gambling machines dominate the casino's gaming space. When I started writing about the casino gambling industry, the prevailing wisdom was that 65 percent to 70 percent of a casino's revenue came from slot machines. That number is now nearing 80 percent, so slot machine play is clearly on the rise.

The casinos know how profitable slot machines are per square foot, and if you pay attention to their advertising materials, you'll notice how much of their advertising focuses on gambling machines. Table games, on the other hand, are shrinking as a percentage of casino market share according to Bestuscasinos.org. Less floor space is dedicated to table games like blackjack, craps, and roulette than ever before. Some of this is because slot machines allow the casino to offer higher jackpots than what would ever be possible at a table game. Of course, the odds of winning one of those huge jackpots can be infinitesimal—along the same lines as winning the lottery in some cases. For the most part, skill doesn't play a big role in table games or gambling machines. You'll find exceptions in both kinds of gambling, though. As a result of the declining floor space to table games, we thought who better than Paul-Son to sell a poker machine, and we should take a look at the slot side of the gaming market with a talking poker machine. For better or worse, that's what we did. My dad and I met John Walsh, the CEO of Intermark Gaming, in 1995 at the World Gaming Show in Las Vegas. He was referred by Doyle Davis, the slot manager at the Stardust Hotel and Casino. John Walsh claimed that he had worked for Bally Slot Machine Company in the past and had a new video gaming device that would revolutionize the casino gaming floor. My dad asked him who he worked for at Bally, and he commented that it was Abe Goodman. Bally Manufacturing, later renamed Bally Entertainment, was an American company that began as a pinball and slot machine manufacturer and later expanded into casinos, video games, health clubs, and theme parks. It was acquired by Hilton Hotels in 1996. Its brand name is still used by several businesses previously linked to Bally Manufacturing, most notably Bally Technologies. My father knew Abe Goodman as did his father before him. As a matter of fact, it was Abe Goodman who first introduced my father to Jimmy Garrett, the casino manager at the Flamingo Hilton. They had become good friends and my father needed his help. When my dad called Jimmy Garrett, he first asked him about his old friend Abe Goodman whom he hadn't seen in years. "He's fine, Paul, just getting up in age like me. He retired last year."

"Jimmy," my father exclaimed, "do you ever remember Abe ever talking about? A guy named John Walsh out of Arizona who worked for Bally's?"

Mr. Garrett didn't seem to remember his name but said, "Let me think about it. Maybe it will come to me later."

"You can think about it on the way when you go with Eric and me this Saturday to Phoenix to see a new slot machine," Dad insisted.

On the Saturday after the gaming show, we picked up Garrett from the Flamingo Hilton and hurriedly drove to Intermark's office in Phoenix. When we first saw and heard the talking video poker machine, my dad and I were impressed, Garrett not so much. He had been in the business for over fifty years and said that he saw just about everything there is, but this was different. The Intermark draw poker machine that we saw and heard was the only one at the time that spoke and could be changed by just "the flick of a switch" from a male voice to a female voice. My dad saw the machine as a "home run" and asked Garrett what he thought of it since he appreciated his casino experience.

"The good news is that I like that the voice can be changed so the customer doesn't get confused or distracted while playing, but has it been tested in the Nevada gaming lab yet? We can't even try it until after they have."

"Not yet," replied Mr. Walsh. "But it has been submitted and should be tested next month."

"I am not licensed in Nevada, but since Paul-Son is, they would have to present the machine for testing."

My dad said to load the poker machine in our car, and we would take it to the testing lab next week. Before we left, my dad walked up to John, nose to nose, and said, "We're here first, so it's only ours to distribute, right John?" He reached out his hand to shake on the deal.

Of course, John obliged by shaking his hand and said, "It's a deal."

The Flamingo Hilton Hotel & Casino, 1985

When my dad shook hands with you on a deal, it was a deal, period. With that, we were on our way back to Las Vegas with a quick stop for lunch in Wickenburg. On Monday morning I met with our patent lawyer, Larry Speiser, and called Lieutenant Rawlings with Nevada Gaming to find out what procedures I had to follow to submit the talking poker machine for approval. Due to Paul-Son's unfamiliarity with how video gaming devices are submitted, it would be a more complicated transaction. However, with my dad's inside help, Paul-Son would get approval in less than two weeks, and less than two months later, we would have over two hundred talking poker machines installed at the Flamingo Hilton. It was quite the sight and especially the sound to hear the dealer of the machine speaking in different masculine and feminine voices at the Flamingo Hilton. The talking poker machines were extremely popular when they were first installed but became problematic after only two weeks. Since I was the only one involved at the beginning with Intermark during their installation, I was also the only one involved in servicing them except the Flamingo Hilton Slot Department, which was a great asset to me.

At 2:00 a.m. on Thursday, I received a disturbing wake-up call from John Straub, the head of the Flamingo Slot Department, that the new poker machines were "running away."

Since I had not heard that saying before and I was still sleepy after just being woken up early in the morning, I asked, "What do you mean they are 'running away'? How can they move?"

John said he would laugh if he could but that there was some mechanical glitch, and the machines were spitting out money from the coin hopper and wouldn't stop. That's a "runaway." He continued by saying that they had shut the power off and on, but it did not stop the runaway. They eventually had to power down all two hundred machines and that I should come over ASAP. He said he had to inform Garrett, and he wasn't happy giving the casino's money away for free. I got out of bed, drove to the Flamingo, and called John at Intermark. He said he didn't know why all the machines were spitting out money like they were and said it must be the casino's wiring problem. I knew the Flamingo wouldn't want to hear that it was their problem and told John to get to Vegas ASAP to fix it and that my dad was going to be pissed off when he found out. My dad liked to go to bed early and get up early in the morning, but it was way too early for me to call him. When I arrived at the Flamingo Hilton, I immediately contacted the slot department and met John near the showroom in front of the normally active talking but now-powered-off machines. John said, "There has to be some kind of mechanical glitch in these machines because none of our others have any problems, and we haven't had any other electrical issues. They all have the same problem." So he assumed they all had the same mechanical glitch. When I looked over my shoulder, I noticed Garrett on his cell phone, and I couldn't help but overhear that he was talking to none other than my father.

When Mr. Garrett handed me his phone, I told my father that yes, I had contacted Intermark, and yes, John Walsh was on his way and should be arriving shortly.

My father hung up the telephone and, within half an hour, was also standing in front of the now-quiet talking poker machines. He was upset and apologized to Jimmy Garrett about the "glitch" and added that we would get an answer right away and take care of it. "Right, Eric?"

"Right, Dad," I replied. I didn't know how long it would take to "fix" our problem, but this time it was serious. It was Paul-Son's reputation at stake. Within a couple of hours, a nervous John Walsh called my dad and me, asking if we could meet up at Paul-Son.

When John arrived at the office, we already had a talking poker machine set up, and my dad had an employee robustly feeding it with coins to duplicate the glitch that had happened last night at the Flamingo. Even though we weren't able to duplicate the problem, John said he had done it. He rubbed his feet furiously on our office carpet and then touched the machine. A slight spark ensued as he put a coin in the acceptor, and it began "running away" just like it had done at the casino.

"It's static electricity, and we have to find another way to further ground and protect the video poker machine."

"And we're finding this out right now? Isn't it a little late?" questioned my father.

"Better late than never, Paul," John quickly replied.

"Well, this is on you, and so is our company's reputation in the gaming industry, John. I expect you to fix this, and fix it fast."

John said he would but would have to return to Phoenix to find a solution. Even though Intermark eventually did fix their "glitch," the novelty talking poker machine never really caught on, or maybe it was just ahead of its time. In today's casino almost every video slot and poker machine talk and unfortunately, they usually don't tell you what you want to hear. I still own an original talking poker machine today as a big dusty souvenir that sits in my garage. At least it will be a "talking" point at my house in the future.

CHAPTER 18

Las Vegas Transformation From "Sin City" to "Family Destination"

In 1989 longtime casino developer Steve Wynn opened the Mirage, the city's first megaresort. Over the next two decades, the strip was transformed yet again. Old casinos were dynamited to make room for massive complexes, taking their aesthetic cues from ancient Rome and Egypt, Paris, Venice, New York, and other glamorous escapes. Casinos and entertainment remained Las Vegas's major employer, and the city grew with the size of the resorts and the numbers of annual visitors according to History.com Editors in 2009, updated in 2020. Southern Nevada witnessed a decade-long boom, experiencing construction and population growth not seen in the United States since the Gold Rush of the 1840s and 1850s. To attract families, resorts offered more attractions geared toward youth but had limited success. The current MGM Grand opened in 1993 with MGM Grand Adventures Theme Park, but the park closed in 2000 due to lack of interest.

Similarly, in 2003 Treasure Island closed its own video arcade and abandoned the previous pirate theme, adopting the new TI name. More than fifteen themed casino-hotels opened their doors throughout the Las Vegas valley, and there was a dramatic diversification of entertainment options, including theme parks (e.g., Circus

Circus' Adventure Dome and the Las Vegas Hilton's Star Trek: The Experience) and stage production shows (e.g., Cirque Du Soleil and EFX).

Various properties exchanged hands, including the Frontier Hotel, Sands, Vegas World (Stratosphere), Holiday Casino (Harrah's), and Aladdin. In Reno, the Silver Legacy Resort & Casino opened on Virginia Street in 1995.

The Silver Legacy in Reno, Nevada

However, with the passage of California's Proposition 5 in 1998, casino-style gambling on Native American reservations was given an open door to compete with northern Nevada casinos. As Nevada entered the twenty-first century, nearly every state had gambling in one form or another and the increased access to Native American casino gaming was dramatically changing the way Nevada approached its tourism economy (sources: Nevada Historical Society, Las Vegas Convention and Visitors Authority, Michael Green [Community College of Southern Nevada], David Schwartz [University of Nevada, Las Vegas Center for Gaming Research], *Roll the Bones: The History of Gambling* by David Schwartz (2006), and *Nevada Magazine* [2006]).

In 1996 Las Vegas continued to grow with the opening of the world's first Hard Rock Hotel, the Stratosphere in April, the Monte Carlo in June, the Orleans in December, and Wayne Newton celebrated his twenty-five thousand performance.

It was hard to believe that sixteen years earlier in September 1980 Newton and Ed Torres, a former chief executive of the Riviera and Newton's longtime friend, bought the Aladdin Hotel for $85 million as equal partners and reopened it the next month. Newton said he decided to take the plunge into casino ownership because his life at that time needed change. For fourteen years he had performed at hotels of the Summa Corporation then the gaming arm of Howard Hughes's empire. Also, at that time, his booking agent, Walter Kane (who was like a father to Newton) died, leaving a void in his life. "I wanted to own a casino, not operate one," Newton told the *Las Vegas Sun* in a 2000 interview. "I didn't want people coming to me because the toilets are backed up. I saw the changes going on in this town with many places doing away with dinner shows. It was different from when I first performed here when I was fifteen." Fast-forward a quarter century to major star Newton looking for help in buying a gaming property. He had invested in the Shenandoah casino in Las Vegas that never got off the ground, toured a Laughlin casino, discussed building a casino in Carson City, and considered buying the Riviera before targeting the Aladdin. The Shenandoah Hotel began as a $29-million project named after the Las Vegas estate of singer Wayne Newton, who was a minority investor in the property. The hotel opened in February 1980.

The Shenandoah Hotel and Casino, 1980

To buy one of the really big places, Newton needed a partner, and Torres seemed to be a perfect choice. But after twenty-one months of running the Aladdin together, Torres and Newton split amid reports that they were constantly fighting. In July 1982, Torres bought out Newton for $8.5 million. Among the things they did not see eye to eye on were employee cutbacks, which Newton opposed. Another tiff was over the size of the shot glasses in their bars. But the straw that broke the camel's back was a dispute over the purchase of a nearby service station on Las Vegas Boulevard that would have to be leveled to give the Aladdin much better access to and from the Strip. Newton was willing to pay the station owner's price of $16 million for the prime Strip property. The property had a few other owners along the way. Frank Sinatra was interested in buying it in 1990, but that deal did not materialize. It was finally imploded in 1998. The Aladdin was rebuilt for $1.4 billion and reopened in August 2000 but did not live up to its new owners' expectations. It was sold to its current owners in 2003 and became Planet Hollywood in April 2007. Newton said owning the Aladdin "was one of the great learning experiences of my life. And I'm one of the few people who owned the Aladdin who can say we made money." Before the Torres-Newton takeover of the Aladdin, a dozen offers were made to buy the resort including a $103 million offer from *The Tonight Show* host Johnny Carson. Just as it appeared Carson's proposal would be accepted, Newton and his former manager Jay Stream outbid him with $105 million. That proposal eventually collapsed, and many months later Newton and Torres acquired the hotel-casino for $85 million.

Then: The Aladdin imploded. Now: Planet Hollywood.

I will never forget May 30, 1983. It was one week after my brother Tommy had passed, and I officially went to work for Paul-Son full time. My first job was to deliver a gift from my dad to Wayne Newton. The gift was a Pac-Man video game console that had been delivered to Paul-Son from the Sands Hotel/Casino. When a limousine arrived on that Monday morning and delivered the Pac-Man arcade console into the Paul-Son showroom, there was a sense of excitement. Everyone first thought that it was a present from my dad for my birthday, but it wasn't for me.

The long story short that was told to me by my dad as I loaded the Pac-Man machine into my pick-up was that Wayne Newton, the king of Brunei, and my dad were playing golf at the Las Vegas Country Club when Wayne Newton said he had to get home to his daughter's birthday party. When Al Fischer said he wanted to send her a video game machine as a present, my dad volunteered and said he have it delivered to Mr. Newton. I was given the address to Wayne Newton's house on Sunset to deliver the Pac-Man machine and did as I was instructed by my dad. I went by myself since my father told me there would be plenty of help to unload the Pac-Man machine, and thank gosh there was because it was heavy.

Wayne Newton and his daughter Erin (*left*)
and her birthday present (*right*)

When I arrived at Wayne Newton's Casa de Shenandoah Ranch, I was amazed. It was a beautifully appointed front entrance with the name of the Ranch on the entry gate. After I was "buzzed" in the front gate, I was met by Mrs. Wayne Newton who asked if I could drive around the back of the house and told me that's where her husband could be found. Mrs. Newton was an attractive Asian woman in her midthirties. Wayne Newton has appeared at numerous hotel-casinos for over sixty years and even owned the Aladdin Hotel for a while.

Elaine Okamura and Wayne Newton were married in 1968 and were married for sixteen years. They have one child, Erin Newton, born on July 25, 1976. They divorced in 1985.

"Mr. Las Vegas"

In 1994, Newton married Kathleen McCrone, a lawyer from North Olmsted, Ohio.

As I drove around the back of the Casa de Shenandoah, I was impressed with the green manicured lawn and the sparkling blue lake but mostly with the four beautiful brown Arabian horses wandering around the estate.

I knew Wayne Newton was successful, but this place was something that didn't even belong in Las Vegas. I had driven by this same entrance countless times while visiting my dad, who lived around the corner on Tobias. I never knew what lay beyond the white walls of this magnificent estate. Upon arriving at the back of the house Mr. Newton greeted me and called out to what he termed as his stage-hands. He instructed us to take the video console machine upstairs. I was just happy that they were there to help us take the Pac-Mac machine to Wayne Newton's daughter's room upstairs! "Nice to meet you, Mr. Newton. I am a fan of yours."

He thanked me and said that he appreciated what I and my dad were doing for his daughter's birthday. "She's asleep, and it's a surprise, so I'll try to be quiet and see you upstairs."

After we dragged the Pac-Man game console up two flights of stairs, we unpacked it and plugged it in just in time. Mr. Newton and his daughter joined us, smiling from cheek to cheek. Mr. Newton thanked me and offered me a tip, which I flatly refused, and said, "My dad wouldn't let me take it, sir. But thanks anyway."

"Okay," Mr. Newton said, "but you can be my guest to my show at the Aladdin."

I remember what my father said about accepting favors, so I never took him up on his offer. Wayne Newton is an amazing performer, and we saw him at almost every hotel while growing up in Las Vegas. One of my favorite songs is "Daddy Don't You Walk So Fast" that Wayne Newton recorded in 1985, and he still sings today at the Flamingo Hotel/Casino.

In 1983, Carnival Leisure Industries, a great customer of Paul-Son, was opening the Cable Beach Casino, the largest casino in the Bahamas. The Cable Beach where the casino would be located is world-famous for its two and a half miles of fabulous beach, sand, and crystal waters and for the myriad upscale resorts that line it with five first-class or luxury resorts, a golf course, nightlife, and the largest casino in the islands of the Bahamas. The only problem was they only gave us one week to deliver their chip order for the casino. Someone in the corporate purchasing office forgot to order their chips and was fired, and we were left in a lurch. The casino manager, George

Negron, assured me that overtime charges were not a problem and that the casino opened in two weeks. When I received their deposit from Federal Express, I decided to hand carry the order to our factory in Mexico. It was the only chance I had to get their chip order produced in time. That meant I would have to hand-carry the chips on a flight to Nassau, and I wasn't convinced that I could still make their grand opening. My dad decided to accompany me to Mexico to work at the plant and help get the order possessed in time. I've never heard my father complain about his health, but this time he did, and he was in pain. For the first time that I can remember, he asked me to drive. On the seven-hour trek to the factory, he told me that he had a toothache and asked me to pull over to the next store where he bought some aspirin for the road.

When we arrived at the Best Western in Yuma Arizona where we normally stayed, we had a brief dinner and went to bed.

Paul-Son Mexican factory number two in San Luis, Mexico.

I could tell my dad was uncomfortable as he kept me awake snoring unusually loud that night. When we arrived at the San Luis factory the next morning, we were greeted by our general manager, Frank Moreno, who asked if we had a safe trip and if we needed anything. My dad immediately replied, "A pair of pliers please, Frank."

Frank obliged my dad's request and fetched a pair that was close by his desk. My father immediately put the pliers in his mouth and pulled his own tooth out! Blood began to spurt out of my father's mouth at once. I immediately grabbed paper towels from the bathroom and handed them to my father, who was now soaked in blood. Frank Moreno yelled out, "Paul, why didn't you tell me you had a toothache? My brother is a dentist. Let me take you to him right now."

"I don't need a dentist now. I'm fine, thank you," quipped my dad.

Within ten minutes Frank's brother, Dr. Eduardo Moreno, was standing in front of my dad with his dental bag. He instructed my dad to sit down and elevate his head so he wouldn't get an infection. He prescribed my dad antibiotics, but he refused any pain medication. Yep, that was my dad.

Once the chip order for Carnival's Cable Beach was completed, I loaded the chips in my suitcase and headed to the closest airport in Yuma, Arizona. Luckily, I arrived safely in Nassau the next day with minimum custom issues, even though I was carrying over two million dollars in chips with me! When I arrived at the Nassau airport, the casino manager, George Negron, was ecstatic as he greeted me. "Welcome to the Bahamas, man," he said as the grand opening of the casino was the day after tomorrow. I was so relieved that I had made it with an extra day to spare! "The CEO of Carnival, along with dignitaries from the local government, will be at the grand opening. But first, we are going fishing."

"Fishing, really, George?" I replied. After we counted in the chips to the new casino cage, Negron told me to check in and that we would have dinner in an hour and go fishing tomorrow. I had previously met George Negron as he had been a casino manager on the Ecstasy, one of Carnival's cruise lines a year earlier, but I never expected to be invited to go fishing.

When Negron picked me up in front of the casino, he was carrying two long sticks with fishing lines and hooks on them. As we got into his well-appointed but simple fishing boat, he immediately put fish bait on each line. I was embarrassed to ask but the only way I had ever fished in the past was with a fishing pole with fishing reels, but these didn't have any. I finally decided to ask George, "How are we supposed to fish without a reel?"

"Oh," he said, "we don't use reels. We use our hands to wind the fishing line."

I was surprised when I dropped my line in the water, but once I caught my first fish, I realized that it was easier than I thought. Even though I enjoyed our time together, I never went line fishing again after that day. The Cable Beach Casino was rebranded in 1988 as the Crystal Palace Casino.

Carnival's Crystal Palace Casino, Nassau, the Bahamas

I made a return trip to the New Crystal Palace in 1988 for Paul-Son with my wife to deliver new chips and set-up a new table game expansion. I was happy to see George Negron again, who was now the general manager. What I found remarkable in the two years that I was gone were the vast improvements that Negron had made to the property, in particular, customer service. When I first went to Crystal Palace to deliver their chips two years before, the room was just okay. But the shower was broken, and sand was coming out of the spout. When I asked room service to repair my shower, it was never done by the time I checked out. Also, when I ordered a roast beef sandwich from the coffee shop, the waiter brought me corned beef, which I don't care for. When I asked the waiter for roast beef, he rudely replied, "We don't have any roast beef, and I thought you would like corned beef." However, this time it was different. When my wife and I arrived at the hotel entrance, we were greeted by security who opened our doors, handed us a newspaper, and welcomed us to the New Crystal Palace. When we checked into our hotel room, it was eloquently appointed. And the food this time, in the same coffee shop, was wonderful, especially the conch chowder.

When I congratulated Negron about his hospitality improvements at the property, his response simply was that "we put everyone to school," and boy did it show. The next time I saw George Negron, he was having a drink at my wedding. Carnival Cruise Lines decided to fold its hand in Nassau and in 1992 put its Crystal Palace Hotel and Casino up for sale after losing $135 million on the 1,500-room resort. Nassau's Crystal Palace Casino closed ahead of the debut of the new Baha Mar resort and casino project that would bring more than 2,000 hotel rooms and the largest gaming and convention facility.

Paul-Son was also the exclusive chip supplier to all of the cruise lines, including Carnival, except for Disney Cruise Lines because it does not have any casinos on any of its ships even though we presented a sample Mickey Mouse blackjack table that was rejected by the Walt Disney Company.

Princess, Carnival, Norwegian, Holland America,
Royal Caribbean casino gaming chips

My dad found happiness again in his personal life when he married Aniela Esswein on June 14, 1973. They had been introduced to each other by Mr. Robert Picardo, half owner of the Golden Gate Casino at the time.

The Golden Gate Casino 1955 and in 1973

They were married on my Dad's fishing boat on Lake Mead. Even though I no longer speak to Aniela, she was a great wife and

friend to my father in his later years and affectionately called him
"Papa Bear." They enjoyed traveling and spending time in Mexico
when Dad wasn't working, which was most of the time. As the
city's original casino, Golden Gate Hotel and Casino brought about
many Las Vegas "firsts." In 1905, the land for Golden Gate (previously Hotel Nevada) was purchased, making it the first casino
in Las Vegas. The Golden Gate Hotel & Casino is located at One
Fremont Street in Las Vegas, Nevada, United States. A part of the
Fremont Street Experience, it is the oldest and smallest hotel (106
rooms) on the Fremont Street Experience. John F. Miller initially
opened a temporary tent hotel—the Miller Hotel—on the property
in 1905 while he planned to construct a permanent hotel structure,
which opened as the Hotel Nevada on January 13, 1906. A casino
operated within the hotel until a statewide gambling ban took effect
in 1909. In 1931, the property was expanded and renamed as Sal
Sagev ("Las Vegas" spelled backward). The casino reopened that year
when gambling in Nevada was legalized again. In 1955, the casino
was renamed the Golden Gate. The entire property was renamed
the Golden Gate Hotel and Casino in 1974. The Golden Gate was
known for its cheap shrimp cocktails, served from 1959 to 2017.
In July 1955, Abe Miller, the property's longtime operator and the
son of John F. Miller, was approved for plans to lease the Sal Sagev's
ground floor to a twenty-three-man group, which would sublease the
floor for $25,000 per month to eight Italian American men, nearly
all of them from Oakland, California. The eight men planned to
open the Golden Gate casino on the ground floor of the Sal Sagev.
Renovations on the new casino were underway that month and were
being financed by the twenty-three-man group, with an estimated
cost of $330,000. Abe Miller was to receive $2,300 per month, as
well as 5 percent of the gambling profits. The Golden Gate casino,
named after the Golden Gate Bridge, opened on the ground floor
later in 1955 while the hotel retained the Sal Sagev name. Italo
Ghelfi, one of the eight partners, operated the casino for nearly forty
years along with Bobby Picardo. The four-story 106-room hotel was
renovated in 2005. By that time, the property was managed by Mark
Brandenburg, Ghelfi's son. Brandenburg later became the owner. In

March 2008, Brandenberg sold a 50 percent interest in the property to Desert Rock Enterprises, the investment company of Derek and Greg Stevens (who also owned the Las Vegas 51s baseball team), and a 19 percent stake in the Riviera Casino. With new money infused by the Stevens, the Golden Gate undertook casino upgrades and hotel room renovations. The following year, the Stevens raised their stake to 60 percent, and Derek took over as CEO with Brandenburg as president. The Golden Gate was the first to serve a $0.50 shrimp cocktail in 1959, now a Las Vegas cliché. The idea came from owner Italo Ghelfi, who based it on Fisherman's Wharf in San Francisco.

In the 1980s the glittery and gaudy capital of American gambling faced more competition for the gambling dollar and yet never have its casinos been more popular and profitable. Las Vegas has responded to the new realities of gaming by trying to transform itself from a sin city into a family entertainment zone where wagering seems as routine as taking in a movie according to Robert Reinhold, special to the *New York Times*, on May 30, 1989. "We are dealing more with the masses of people now," said the casino's part owner, Michael Gaughan, whose family has run casinos here since 1951. "In the early days, we had only a few slot machines for the wives." Even as other parts of Nevada have suffered from out-of-state gambling competition, the Las Vegas Strip booms. Despite new competition from Atlantic City and lotteries run by twenty-eight states and the District of Columbia that drew an estimated $15 billion to $17 billion last year, the number of visitors to Las Vegas swelled to $17.2 million last year, nearly a 50 percent increase over 1982. And since 1984, gross casino revenues in Clark County (mainly Las Vegas) have grown from 41 percent to 44 percent of the American casino gambling total. In 1988, casinos here raked in $3.1 billion before taxes and expenses. Las Vegas has benefited mightily from the sea change in American attitudes that have brought gambling out of the shadows of immorality and crime. Las Vegas has skillfully positioned and promoted itself as a convention, entertainment, sports, and family destination—a warm oasis in the desert offering much more than just gambling. As such, Las Vegas was in a good position to cater to the new generation of gamblers in the view of William R. Eadington, a leading gaming authority at the University of Nevada in Reno. In contrast to the hardened high rollers of the past, he said that the newcomers tend to be people for whom the gambling was "incidental" to a weekend "escape from everyday life" that might also include boating on Lake Mead. In the casinos, computerized slot and poker machines installed in the last decade are crowding out the craps and other "table" games because the new generation, weaned on Pac-Man and Asteroids video games, was more at ease with them than sitting before a dealer glowering at their mistakes. "They feel much more comfortable with the machines. Society has become much more computer-oriented," said John V. Giovenco, president of the Hilton Nevada Corporation. Lurking in the background are many threats, not least of which is the new gambling competition, from government-run lotteries; relaxed federal laws on Indian gaming; casinos in Atlantic City, Puerto Rico, Canada, and on cruise ships; legal card clubs in California and other states; and now from the prospect of full casinos in South Dakota, Indiana, Iowa and Ohio. Indeed, the boom here did not extend much beyond the Strip, and Nevada officials are worried that the state's fifty-year-old near-monopoly on legal gambling is being eroded. Casino growth and profits are decidedly sluggish in Reno, South Lake Tahoe, and Downtown Las Vegas. Before-tax profits are highest on the Strip and in the thriving new town of Laughlin on the Arizona border, which also promotes itself as a resort boom that is fueled by more than gambling. For now, Las Vegas appears confident it can withstand the new competition with its mass of entertainment, services, transportation, and trained employees that took half a century to build up. "People are not going to drive to Gary, Indiana, or Deadwood, South Dakota, simply for the gambling," said Sig Rogich, an advertising man here who created the new campaign depicting Las Vegas as a diversified resort rather than just a gambling center.

The "Mafia/Rat Pack" Las Vegas of the mid-twentieth century came to a gradual end in the 1980s with the aging out of the World War II generation, the decline of organized crime elements, and the rise of baby-boomer entrepreneurs who began a new chapter in the city's history, the so-called megaresort era. Las Vegas began to become a more commercialized, family-oriented place with large corporations coming to own the hotels, casinos, and nightclubs in place of Mafia bosses. The megaresort era kicked off in 1989 with the construction of the Mirage. Built by developer Steve Wynn, it was the first resort built with money from Wall Street, selling $630 million in junk bonds. Its 3,044 rooms, each with gold-tinted windows, set a new standard for Vegas luxury and attracted tourists in droves, leading to additional financing and rapid growth on the Las Vegas Strip. More landmark hotels and other structures were razed to make way for ever larger and more opulent resorts. More than 11,000 new hotel rooms were under construction in Las Vegas, and 34,000 more were planned. By 1992, Las Vegas would have six of the world's seven largest hotels. With 61,000 rooms it competed effectively with New York and San Francisco for major conventions. There were title fights, golf tournaments, rodeos, the Wet'n'Wild aquatic park for children, and new retirement complexes. Still, gambling ultimately drove everything. Going up on one end of the Strip was the massive Excalibur Hotel and Casino, four twenty-eight-story towers on 117 acres, 4,032 rooms in a modern-day version of a medieval castle with turrets, battlements, and moats that would be the world's largest hotel. Abetted by technology, much gambling has changed apart from the eternal verity that the average gambler goes home poorer than when he arrived. In 1983, for the first time, the betting on slots exceeded that on table games in Nevada. There are now more than 122,000 electronic game machines statewide. Last year, machines represented 46 percent of the Strip action up from 20 percent in 1976. Fading fast is craps, a dice game preferred by the World War II generation. Having once scorned them, the casinos now pamper regular slot players with special "slot hosts" who offer them drinks and take their names and addresses. The allure is heightened through big cumulative jackpots and the "Megabucks"' and "QuarterMania" games by which thousands of slots are connected to a central computer at International Game Technology in Reno so slot players statewide can compete for the same huge jackpot like a lottery. Meanwhile, casinos are bending over backward to initiate newcomers, training dealers not to embarrass novices. Most casinos offer free gambling lessons. The Las Vegas

Hilton even offered a special low-stakes blackjack "learning center" with a $5 maximum, where a friendly dealer will tell you when you are doing the wrong thing. A driving force behind the broadening of Las Vegas's appeal has been the Convention and Visitors Authority, the authority that widely promotes it as a family destination in television and newspaper advertising nationwide. It has also encouraged the development of theme parks near the Strip for youngsters. "In the last five years, our family activity has doubled," said the executive director, Frank C. Sain (Nagging Fears of Bust, Image Struggle Goes On). But many here worry that the gambling and tourism boom cannot last. "Any market will become saturated, so we need to balance our economy so it doesn't become like Texas with oil," said Douglas R. Bell of the Clark County Community and Economic Development Department. Given its image of tawdry garishness and once-well-known links to organized crime, Las Vegas has never had much success in attracting other industries. But a new push is having some success, promoting low costs, no personal or corporate income taxes, proximity to the huge markets of Southern California, good transportation, weak unions, pleasant climate, and good recreation. But Las Vegas continues to struggle against its image—an image not helped by statistics showing that Nevada ranks highest among the states in teenage suicides, third in the rate of abortion, and highest in per capita consumption of alcoholic beverages, although some of this must be attributed to visitors. "Image is the ultimate issue we have to contend with," said Mr. Bell. Still. Tourism and gambling overwhelm the diversification efforts. "Gaming is going to be the number one industry here for a long time," said Dennis L. Amerine of the Nevada Gaming Control Board. "It's healthy to try to diversify, but I don't see any significant impact on revenues. Nothing is going to take the place of gambling." But everybody here knows Las Vegas is vulnerable should California adopt casino gambling or go for video lottery machines with instant payoffs.

CHAPTER 19

Vegas Reimagined

Las Vegas transforms again from "family-friendly" to "luxury resorts."

The turn of the twenty-first century saw Las Vegas and the Strip invest in what made it famous in the first place—a return to its more sinful roots. According to a Las Vegas Convention and Visitors Authority spokeswoman, "There's some appeal for families, but Las Vegas is a destination that's best suited for adults" (Lee 2004, 1). This shift in marketing was perhaps most apparent in new TV spots with the tagline "What happens here stays here." Unlike in previous years, though, this time Las Vegas would reinvent itself as a luxury destination, an adult playground where those with wealth could trade up (Yeoman and McMahon-Beattie 2018), living out their dreams and fantasies surrounded by extravagance. With rising incomes and increased personal propensity, many guests became more demanding, seeking out quality innovation, premium choices, and increasingly personalized customer service (Yeoman and McMahon-Beattie 2014). As a result in the late 1990s, the more family-friendly theming was removed from both the Luxor and MGM Grand resorts (Lee 2004).

In 1998 the Bellagio opened its doors, a resort steeped in classical elegance inspired by the Lake Como town in Italy. Soon the Venetian, Palazzo, Wynn, Encore, CityCenter, and the Cosmopolitan would follow in its footsteps, all representative of the trend toward a higher degree of opulence and luxury in Las Vegas (Richard 2018).

Amid all the glitz and glamour of the luxurious resorts that were transforming the Strip was an ongoing trend, perhaps apparent to longtime visitors of Las Vegas, a shift in revenues away from gaming toward other lines of business. It was a trend that was accelerated by the Great Recession and its lasting impact on Las Vegas and its casinos. An understanding developed that for the city to survive and remain successful, even though gaming was an important source of profits, it could not remain the only source of revenue. Resorts had to work hard to encourage guests to visit their adult playground with more opulent bars and lounges, bigger and better clubs with world-renowned DJs, fine-dining restaurants in collaboration with celebrity chefs, and more exciting and dazzling shows and entertainment. As new luxury resort construction continued in Las Vegas, older casinos were also being rebranded and had to order new chips and gaming supplies from Paul-Son.

Now not unlike the casinos, as resort theming changed from family-friendly to luxury, Paul-Son became more dependent on replacement orders. To do so, Paul-Son expanded our manufacturing operations in Mexico once again.

In early 1997, Paul-Son acquired a 66,400-square-foot playing card plant located adjacent to its San Luis facility, allowing the company to consolidate its playing card operations in Mexico—a move that it hoped would make its playing cards more competitive in the marketplace. As a result, my dad spent more and more time at the Mexico factory. He used to say, "We need to spend more time in fields," referencing the need to spend more time on the factory floor. It was not unusual for the sales team in Las Vegas to complain about either the delivery time or some minor quality issue out of the factory. It was also not unusual for the production team in Mexico to complain about the short lead time they got from sales to produce the product for the customer. This upset my father, so he decided to teach them both a lesson. One day he insisted that the two teams trade place. So the sales department went to Mexico with him and tried to produce the product, and the production team was sent to Las Vegas with our sales manager. I don't believe Paul-Son sold or manufactured any product during that two-week experiment. However, once each team returned to their perspective job, they never complained to me again.

The Paris Las Vegas is a hotel and casino located on the Las Vegas Strip in Paradise, Nevada. It is owned and operated by Caesars Entertainment Corporation and has a 95,263-square-foot casino with over 1,700 slot machines. The theme is the city of Paris, France. It includes a half scale, 540-foot-tall (164.6-meter) replica of the Eiffel Tower. The Paris Hotel & Casino also has a sign in the shape of the Montgolfier balloon, a two-thirds-size Arc de Triomphe, a replica of La Fontaine des Mers, and a 1,200-seat theater called Le Theatre des Arts. The front of the hotel suggests the Louvre, Musée d'Orsay, and the Paris Opera House. The Paris is linked via a promenade to its sister property, Bally's Las Vegas, through which it is linked to the Las Vegas Monorail at the Bally's & Paris Station. In May 1995, Bally Entertainment, owner of the adjacent Bally's Las Vegas, announced the projects at a shareholders meeting. Paris was designed by architectural companies Leidenfrost/Horowitz & Associates, Bergman Walls & Assocciates, and MBH Architects. Paris Las Vegas opened on September 1, 1999, with fireworks being shot from the Eiffel Tower. French actress Catherine Deneuve flipped a switch, turning on all of Paris's lights, including the various crystal chandeliers in the main lobby.

$100,000—the highest-value casino chip?

This chip rarely sees the light of day, and usually only comes out for players with a million-dollar credit limit or more. It was our distinct pleasure to fondle it for a full three seconds before we were tackled by a Paris Las Vegas security guard. (We probably shouldn't have shared that we did sleight-of-hand magic in a former life.) As we got a closer look at this majestic $100,000 chip, we noticed a little speck on it and were ready to photoshop it away but then realized it wasn't a speck after all. It's a computer chip adhered to the baccarat chip for top secret security reasons. See it? Here's a close-up.

It's a computer chip adhered to the baccarat chip for top secret security reason. A bonus factoid: from what we hear, next door to Paris, Planet, Hollywood, all the chips have these security devices, called radio-frequency identification tags (or "RFID tags"). RFID tags, used for years to track livestock, are useful in detecting fake chips. The $100,000 chip is usually reserved for baccarat or mini-baccarat in a high-limit salon. During our quest for the biggest chip, we also asked what the maximum bet would be at blackjack at, say Caesars Palace. The answer: a guest could bet $25,000 a hand, three hands at a time. So that's a maximum of $75,000 a pop. (A guest can also bet $50,000 on one hand. That's said to be the highest one blackjack-hand bet accepted in Las Vegas.)

For what it's worth, the maximum bet at Planet Hollywood's baccarat tables is a whopping $200,000.

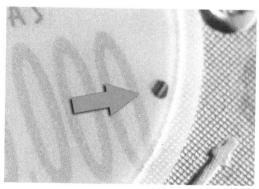

Paul-Son anti-counterfeit chip.

Paul-Son manufactured the chips for Paris including the high-value $100,000 chips which were the highest value chips that Paul-Son manufactured. In addition to Paris we manufactured $100,000 chips for some of the most luxury resorts including the Aria, Bellagio, Dunes, Caesars Palace, MGM, Mirage, and Wynn in Las Vegas. The typical size of standard casino gaming chips is thirty-nine millimeters. However, the highest value chips and particularly the Baccarat chips were either forty-three millimeters or a rectangle/oval gaming plaque that the Dunes Hotel and Casino and Caesars Atlantic City offered.

However, the largest denomination chip Paul-Son ever manufactured were some one-million-dollar chips for Caesars Palace for a high roller that were never circulated. I don't believe the chips to this day were ever offered by the casino.

Some Casinos offered their casino patrons a plaque for their grand opening celebration. These marketing plaques, however, typically did not have any value.

Not only were these plaques taken by casino patrons but also chip collectors, which have become more popular over the years.

Casino chip collecting is the practice of intentionally taking casino chips (also called "checks") from casino premises or trading or collecting online or in person for collection. Casino chip collecting is a variety of exonumia or coin collecting. Before it became a more serious hobby, casino chip collecting was simply a case of people keeping them as souvenirs from a casino they may visit. The biggest boost to the hobby came with the creation of the online auction site, eBay. eBay has now become the most popular way to collect and trade casino chips with listings in the casino category regularly, including more than twenty thousand items for sale. Casino chip collecting became increasingly popular during the 1980s as evidenced by the sale of chips through several casinos and collecting newsletters. Bill Borland's *Worldwide Casino Exchange* (early 1980s) had a casino story each issue and dozens of old chips for sale. Likewise, Al W. Moe's *Casino and Gaming Chips* magazine ran for several years in the mid-1980s and attracted hundreds of subscribers. Each issue featured stories and pictures from old Nevada casinos and included photos of old, collectible chips. Archie Black established the Casino Chip & Gaming Tokens Collectors Club (CC&GTCC) in 1988 in response to the continuing evolution and popularity of chip collecting. Membership in the club includes an annual subscription to the club's magazine, *Casino Collectible News*, now in its twenty-sixth year. The magazine has won six First Place Awards from the American Numismatic Association for Outstanding Specialty Numismatic Publication. The club held its first annual convention at the Aladdin Hotel and Casino in 1992. The twenty-second annual convention wrapped up in June, and the twenty-third annual convention was held at South Point Hotel, Casino & Spa from June 25 to 27, 2015. The South Point Hotel, Casino & Spa now hosts the CC&GTCC every year. As the number of collectors grew, the creation of an official grading system was viewed as being a useful tool in part of the process to help determine the collectible value of the chips as opposed to the face value they can also represent. In 2003, members of the CC&GTCC's Standards and Archives Committee agreed on a grading system that would be used worldwide. There are many published price guides; but two, in particular, are more widely used by casino chip collectors. *The Official U.S. Casino Chip Price Guide*, now in its fourth edition, covers chips from casinos in Nevada, Atlantic City, New Jersey, Colorado, Deadwood, South Dakota, and the several Midwest States that permit Riverboat casinos. *The Chip Rack*, now in its fifteenth edition, attempts to include all chips and checks issued by casinos in the State of Nevada. Some chips are considered high-value and have a listed value as high as $50,000. During their 2014 convention, a $5 chip from the Lucky Casino sold for $52,500, and a $5 Paul-Son chip from the Golden Goose Casino sold for $75,000!

My dad and I supported the chip collectors in Las Vegas and attended their convention for many years. We would often receive calls from chip collectors all over the world asking about the value chips, or whether we were making any new chips. Most chip collectors would somehow know when new chips were delivered, so they could be there to grab them first. When my dad wasn't working in Mexico, he and his wife Aniela helped at Asilo de Ancianos, a home for impoverished and elderly Mexican women.

My dad was also a contributor to several orphanages in Mexico, where the Paul-Son factory is a chief source of income to the people of San Luis, Mexico. My family (Grandmother Pat, Mother Jean, and wife Cathy) all attended the dedication to the senior home ceremony in 1992 that my father held for my late brother Tommy Endy.

Many of our customers wanted to tour the factory where their chips were made, so my father was the official tour guide when he was needed, and he often took them fishing after the tour of the factory. As his wealth grew, my dad spread it around to numerous charities, especially those who helped young people. He was a past chairman and member of the Board of Directors of WestCare, a nonprofit drug rehabilitation program. His other charitable causes included the Boy Scouts, the UNLV, and Chaparral High School baseball teams. In 1984 the Men's National AAU Basketball Championships held in Las Vegas was dedicated to my late brother, Tommy.

THOMAS D. ENDY

1953 — 1983

"If you have anything really valuable to contribute to the world, it will come through the expression of your own personality—that single spark of divinity that sets you off and makes you different from every other living creature."
BRUCE BARTON

Remembering Las Vegas's first national basketball champions by
Ron Kantowski, *Las Vegas Review-Journal*, April 1, 1984.

In the article "Remembering Las Vegas' first national basketball champions," Paul Son-Dice of Las Vegas (led by former UNLV Rebels Armon Gilliam, Sudden Sam Smith, and Greg Goorjian) won the 1984 AAU men's national basketball championship on home turf. The Amateur Athletic Union is a youth sports organization with groups of players that get together and form independent teams that compete in AAU tournaments against other teams. Since it was first created, the goal of AAU has been to advance the development of youth sports and physical fitness programs. Armon Gilliam, number 35, the former UNLV great, signed his name above the long list of former AAU national champions. In its heyday, the AAU national championship was about as good as it got, outside of the NCAA Tournament and the NIT and the NBA on CBS. Former AAU MVPs include Tom Meschery, Bob Boozer, Don Kojis, Larry Brown, Cazzie Russell, and Darnell Hillman, all of whom played in the pros. After winning the AAU title the year the AAU championships were played at UNLV, Larry Keever said Paul-Son Dice received an invitation from Dale Brown to play his Louisiana State team in Baton Rouge.

By then, Gilliam (who died in 2011 at age of forty-seven while playing pickup basketball) was dominating the paint for the Rebels and the team pretty much had disbanded. The AAU tournament was in memory of my late brother and Paul Endy's son Tom Endy. Tom was a basketball fan and loved going to both UNLV basketball and football games.

Paul-Son Dice won the 1984 AAU basketball Championship in 1984 the year it was held in Las Vegas. Team members included (*front row, left to right*) Sam Smith, Melvin Washington, sponsor Paul Endy, Greg Goorgian, Terry Manghum; Coach Larry Keever Bobby Joe Jacobs, Melvin Bennett, Keith Starr, manager Mike Pilz (*middle row*); Chris Jackson, Allen Holder, Armon Gilliam (*back row*).

The University of Nevada, Las Vegas (UNLV), was officially established in 1957 with the construction of Maude Frazier Hall. Despite its short history, UNLV has seen dramatic growth in all areas over the years. More than 120 graduate and underrate programs are offered to a student body that reached over 19,500 in fall 1991. UNLV's class of 2000 numbered approximately 3,744 as compared with 3,071 in 1999.

The figure for 2000 included students who completed their degree work in August 1999, December 1999, and May 2000. The increase in undergraduate degrees was approximately 22 percent while the number of graduate degrees climbed about 23 percent. UNLV has over 600 facility members, 73 percent of whom held doctoral degrees.

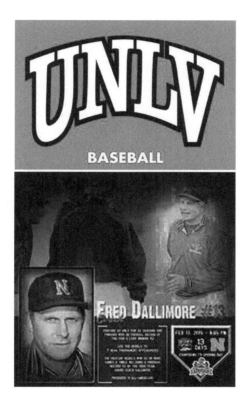

One of the winningest coaches in college baseball history, Fred Dallimore, led UNLV for twenty-three seasons and compiled an overall record of 794–558–2 (0.587). He averaged a stunning 34.5 wins per season. In 1994 the UNLV baseball team gave my dad the distinguished individual award for his contributions.

My dad was friends with UNLV Baseball coach Fred Dallimore, who is the only man to ever become synonymous with UNLV baseball. In fact, it was he who almost single-handedly built the program according to my dad. Even though my father preferred UNLV baseball, I preferred UNLV basketball and we had season tickets for many years. I attended almost every UNLV game during the most exciting Jerry Tarkanian years at UNLV. Basketball games at that time were played at both the Las Vegas Convention Center and the Thomas and Mack Center where we enjoyed watching Coach Tarkanian and UNLV Runnin' Rebels.

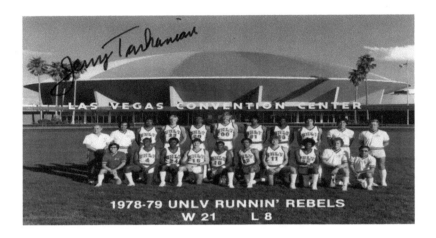

The 1990–1991 UNLV Runnin' Rebels basketball team represented the University of Nevada, Las Vegas in NCAA Division I men's competition in the 1990–1991 season. The Runnin' Rebels, coached by Jerry Tarkanian, entered the season as defending national champions and entered the 1991 NCAA tournament unbeaten but lost in the national semifinal to eventual champions Duke when Anderson Hunt's desperation three in the final seconds bounced off the backboard and into the hands of a Duke player, Bobby Hurley, ending a forty-five-game winning streak that dated back to the previous season. They had been the last team to finish the regular season unbeaten before St. Joseph's did it in 2004. They were the last team to enter the NCAA tournament unbeaten until Wichita State did it in 2014 and Kentucky in 2015. My dad enjoyed having dinner at Piero's restaurant with the owner, Freddy Glusman, who was good friends with Coach Tarkanian. Almost every time we had dinner at Piero's, we saw and always spoke to "Tark the Shark" as he was affectionately called.

My favorite restaurant growing up in Las Vegas was the Alpine Village German restaurant on Paradise which is now closed. The Alpine Village was located at 3003 Paradise Road across the street from the Las Vegas Hilton. This famous place began serving German food in a downtown location in 1950 then moved four times before settling into its final location on Paradise in 1970. The Alpine Village had a traditional dining room upstairs and a sing-along piano Rathskeller where traditional Bavarian-style singing and stein raising in the basement of the 250-seat dining room. One of the most memorable items of the Alpine Village Inn was their famous chicken soup and the seasoned cottage cheese (https://www.lasvegas360.com/2262/apline-village-inn/). When I was in TIME and Jubilation, we used to frequent the Rathskeller after performing at various functions in Las Vegas.

CHAPTER 20

Paul Endy is inducted into the Gaming Hall of Fame

The Gaming Hall of Fame
American Gaming Association

Gambling has a long and fascinating history, but it's only recently that those in the profession have chosen to honor their colleagues with exemplary careers with election to the Gaming Hall of Fame. Induction into the Gaming Hall of Fame is the highest honor accorded by the gaming-entertainment industry. Each year, two or more individuals who have distinguished themselves through significant contributions to the gaming-entertainment industry receive this honor. Created in 1989 with the induction of gaming industry legends Warren Nelson, Jay Sarno, William Harrah, Grant Sawyer, and E. Parry Thomas, the Gaming Hall of Fame now holds more than sixty members, including such industry giants as William Boyd, J. Terrence Lanni, and Steve Wynn. The AGA solicits nominations from its members, and then AGA staff and members of the board of directors confer to make the final selections. Over the years, the Hall of Fame's mark of distinction has been expanded in recent years to include culinary visionaries and entertainment legends such as Wolfgang Puck, Frank Sinatra, Wayne Newton, and Debbie Reynolds, who have helped shape the American gaming industry.

This exhibit chronicles the lives of those who have been inducted into the Gaming Hall of Fame. Las Vegas has been an enduring presence in the USA and the world for the past one hundred years. Paul Endy Jr. followed his father into the card-and-dice business.

After working for T. R. King & Co., a California gaming-supplies distributor and dice manufacturer for several years, Endy moved to Las Vegas and bought a bankrupt dice company in 1963. Endy renamed the company Paul-Son and began tailoring cards and dice to meet the needs of the growing Nevada casino industry. As the gaming industry expanded geographically throughout the United States in the 1980s and 1990s, Paul-Son opened new offices to keep pace. Paul-Son also went beyond just cards and dice, manufacturing casino furniture and other products as well. Also, Endy explored new technologies, including high-tech security features and improved graphics applications. In 1994, Paul-Son went public and in late 1998, Paul Endy stepped down as the company's CEO after thirty-five years at the helm. Two years later, Paul-Son was acquired by Bourgogne et Grasset, a French gaming manufacturer, which later renamed itself Gaming Products International. Paul Endy's career spanned some of the most dynamic decades in the history of the gaming industry, and his company helped to fuel the casino boom of the 1990s. He passed away in 1999 and was remembered, along with his wife Aniela, for contributing to a variety of civic and educations philanthropic endeavors.

Paul Endy Industry Leader proposed 1996 Inductee Paul Endy was inducted into the Gaming Hall of Fame October 3, 1996.

Over its relatively short history, Las Vegas has been influenced by a variety of factors from its geology to government and private infrastructure projects, to the economy, and the efforts of business visionaries and their corporations to reimagine the city. No one has influenced the city of Las Vegas and the gaming industry as a whole more than Paul Endy has done. As a result, I was able to get him inducted into the Gaming Hall of Fame in 1996 along with Donald Carano and Michael Rose. I was able to get my father inducted into the Gaming Hall of Fame on October 3, 1996, as he was a true legend in the gaming products industry. The induction was held at Caesars Palace, and almost all Paul-Son employees attended the event. Las Vegas holds a special place in our imaginations, an impossible city in the desert built by mobsters where A-list celebrities frequent, the elite party, and the world-renowned perform. It's a city that never sleeps with a 24-7 party of gambling, booze, music, and entertainment. An ever-adapting city, Las Vegas has reinvented itself time and again when necessary to survive and prosper. My father helped Las Vegas and made the gaming industry "grow larger by serving better." My dad was also a member of Zelzah Shrine Temple, Elks, Optimists International, Masons, and Scottish Rite. He was named 1990 Man of the Year by the San Luis Social Assistance Organization.

According to Darlene Terill, director of Special Projects for WestCare, "Paul Endy had a special place in his heart for our children and would often make a point of bringing his Hummer limo, pack it with the kids and take them to McDonald's and let them order whatever they wanted." WestCare, which was started in 1973, handles more than twenty-one thousand cases each year involving adult victims of substance abuse, high-risk youth, and families in crisis. It operates programs in Nevada, Arizona, and California. My Dad and his wife were honored for making numerous contributions to WestCare programs and were recognized at the organization's annual fund-raising dinner on March 26, 1996, at the Riviera Hotel and Casino.

LAS VEGAS SUN

WestCare to honor LV couple on Friday, March 1, 1996

WestCare, a private nonprofit agency devoted to the prevention and treatment of alcohol and drug abuse, is honoring a local couple for their longtime support.

Aniela and Paul Endy Jr., who have made numerous contributions to WestCare programs, were recognized at the organization's annual fund-raising dinner at the Riviera Hotel and Casino. Paul Endy founded Paul-Son Gaming Supplies, the nation's largest manufacturer of gaming tables, betting chips, and dice. Aniela Endy was an elementary school teacher. In addition to their work for WestCare, the Endys are supporters of Chaparral High School baseball, UNLV baseball, and the Boy Scouts of America. They also sponsor and support the Asilo de Ancianas, a home for elderly women and an orphanage in Guaymas, Mexico. WestCare, which started in 1973, handles more than twenty-one thousand cases each year involving adult victims of substance abuse, high-risk youth, and families in crisis. It operates programs in Nevada, Arizona, and California.

The Riviera Hotel and Casino opened in 1955 and imploded in 2016.

The Riviera Hotel was one of the oldest and well-known casino resorts on the Las Vegas Strip. It was officially opened on April 20, 1955, and it stopped operating in May 2015 after being bought by the Las Vegas Convention and Visitors Authority, which was imploded as part of the billion-dollar project of expanding the convention center. The hotel had over two thousand rooms, which were distributed among its two towers, the twenty-four-story Monaco Tower and twenty-two-story Monte Carlo Tower. The Riviera Hotel was a proposal by William Bischoff, a Detroit mobster, and was known as Casa Blanca, a casino by that time. In 1952 the casino received its gaming license, but later Bischoff left the project. Samuel Cohen, a Miami businessman, took over the project. Around March 1955, he was said not to be part of the group that invested in the project, but there was some indication that he was still involved. And other members like Marx Brothers Harpo and Gummo had minority interests during its opening. Just three months after its opening, the Riviera went bankrupt. In turn, previous managers of the Flamingo Hotel took over its management. Greenbaum, a part of the management, started embezzling the casino due to his gambling and drug addictions. In December 1958, he and his wife were murdered in their home. Thereafter, Sidney Korshark, a mob fixer, was the major manager of the resort. In June 1968, a group of bankers and some investors associated with Parvin-Dohrmann Corp. purchased the Riviera; and in 1969 the Riviera was sold to the Parvin-Dohrmann Corp. not to be stopped by the Nevada Gambling Control Board since the company's failure to report the change in ownership earlier on. In 1969 Dean Martin was hired to perform at the casino and was offered 10 percent of the interest in the resort. He later withdrew from the deal after the management denied him the opportunity to reduce his two nightly shows to one, and they bought back his shares.

My dad's favorite entertainer in Las Vegas, without a doubt, was Dean Martin and the Rat Pack with Frank Sinatra and Sammy Davis Junior. We saw Dean Martin perform at the Riviera, Bally's, and the Sands Hotel and Casino. Dean Martin (born Dino Paul Crocetti [June 7, 1917–December 25, 1995]), was an American actor, singer, and comedian. One of the most popular and enduring American entertainers of the mid-twentieth century, Martin was nicknamed "the King of Cool" for his seemingly effortless charisma and self-assurance. Martin gained his career breakthrough together with fellow comedian Jerry Lewis, billed as Martin and Lewis, in 1946. They performed in nightclubs and later had numerous appearances on radio, television, and in films. Following an acrimonious ending of the partnership in 1956, Martin pursued a solo career as a performer and actor. Martin established himself as a notable singer, recording numerous contemporary songs as well as standards from the Great American Songbook. He became one of the most popular acts in Las Vegas and was known for his friendship with fellow artists Frank Sinatra and Sammy Davis Jr. who together formed the Pack. Starting in 1964, Martin was the host of the television variety program The Dean Martin Show, which centered on Martin's singing talents and was characterized by his relaxed, easy-going demeanor. From 1974 to 1984 he was the roastmaster on the popular *Dean Martin Celebrity Roast*, which drew notable celebrities, comedians, and politicians. Throughout his career, Martin performed in concert stages, night-clubs, audio recordings and appeared in 85 film and television productions. His relaxed, warbling, crooning voice earned him dozens of hit singles, including his signature songs "Memories Are Made of This," "That's Amore," "Everybody Loves Somebody," "You're Nobody Till Somebody Loves You," "Sway," "Ain't That a Kick in the Head?" and "Volare." Dean Martin was by far the most popular entertainer to headline a showroom in Las Vegas. When he performed at Bally's, he performed more concerts in the 1,400-seat showroom than any other performer. On June 11, 1995, Dean played to his one millionth fan. He was quoted as saying, "I'm not trying to prove anything. I'm just singing and working and having a good time. Ain't that enough?"

We saw Dean Martin perform at the Sands
in the 1960s and Bally's in 1995.

In 1973, a Boston travel company, AITS Inc., managed by Meshulam Rikilis and Isidore Becker, bought the Riviera for $60 million. In 1983, the resort filed for Chapter 11 and appointed Jeffery Silver as the CEO with the hopes of him making the resort great again. Silver observed that it was better for him to target middle- and working-class gamblers other than high rollers. The resort went ahead with suffering of constant bankruptcy from 1988 to 1991, and was revived in 1993 as Riviera Holdings Corporation, but this time owned by its previous creditors. I have taken my dad's place at the table helping WestCare's community action counsel with Darlene Terril, director of development for Nevada.

In October 1998, my father was on a fishing trip in Mexico when he suffered a severe stroke. Just as he had done so many times, he took a group of friends with him, driving eleven hours and forty-four minutes (739.2 miles) from Las Vegas to San Carlos, Mexico.

When I got the telephone call from Michael Cox, my dad's CPA, who was with him on that fateful day, I was shocked. Cox had explained that my father was piloting his boat when he collapsed on the floor. Since the boat was about an hour from shore there was a mad rush to get my Dad to a hospital. Unfortunately, by the time they got him to a doctor, it was too late. The doctor wasn't able to give him an anti-stroke drug in time, and he was unresponsive. We eventually transported him to USC Medical Center in Southern California to be hospitalized. Since my father was mostly unresponsive, I stepped in as chief executive officer on an interim basis while my father recovered. While my dad was attempting a recovery at USC, I was running the company, traveling back and forth to the Mexico factory, dealing with our public shareholders, and flying back and forth to visit my father in Los Angeles. We eventually moved him back to Las Vegas's Sunrise Hospital for further rehabilitation. However, his mental condition continued to deteriorate as did his kidneys. Many of his friends and especially some Paul-Son employees believed he was getting better and would be back to run the company, which is what they preferred over me becoming CEO. What they didn't realize was that I missed him and wanted my dad back! Unfortunately, every time I went see him, he was continually getting worse and eventually wasn't able to remember his own name. When he lapsed into a coma, we said our goodbyes and transferred him to a hospice. In April 1999, when my father died, I became the permanent CEO of Paul-Son and sought to continue his legacy. In doing so, I had to make significant changes to streamline the company. After his death, there was so little time to grieve for my dad. Once I took care of the funeral costs, his wife handled most of the other funeral arrangements. Our son Daren played piano at my father's funeral, which was so touching. However, I had a public company to look after, and there were storms a brewing in Las Vegas. Paul-Son had posted a string of quarterly losses, and its overhead was way too high.

LAS VEGAS
REVIEW-JOURNAL

Eric Endy runs the world's largest live gaming supply distributorship.

After meeting with the board of directors, we hired a new CFO, further analyzed the financials, and decided to pursue strategic alternatives—a fancy way of saying we might consider selling the business. A former competitor of ours, the Bud Jones Co., had been purchased just a year earlier by the French company Establissements Bourgogne et Grasset SA. I didn't recognize the caller when my secretary passed me the telephone to me in November of 2000. It was the investment banker for Establissements Bourgogne et Grasset SA (aka B & G). He told me he had seen our press release and wanted to know if we were interested in a buyout from B & G. I of course responded that we were possibly interested. I told him I would speak to my board and get back to him as soon as possible. B & G was especially interesting to me because they had a huge footprint outside the United States and had been issued a patent for RFID readers for gaming chips for security and table management. At the time, more and more casinos were requesting better security devices and a more efficient way to track players to issue them comps for gambling. The CIS device that B & G possessed along with readers strategically placed under the layout could potentially accomplish what the casinos were requesting. It would also solve the problem that our chips were getting destroyed in the roulette chip sorting devices. Also, Macau approved legalized gaming, and according to our sales manager, B & G chips were the only ones used in Macau.

CHAPTER 21

Paul-Son Becomes Gaming Partners International

In January 2001 we signed a letter of intent to combine with the French company Establishments Bourgogne et Grasset SA and its subsidiary, the Bud Jones Company Inc. B & G was founded in 1923 and primarily served casinos in Europe and the Far East, providing plaques, jetons, chips, roulette wheels, layouts, tables, and accessories and equipment. In October 2000, B&G acquired Bud Jones, a competitor who was a Las Vegas-based company founded in 1965 that manufactured and distributed casino gaming equipment and accessories. I believe to this day that B & G was under the impression that the Bud Jones Company Inc. had the majority of the casino supply business, but they did not. Paul-Son did. As a matter of fact, at one time Paul-Son had 90 percent United States casino chip market; but Bud Jones, through a John Huxley distributorship, had a better percentage in the international market. By merging operations, we hoped to become the leader in the global casino table game market. The merger fell through at the time, however, and in April 2001 we placed a demand on B & G for a $1 million termination fee, which was part of the letter of intent. It took more than a year before we could iron out the terms of a new deal. In April 2002 we finally reached an agreement which, in September, the Paul-Son stockholders approved. Although B & G and Bud Jones became subsidiaries of Paul-Son Gaming Corporation, the transaction was really a reverse merger. In January 2001, we signed a letter of intent to combine with the French company B & G and its subsidiary, the Bud Jones Company Inc. As a result of the merger, I continued to help the company as a board member and shareholder; however, the new CEO of the company rarely asked for my help. The company continued to grow by acquiring TK Dice and Gemaco Playing Card Company—yes, the same one that we distributed back in 1978. I guess history really does repeat itself.

Wynn Macau opened in 2006.

Two years later in 2008, my wife opened Las Vegas Chinese School teaching Mandarin Chinese and bilingual after-school homework help. I even took a Chinese language class for the second time since it was such a difficult language for me to learn.

拉斯維加斯中文學校
張曉琴 校長

中文繁體 简体 1-12冊 課後輔導 學前班, 英數輔導
各科家教, 繪畫 電腦, AP 中文班 中文考級
成人中文會話 暑期班

電話: (702) 476-9888   傳真: (702) 476-0888
網址: www.lasvegaschineseschool.com
地址: 6284 Spring Mountain Road Las Vegas, Nevada 89146

Las Vegas Chinese School

*Chinese Traditional and Simplified, After school,
Preschool, English & Math Enrichment,
Private Tutoring in all Subjects, Painting,
Computer , AP Chinese, Chinese
Summer Camp, & Adult Conversation*

(702) 476-9888

Email: lvcs999@gmail.com • Fax: (702) 476-0888
Website: www.lasvegaschineseschool.com

Cathy Endy
Principal

6284 Spring Mountain Road Las Vegas, Nevada 89146

MGM Macau opened in 2017.

Macau, also spelled Macao (/məˈkaʊ/; 澳門; Cantonese: [ōu. mǔːn]; official Portuguese: [mɐˈkaw] Macau), is officially the Macao Special Administrative Region of the People's Republic of China. It is a city in the western Pearl River Delta by the South China Sea and is a special administrative region of China and maintains separate governing and economic systems from those of mainland China. With a population of 667,400 and an area of 32.9 square kilometers (12.7 square miles), it is the most densely populated region in the world. Macau was formerly a colony of the Portuguese Empire after Ming China leased the territory as a trading post in 1557. Macau has a capitalist service economy largely based on casino gaming and tourism. It is the world's eighty-third largest economy with a nominal GDP of approximately MOP433 billion (US$53.9 billion). Although Macau has one of the highest per-capita GDPs, the territory also has a high level of wealth disparity. Macau's gaming industry is the largest in the world, generating over MOP195 billion (US$24 billion) in revenue and about seven times larger than that of Las Vegas. Macau's gambling revenue was $37 billion in 2018. Casino gambling was legalized in 1962, and the gaming industry initially operated under a government-licensed monopoly granted to the Sociedad de Turismo e Diversões de Macau. This license was renegotiated and renewed several times before ending in 2002 after forty years. The government then allowed open bidding for casino licenses to attract foreign investors. Along with an easing of travel restrictions on mainland Chinese visitors, this triggered a period of rapid economic growth. From 1999 to 2016, Macau's gross domestic product multiplied by 7, and the unemployment rate dropped from 6.3 to 1.9 percent. The Sands Macao, Wynn Macau, MGM Macau, and Venetian Macau were all opened during the first decade after the liberalization of casino concessions.

Casinos employ about 24 percent of the total workforce in the region (footnote 94).

"Increased competition from casinos popping up across Asia to lure away Chinese high rollers and tourists" in Singapore, South Korea, Japan, Nepal, the Philippines, Australia, Vietnam, and the Russian Far East led in 2019 to the lowest revenues in three years. B & G would give Paul-Son the opportunity that we needed to sell outside the United States, in particular to Macau whose revenues had already exceeded the Las Vegas Strip. We would open a GPIC office in Macau in 2012.

Today more than half of the USA is within a ninety-minute drive of a casino. With total casino win down 7 percent on the Strip since 2007 the percentage of income from gambling is at an all-time low of 34 percent (Schwartz 2017). Since 2007 more than 17,000 rooms have been added in Las Vegas, with over $10 billion reinvested into the industry, adding new restaurants, convention and meeting spaces, entertainment venues, and world-class amenities (Heilman 2013). If the current pattern continues, it is even predicted that by 2020 rooms revenue will surpass that of gaming (Schwartz 2017) with food and beverage and entertainment continuing to be valuable sources of revenue for the traditionally casino-oriented corporations that now control a majority of the Strip and the greater Las Vegas area. In this environment, Las Vegas had to adapt to survive. Business as usual, where nongaming divisions were loss leaders handing out copious amounts of complimentary rooms and buffets, would no longer suffice. Steve Wynn remarked on the situation bluntly:

> The pattern is this: Gaming is a passive activity. It has no value. One roulette table is exactly the same as every other damn roulette table. The driver in our business is the non-casino activity. The driver in our business is the experiential value of the enterprise. (Tomaselli 2016, 1)

As a result of the changing atmosphere of casinos in the US and, in particular, the growth of casinos outside the United States, I decided I needed help, especially since my dad was gone; and I believed the reverse merger was the best alternative. Also, I was told by my estate lawyer that I would be responsible as the trustee of his living trust for over three million in estate taxes. The problem was that there wasn't any significant cash in his account, and the rest of his estate was paper stock. If the reverse merger were to go forward, I would need to work out a deal with the French to get some liquidity from Paul-Son stock because what was my dad's estate problem was now mine. Now I couldn't wait for the merger to happen! Once our board and our investment banker agreed in principal to the merger, I was both excited and afraid. A reverse merger wouldn't be great for me financially, but it would be for the company, and that was more important now that we were public. However, for the merger to even happen, I was told that we would have to cut our losses, reduce our overhead, and at least break even. That's exactly what we did even if it meant I was the bad guy! Before his death, my father went on a hiring spree at Paul-Son. He would often hire someone, tell me to fire them and then rehire them. At one time it became so difficult for me that I considered leaving the company. However, my dad and I made up and he had a better understanding of company policy. Also, my father thought his life might be in jeopardy because of another arrest that was made by a toy company in China attempting to counterfeit $100 Empress Cruise Lines. Once again, Jerry West was able to make an arrest and stop the potential counterfeiting. However, there were some threats made against the company according to Jerry West. The forging of casino chips is an age-old problem, but in recent years the scammers have become much more sophisticated, forging not only chips but also playing cards and dice. In the Philippines, South Korea, and especially in China, factories exist for cloning and copying all sorts of gaming equipment; but scammers obviously believe there is much more profit in the manufacture of gaming chips. In June 2005 a group of four Chinese men was arrested for covertly photographing the playing cards on a mini-baccarat table in an Australian casino so they could forge the playing cards and reintroduce them into the game at a later date through the method of hand mucking. The minicamera was concealed in a packet of slimline cigarettes. However, in the last decade with the expansion of casinos worldwide and the conversion of many countries in Europe into the euro currency, huge profits have been realized by gaming chip and card manufactures. This has enabled these chip and card companies to invest in new technology to combat the forgers. Certain card manufacturers are now offering playing cards with the casino's own logo designed in infrared on the face of the card and electronic baccarat shoes can be purchased. These shoes can read the cards as they are drawn from the shoe and correct dealer errors before they are about to be made. These security baccarat shoes work with an optical reader that identifies all the cards drawn, reading a bar code on the surface of the cards. The security baccarat shoe has the baccarat rules set in the firmware, so after identifying the cards as they are drawn it determines who the winner is—player, banker, or tie. This is immediately displayed on the digital table display unit. The software includes the possibility to adjust the game to the way each casino plays. It can be adjusted to the way to deal with burn cards (autoburn, static burn, manual), how to manage overdrawn cards or if you want to play face up or face down. If there is an incident occurring, an alarm will go off. The main benefit of these security baccarat shoes is the security that it brings to the game as it minimizes enormously dealing errors and cheating. It prevents card mucking and card swapping or rogue cards being introduced into the game. It also prevents the possibility of drawing two cards at the same time. At the time of writing, 750 of the smart shoes are employed throughout various casino baccarat tables in Macau. Chip manufacturing companies have been hard at work to bring efficient and cost-effective RFID (radio-frequency identification) solutions to the table games industry. Devices incorporated onto gaming tables to fight counterfeiting and fraudulent chips being introduced at the very first point of entry in the casino, the tables, and at all points of exchange. RFID chip security technology includes RFID embedded casino currency (gaming chips and plaques), hardware, and software that allows the operator the flexibility to track and verify gaming chip authenticity for its casino almost instantly, which can eliminate the possibility of counterfeit chips or errors in chip counts. RFID technology allows casinos the ability to track individual chips throughout the gaming floor and with special readers and software, follow payments, fills and credits, table drops, tips, win, and losses per table at any time of the day. This almost eliminates the possibility of theft and any counterfeiting attempts.

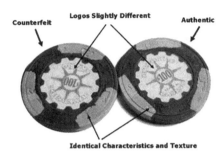

In late December 2008, the Argosy Casino in Kansas City, Missouri, US, during an investigation of the total chip stock, discovered one thousand one hundred, $100 fake chips during a monthly inventory. Just how this many chips remained undetected is a mystery. It seems that a cashier discovered the chips. While attempting to put them into racks, she noticed that the thickness of the chips was too great. A thirty-six-year-old man was later taken into custody, but until now there is no news of him being charged. The man is under investigation, accused of making hundreds of fake $100 chips then cashing them in for more than $100,000. The general manager of the casino said that the counterfeit chips were of such good quality that they were difficult to spot. Even more recently, just in April of 2009, the Crown Casino Melbourne realized through a routine check that they had over thirty-six one-thousand-dollar chips. A gaming floor worker raised the alarm as she handled one of the chips in a high-security count room. In a casino that size, it may be easier to pass forged chips without them being noticed. This called for a complete inventory of more than $13,700,0000 worth of chips, eventually leading to the discovery of all of $42,000 worth of forged chips. A recall and a completely new and improved set of $1,000 chips have since been issued.

It has not been announced how or when the fake chips were brought into the casino, and it is not known how long the chips have been in circulation on the gaming floor. Police are investigating and casino surveillance crews are reviewing hours of gaming table video recordings in a bid to discover the counterfeiting masterminds. No prizes will be awarded for guessing the nationality of the criminals involved.

Since my father was concerned about his safety after removing any counterfeit threats, he hired two security guards, my aunt Dorothy (my uncle Charlie's wife) to work in accounting, and a new investor relations "guy" out of Cleveland, Ohio, who caused me more problems than I already had. He claimed he represented a group of investors, and they weren't happy with the results of the company and that I needed his help. As a result, I was put in a position to put one of the investors on our board. Even though I was opposed to this recommendation, I was advised by my legal counsel that it was the right decision going forward. It was a decision I would later regret. To bring the company back to at least breakeven, I knew whatever I did wouldn't be appreciated or liked. I fired or laid off over ten people in the Las Vegas office, not including my own aunt Dorothy, who was laid off by our CFO, John Gardner. After John let my aunt Dorothy go, I never spoke to her or my uncle Charlie ever again. In 1998, Uncle Charlie went on to open a competing chip company called the Blue Chip Company, which was purchased by GPIC in 2000. With the support of my board, I fired the two security guards, terminated the investor relations guy, and closed the Louisiana office and one Mississippi office to further reduce costs and consolidate operations. When I fired the investor relations guy, I was sued and had to settle in arbitration by giving him some of my father's shares, which my father supposedly promised him for helping the company. I don't believe my father ever promised him anything. but I didn't want a lawsuit either.

I was told by my attorney that "there will be people crawling out of the woodwork that you've never seen before that are going to want something." Unfortunately, there wasn't anything in the estate except my dad's paper stock, and the IRS wanted $3 million in estate taxes. However, Mike Bonner was correct as I began receiving calls either from relatives or other people that I didn't know who wanted something. I would hire an IRS attorney to help me deal with my IRS problem since I had received a letter from them putting demand on my house. I eventually moved the IRS dispute to Los Angeles where I was able to reach a more favorable resolution and at least keep our house.

Former gaming partners International Board and Gemaco managers

A thank-you for serving on the board of GPIC

Mr. Alain Thiefry, former GPIC CEO, and Yasushi Shigeta Angel, chairman and CEO

CHAPTER 22

GPI Becomes a Division of Angel

 Gaming Partners International

An article from *PR Newswire* states:

> NORTH LAS VEGAS, Nevada, May 1, 2019 /PRNewswire/—Gaming Partners International Corporation (GPIC) ("GPIC") today announced the completion of the closing of the previously announced merger contemplated by the

Agreement and Plan of Merger, dated as of November 27, 2018, with Angel Holdings Godo Kaisha ("Angel") and AGL Nevada Corporation ("Merger Sub"), pursuant to which GPIC became a wholly owned subsidiary of Angel.

GPIC stockholders were entitled to receive $13.75 in cash, without interest, for each share of GPIC common stock that they held immediately prior to the effective time of the merger. They will receive letters of transmittal and forms with instructions on how to claim their cash payment of $13.75 per share.

As previously announced, trading of GPIC common stock on NASDAQ was suspended after the close of trading on May 1, 2019, and NASDAQ filed a notification of removal of listing and registration on Form 25 with the United States Securities and Exchange Commission ("SEC") with respect to GPIC's common stock. GPIC intends to deregister its common stock and to suspend its reporting obligations under the Securities Exchange Act of 1934, as amended, by promptly filing a Form 15 with the SEC.

Angel manufactures and supplies playing cards and card games for both the gaming industry and the retail market. A world leader in casino playing cards and table game equipment, Angel's many groundbreaking innovations include the best-selling Angel Protect Pre-Shuffled Cards, and the Angel Eye® series of electronic shoes. Angel's principal business office is in Kyoto, Japan, with manufacturing facilities in Japan and Singapore. Angel also has offices in the United States.

On February 11, 2020, the World Health Organization announced an official name for the disease that is causing the 2019 novel coronavirus outbreak first identified in Wuhan, China. The new name of this disease is coronavirus disease 2019, abbreviated as COVID-19. In COVID-19, *CO* stands for "corona," *VI* for "virus," and *D* for "disease." Formerly, this disease was referred to as 2019 novel coronavirus or 2019-nCoV. There are many types of human coronaviruses including some that commonly cause mild upper-respiratory tract illnesses. COVID-19 is a new disease caused by a novel (or new) coronavirus that has not previously been seen in humans. The name of this disease was selected following the World Health Organization (WHO) best practice external icon for the naming of new human infectious diseases.

In March 2020, the Las Vegas Strip is closed.

Not unlike in 1963, most of the businesses on the Vegas Strip and Fremont Street shut down in mid-March when Steve Sisolak, the Nevada governor, ordered the closure of all nonessential businesses. This is the first time the entire strip has been shut down since the JFK assassination in 1963. Even the devastating mass shooting of President John F. Kennedy in 1963 only resulted in only a partial closure of the Strip.

As of June 4, 2020, an astonishing 6.6 million people in the world have COVID-19; and there have been 393,000 deaths. In the United States there have been 1,923,637 COVID-19 cases and 110,721 deaths. In Nevada, there have been 9,090 COVID-19 cases and 429 deaths. The effects on the local and state economy are expected to be catastrophic. Las Vegas saw 42.5 million visitors in 2019, and the Las Vegas Convention and Visitors Authority estimates that the city hosted 3 million visitors in February alone. The Strip and Fremont Street aren't totally empty, of course. All the left-behind establishments are carefully watched by security guards, some of whom will try to stop photos being taken from a casino with caution tape strung across its entrance.

The economic indicators for the state of Nevada as a whole, which relies just as heavily on tourism, are devastating. The Nevada Resort Association (NVA) has warned the state has lost an estimated $2 billion from canceled meetings and conventions and could lead to $39 billion in economic losses overall. The NVA says that one in three jobs in Nevada are connected to the tourism industry, responsible for $20 billion in annual wages and salaries. "No other state in America depends on travel and tourism at the magnitude Nevada does," the association warns (https://www.theguardian.com/us).

As a result of the coronavirus, all Las Vegas Casinos have been temporarily closed, as have our lives temporarily. We now have to spray our groceries or anything we buy from the outside. It is also recommended by both the Center for Disease Control and Prevention and the World Health Organization that we wear face masks whenever we are around others or go outside.

Mr. Las Vegas says, "Please wear a mask."

Since I started writing this biography about my dad, Nevada governor Steve Sisolak announced Tuesday night, May 2, 2020, that he would allow casinos to reopen on June 4, welcoming tourists to return to the glitzy gambling mecca of Las Vegas. "We welcome the visitors from across the country to come here to have a good time, no different than they did previously. But we're going to be cautious," Sisolak told the reporters. As part of a broad shutdown to stop the spread of the coronavirus, Sisolak took the unprecedented step ten weeks ago of shutting casinos that typically draw millions of tourists to Las Vegas and power the state's economy. By allowing the casinos to reopen, with new rules on physical distancing and sanitizing, Sisolak said Nevada would again welcome visitors. However, he would be prepared to close down again if there is a spike in cases. "We've taken every precaution possible. I don't think you're going to find a safer place to come than Las Vegas especially with the protocols that we've put in place. We'll have the testing in and contact tracing in place by that time," Sisolak said. "We're encouraging visitors to come and enjoy themselves and have a good time" (Associated Press 2020).

Las Vegas casinos welcoming guests after long shutdown — BLOG

Mr. Las Vegas welcomes guests back to Las Vegas with a mask.

Wynn & Encore Las Vegas welcomes guests back on June 4, 2020.

**Vegas Casinos Are Reopening
& Wayne Newton Showed Up
in a Tuxedo + Face Mask**

From the first cheers on Fremont Street at 12:01 a.m. Thursday to the quiet hum of traffic at midnight Friday, *Review-Journal* photographers captured the reawakening of Las Vegas after the coronavirus pandemic shuttered the city's casinos for seventy-eight days. Revelers on the Strip found sights both familiar (showgirls, flowing fountains and the bubbly blips and binges of slot machines) and newfangled (face masks, sanitizing stations, and temperature checkpoints). As Nevada begins to reopen, there is uncertainty among workers, residents, and tourists about what a post-pandemic Vegas will look like. The hospitality-centered economy has been strained under the shutdown and has pushed the state government into deficits, stripped its primary tax revenue, and drained the unemployment fund dry. Now many are worried the public and private sectors can't hold out for much longer. Although Nevada has appeared to reach a plateau in COVID-19 cases, many fear the possibility of a second wave, particularly in the "petri dish" environment of casinos. For MGM Resorts, whose Las Vegas properties include Bellagio, MGM Grand, Mandalay Bay, and New York-New York, that means enacting a "Seven-Point Safety Plan" that calls for employee screening, thermal temperature scanning, social distancing, enhanced cleaning protocols, and handwashing stations on casino floors. Employees will be required to wear masks, while guests will be encouraged to do so. In some parts of the resort, like at roulette tables, guests will be required to wear masks. Never before were casino (https://www.theguardian.com/us-news/2020/may/15/las-vegas-reopening-casinos-workers) employees or casino patrons allowed to wear face coverings for the obvious reasons that a robber wears a mask to rob a bank. Since my dad said casinos were America's banks, he would have been shocked to see casinos offering masks to their customers. Some casinos even have plexiglass dividers so the dealer and each player is protected from COVID-19, which is still upon us (*Review-Journal*).

Bellagio's plexiglass not in cards for all poker rooms

The Bellagio is the only room in Las Vegas with six-handed games because it has installed plexiglass dividers between players.

We are happy that once again Las Vegas and our lives are trying to get back to a "new" normal; however the coronavirus is still with us. My dad would have been shocked to see that Las Vegas was "closed" but even more elated that Las Vegas had re-opened.

Even though casinos are cleaning and sanitizing their chips, dice, and playing cards, you can bet that they will need to order new Paul-Son gaming chips soon.

Paul-Son chips are sanitized before they are recirculated onto the gaming floor at TI on Thursday, June 4, 2020, in Las Vegas (Benjamin Hager, *Las Vegas Review-Journal*).

Las Vegas is now open.

Dad, rest in peace. Paul-Son is in good hands
with an Angel and the Japanese.

BIBLIOGRAPHY

1948. "Las Vegas Hotel Opening Slated." August 31, 1948.

1948. "Las Vegas Neon Sign Co. Will Erect Spectacular Display." *Deseret News*, August 27, 1948. https://www.newspapers.com/newspage/595012169/.

1954. "Shows to start at midnight for new Showboat." *Billboard*, September 4, 1954. https://books.google.com/books?id=LS-MEAAAAMBAJ&pg=PA34#v=onepage&q&f=false.

1955. "License Okehed For New Casino." *Nevada State Journal*, July 27, 1955. https://www.newspapers.com/clip/11639905/nevada-state-journal/.

1955. "Nevada Gaming Control Board in First Meet: Lengthy Program Topped by Lease Of Vegas Hotel." *Reno Gazette-Journal*, July 27, 1955. https://www.newspapers.com/clip/11639820/reno-gazette-journal/.

1957. "Pioneer Southern Nevada Rancher Taken by Death." *Reno Gazette-Journal*, February 14, 1957. https://www.newspapers.com/clip/11639856/reno-gazette-journal/.

1961. "New Thunderbird Director Elected. September 15, 1961.

1967. "Architect appointed for Las Vegas Hotel." *Los Angeles Times*, July 9, 1967. https://www.newspapers.com/clip/21842226/architect-appointed-for-las-vegas-hotel/.

1969. "'Backward' Wife Leaves Sal Sagev. *Pittsburg Press*, April 12, 1969. https://www.newspapers.com/clip/11640153/the-pittsburgh-press/.

1974. "Museum-Casino Destroyed by Fire on Vegas 'Strip.'" *Daily Herald*, May 22, 1974. https://www.newspapers.com/clip/8636642/the-daily-herald/.

1975. "Arson claimed in casino fire." *Independent*, June 19, 1975. https://www.newspapers.com/clip/8636843/independent/.

1978. "New hotel-casino under way in Vegas." *Reno Gazette-Journal*, June 21, 1978. https://www.newspapers.com/clip/8636892/reno-gazette-journal/.

1992. "Luxor Casino: 30-Story Pyramid." *Chicago Sun Times*, April 26, 1992. https://web.archive.org/web/20121105085312/http://www.highbeam.com/doc/1P2-4107334.html.

1998. "LV Country Club presents challenge." *Las Vegas Sun*, October 12, 1998. https://lasvegassun.com/news/1998/oct/12/lv-country-club-presents-challenge/.

1999. "Mark Keppel High School." December 31, 1999. https://www.mkhs.org/apps/pages/index.jsp?uREC_ID=62613&type=d&termREC_ID=&pREC_ID=97013.

2000. "Three Nevada casinos dropping 'Hilton' name." *Las Vegas Sun*, August 15, 2000. https://lasvegassun.com/news/2000/aug/15/three-nevada-casinos-dropping-hilton-name/.

2000. "Vegas Vic Lives." *Las Vegas Sun*, June 25, 2000. https://lasvegassun.com/news/2000/jun/25/vegas-vic-lives/.

2003. "Stardust memories." *Las Vegas Sun*, May 22, 2003. https://lasvegassun.com/news/2003/may/22/stardust-memories/.

2004. "Showboat-turned-Castaways has storied LV history." *Las Vegas Sun*, January 30, 2004. from http://www.lasvegassun.com/news/2004/jan/30/showboat-turned-castaways-has-storied-lv-history/.

2005. "Castaways cast down." *Las Vegas Business Press*, October 31, 2005. https://web.archive.org/web/20060427064032/http://www.lvbusinesspress.com/articles/2005/10/31/news/news06.txt.

2008. "MGM Grand Fire in Las Vegas November, 1980." *Cardinal News*, July 12, 2008. https://www.arlingtoncardinal.com/2008/07/mgm-grand-fire-in-las-vegas-november-1980/.

2007. "The Fabulous Flamingo Hotel History in the 1950s." *Classic Las Vegas*, October 5, 2007. https://web.archive.org/web/20150412010923/http://classiclasvegas.squarespace.com/a-brief-history-of-the-strip/?currentPage=7.

2007. "The Fabulous Flamingo Hotel History—The Wilkerson-Siegel Years." *Classic Las Vegas*, September 23, 2007. https://web.archive.org/web/20160111084052/http://classiclasvegas.squarespace.com/a-brief-history-of-the-strip/2007/9/23/the-fabulous-flamingo-hotel-history-the-wilkerson-siegel-yea.html.

2009. "New Wynn resort, Encore, opens in Vegas with Sinatra restaurant." *Pittsburg Post-Gazette*, January 8, 2009. http://www.post-gazette.com/stories/sectionfront/life/new-wynn-resort-encore-opens-in-vegas-with-sinatra-restaurant-288950/.

2010. "Mob Museum promoted on 60th anniversary of Kefauver hearing." *Las Vegas Review-Journal*, Nobember 16, 2010. https://www.reviewjournal.com/news/mob-museum-promoted-on-60th-anniversary-of-kefauver-hearing/#:~:text=Officials%20noted%20the%2060th%20anniversary, in%20Las%20Vegas%20was%20held.&text=%22Las%20Vegas%20was%20what%20was%20called%20an%20'open%20city.

2014. "The Kefauver Committee in Las Vegas." *The Mob Museum*, November 11, 2014. Last updated November 15, 2017. https://themobmuseum.org/blog/the-kefauver-committee-in-las-vegas/.

2015. "Bob Stupak Business ventures." August 10, 2015.

2015. "Foxwoods to celebrate Frank Sinatra's centennial birthday throughout December." *Casino City Times*, November 15, 2015. http://www.casinocitytimes.com/news/article/foxwoods-to-celebrate-frank-sinatras-centennial-birthday-throughout-december-215355.

2016. Arcuri, Nancy. April 19, 2016.

2017. "Golden Entertainment Completes Acquisition of American Casino & Entertainment Properties for $850 Million." *Business Wire*, October 23, 2017. https://www.businesswire.com/news/home/20171023005426/en/Golden-Entertainment-Completes-Acquisition-American-Casino-Entertainment.

2019. "Luxor Las Vegas is a 30-story hotel and casino situated on the southern end of the Las Vegas Strip in Paradise, Nevada." *Hotel News Group*, April 14, 2019. Edited April 17, 2019. https://

hoteldarnews.ir/en/training/luxor-las-vegas-is-a-30-story-ho-tel-and-casino-situated-on-the-southern-end-of-the-las-vegas-strip-in-paradise,-nevada-/7992.

Arak, Mark. 1985. "Lily Lee Chen: Her Roots--and Perhaps Her Political Goals--Lie Beyond Monterey Park." *Los Angeles Times*, November 14, 1985. https://www.latimes.com/archives/la-xpm-1985-11-14-ga-2678-story.html.

———. 1987. "Monterey Park: Nation's 1st Suburban Chinatown." *Los Angeles Times*, April 6, 1987. https://www.latimes.com/archives/la-xpm-1987-04-06-mn-135-story.html.

———. 1985. "Stronger Rules on English in Signs Pushed by Council." *Los Angeles Times*, December 5, 1985. https://www.latimes.com/archives/la-xpm-1985-12-05-ga-633-story.html.

Autoridade Monetária De Macau. "Monetary Authority Annual Report 2017." https://www.amcm.gov.mo/files/research_and_stats/annual_reports/2017/en/ii.2.2.pdfMonterey Park Bruggemeyer Library—The Citizen's Voice.Barbary Coast.

Batterys—Dans. 2011. "Las Vegas, Nevada." *OverBlog*, June 18, 2011. http://batterys.over-blog.com/article-las-vegas-ne-vada-77056609.html.

Benston, Liz. 2007. "The Luxor's New Threads." *Las Vegas Sun*, July 22, 2007. https://lasvegassun.com/news/2007/jul/22/the-luxors-new-threads/.

Berthelsen, Christian. 1999. "Frederic Hsieh Is Dead at 54; Made Asian-American Suburb." *New York Times*, August 20, 1999. https://www.nytimes.com/1999/08/20/us/frederic-hsieh-is-dead-at-54-made-asian-american-suburb.html#:~:text=-Frederic%20Hsieh%2C%20the%20entrepreneur%20who,lived%20mostly%20in%20Hong%20Kong.

Bet Us Casinos. https://www.bestuscasinos.org/blog.

BlogTalkRadio. 2009. "Dean Martin's Diva Daughter: Elvis Called My Dad 'The King of Cool.'" *BlogTalkRadio*, July 23, 2009. https://blog.blogtalkradio.com/celebrities/dean-martins-diva-daughter-elvis-called-dad-the-king-cool/.

Bloomberg. "Halo Industries." https://www.bloomberg.com/profile/company/HMLOQ:US.

Bracelin, Jason. 2020. "By the Seat of our Pants." *Las Vegas Review-Journal*, June 7, 2020. https://www.reviewjournal.com/business/casinos-gaming/treasure-island-go-behind-the-scenes-at-the-resorts-reopening-2047483/.

Bronson, Brittany. 2020. "'We're on virus time': Las Vegas on edge amid reopening gamble." *Guardian*, May 16, 2020. https://www.theguardian.com/us-news/2020/may/15/las-vegas-reopening-casinos-workers.

Burbank, Jeff. 2014. *Lost Las Vegas*. Pavilion Books.

Bureau, US Census. American FactFinder-Community Facts. https://web.archive.org/web/20140808043521/http://www.census.gov/2010census/popmap/ipmtext.php?fl=06:0648914.

Cantarini, Martha Crawford, and Chrystopher J. Spicer. 2010. *Fall Girl: My Life as a Western Stunt Double*. McFarland & Company.

Cards Chat. "The History of Poker Chips." https://www.cardschat.com/history-poker-chips.php.

Casino Chips World. "The History of USA Poker Chips." https://casinochipsworld.com/all-poker-chips-history.htm.

CasinoCyclopedia. "The Paddlewheel Hotel and Casino." https://casino.fandom.com/wiki/The_Paddlewheel_Hotel_and_Casino.CDC. "Covid Data Tracker." https://www.cdc.gov/covid-data-tracker/#cases.

CBS News. "TV Guide Names Top 50 Shows." https://www.cbsnews.com/news/tv-guide-names-top-50-shows/.

Chuckmonster. 2007. "The Tale of MGM Grand Atlantic City, Borgata and Le Jardin." *Atlantic City Tripping*, November 19, 2007. http://www.atlanticcitytripping.com/cityboom/blog/2/the-tale-of-mgm-grand-atlantic-city-borgata-and-le-jardin/. Clark County Nevada. "MGM Hotel Fire, November 21, 1980." http://www.clarkcountynv.gov/fire/Pages/MGMHotelFire.aspx.

CIA (Central Intelligence Agency). 2016. "Life Expectancy at Birth." Published January 20, 2016. https://www.cia.gov/LIBRARY/publications/the-world-factbook/rankorder/2102rank.html.

———. 2019. "The World Factbook." April 12, 2019. https://www.cia.gov/library/publications/resources/the-world-factbook/geos/mc.html.Clarke, Norm. 2008. "Jacko turns down Wynn Encore gig." *Las Vegas Review-Journal,* November 2, 2008. https://www.reviewjournal.com/news/jacko-turns-down-wynn-encore-gig/.

CN Tower. https://www.cntower.ca/en-ca/plan-your-visit/tickets/tower-experience.html.

Cohen, Mitchell. 2019. "Lost Signs of Las Vegas—Part 1." *Neon Museum*, November 15, 2019. https://www.neonmuseum.org/the-collection/blog/lost-signs-of-las-vegas-part-1.

Collectors Weekly. "Vintage/Antique Thunderbird Hotel & Casino $25 Poker Chip." https://www.collectorsweekly.com/stories/124140-vintage-antique-thunderbird-hotel-and-casi.

Comedy Central. 2004. "Comedy Central's 100 Greatest Stand-Ups of All Time." Published April 17, 2004. https://web.archive.org/web/20040605175309/http://www.comedycentral.com/tv_shows/100greatest/list.jhtml.Craft, Byron. 2014. "The Men Who Made Las Vegas—Bob Stupak—The Polish Maverick." *StripLV*, 2014. https://web.archive.org/web/20160811120841/http://striplv.com/archives/19-articles/featured/517-the-men-who-made-las-vegas-bob-stupak-the-polish-maverick.html.

Craps Maps. "El Cortez Hotel & Casino." https://crapsmaps.com/listing/el-cortez-hotel-and-casino/.

Croghan, Lore. 2004. "Trump Hotels Deal with Credit Suisse First Boston is Dead; Donald Trump Claims Bondholders Will See a Happy Ending!" *Hotel Online*, September 24, 2004. https://www.hotel-online.com/News/PR2004_3rd/Sept04_TrumpCreditSuisse.html?__cf_chl_captcha_tk__=73a1579913f5f-05de81ccc12badd75488083e09e-1612767014-0-Ac1LkLT-GToStNrVhDh_DWmmO60oC3QfnoQSSMOxf55hNv7N N5qBLGGHZqNpLOrk5OqZTG2zFiErDFT5ipF7uMRV UGjJ3y5GkPHaWrSuOxDtXe53eHOoupwhsQDYPOpciX 6UZTzuO2LkPeqk5doRgqg8XM78C-UxVXdGkuL54uw-w6YuVp6cqKZeXte8e6z16O1sGj2vEQ892dmCbB9VGQo_jSoKr8S2OgXgDFR5kMHyW_jTMr8YAUgTxHwbME-Hs0-ydoAja5EIjqtpGVYT9_Bb3P3lSepbQA2YrJmTxVjk5K rw5Ttaeldq1avfW-Yzpc5_y08Qnk9ThYUSbyaQuQBo0G-

c6ELLZZxdUCh2cWtDlPsgmlFKU8hJGF4Qsan2P5divak-
tAHs2eoZfhjm65yLcDJ-x_SWlKzezvaX430dzpYHiXaaoBc
T3jdgBL55oUA547e6xBUk6YKl6iNd6Rg0zvhU4hWyUnj
mj1ZH5Se7jcGqpRByxM7kh-GPswLC4Ri7IeRkYEMiwJx
UacjgrtQNdEUFv8yx16_pX2bhUFI4NZqD0XNOkG2H-
vdBSEsQ-7YIX9KeILrnOuvM3muItqlKnjOYfV28M8sikRa-
gHYRUsaebFZ0gjjxjQ3TwTCjI3qpWyQElovF3cb-wdMIH-
dWt5vJGio.

CTBUH (Council on Tall Buildings and Urban Habitat). "Eiffel Tower, Paris Las Vegas." http://www.skyscrapercenter.com/building/eiffel-tower-paris-las-vegas/14040.

Curtis, Anthony. 2014. "Cromwell casino opens in Las Vegas." *AZ Central*, May 2, 2014. Updated May 2, 2014. https://www.azcentral.com/story/travel/2014/05/02/vegas-cromwell-casino-opens/8613107/.

———. 2014. "Question of the Day—01 October 2014." *Las Vegas Advisor*, October 1, 2014. https://www.lasvegasadvisor.com/question/2014-10-01/.

Darian-Smith, Eve. n.d. "Indian Gaming." *Britannica*. https://www.britannica.com/topic/Indian-gaming.

Dean Martin. https://deanmartin.com/.

Dombrowa, Beth. 1999. *The Las Vegas Millennium Edition: Southern Nevada Enters the 21st Century*. Pioneer Publications.

du Cros, Hilary. 2009. "Emerging Issues for Cultural Tourism in Macau." *Journal of Current Chinese Affairs*.

El Cortez Hotel & Casino. "El Cortez Hotel & Casino Timeline." https://elcortezhotelcasino.com/about-us/timeline/.

Emporis. "Bellagio." https://www.emporis.com/buildings/122235/bellagio-resort-casino-las-vegas-nv-usa.

Erheriene, Ese. 2019. "Casino Upstarts Give U.S. Operators a Run for Their Money in Asia." *Wall Street Journal*, May 7, 2019. Updated May 6, 2019. https://www.wsj.com/articles/casino-upstarts-give-u-s-giants-a-run-for-their-money-in-asia-11557145039.

Excalibur. https://excalibur.mgmresorts.com/en/entertainment/fun-dungeon.html.

Frazier, Donald. 2012. "Chinese Players Find Good Fortune in Las Vegas." *Forbes*, March 28, 2012. https://www.forbes.com/global/2012/0409/feature-visitors-mgm-grand-find-good-fortune-in-las-vegas.html?sh=20c28ed05333.

Fabricant, Florence. 2005. "Atlantic City Is in on the Bet." *New York Times*, October 26, 2005. https://www.nytimes.com/2005/10/26/dining/atlantic-city-is-in-on-the-bet.html.

Fact Republic. "Frank Sinatra." https://factrepublic.com/facts/31241/.

Fun Dungeon.

Gambling Sites Online. "The Gambling History of Reno." https://www.gamblingsitesonline.org/casino/articles/gambling-history-of-reno/.

Gaming History—Week of April 03, 2016. http://museumofgaminghistory.org/mogh_history.php?sd=1459656000.

Gaming History—Week of July 01, 2018. http://museumofgaminghistory.org/mogh_history.php?sd=1530417600

Gaming History—Week of May 01, 2005. http://museumofgaminghistory.org/mogh.php?p=history&sd=1114920000.

Gaming History—Week of November 13, 2011. http://museumofgaminghistory.org/mogh.php?p=history&sd=1321160400.

Gaming History—Week of November 15, 1998. http://museumofgaminghistory.org/mogh_history.php?sd=911106000.

Gaming History—Week of September 01, 2002. http://museumofgaminghistory.org/mogh_history.php?sd=1030852800

Gaming History—Week of September 03, 1954. http://www.museumofgaminghistory.org/mogh.php?p=history&sd=1851566400

Gaming Partners International Corporation. 2019. "GPIC Completes Closing of Acquisition by Angel." *PR Newswire*, May 1, 2019. https://www.prnewswire.com/news-releases/gpic-completes-closing-of-acquisition-by-angel-300842253.html.

Giesler, Marsha. 2016. *Fire and Life Safety Educator: Principles and Practice.* Jones & Bartlett Learning.

Girl, Garage. 2016. "Top 50 TV Cars of All Time: No. 7, Vega$ 1957 Ford Thunderbird." *Rod Authority*,

October 26, 2016. https://www.rodauthority.com/news/top-50-tv-cars-of-all-time-no-7-vega-1957-ford-thunderbird/.

GM Dice. 2019. "7 Surprising Facts About How Dice Are Made." Published August 19, 2019. https://www.gmdice.com/blogs/dnd/how-are-dice-made.

Goertler, Pam. 2007. *The Las Vegas Strip: The Early Years*. http://www.ccgtcc-ccn.com/LV%20Strip%20The%20Early%20Years.pdf.

Golden Gate Hotel & Casino. "Las Vegas Firsts at Golden Gate Hotel & Casino." https://www.goldengatecasino.com/blog/las-vegas-firsts-at-golden-gate-hotel-casino/.

Golden Globe Awards. "Red Foxx." https://www.goldenglobes.com/person/redd-foxx.

Goldstein, Matthew, Tiffany Hsu, and Kenneth P. Vogel. 2018. "Stephen Wynn, Casino Mogul, Accused of Decades of Sexual Misconduct." *New York Times*, January 26, 2018. https://www.nytimes.com/2018/01/26/business/steve-wynn-sexual-misconduct-claims.html.

GPSMyCity. "Gangster Attractions Tour (Self-Guided), Las Vegas." https://www.gpsmycity.com/tours/gangster-attractions-walking-tour-2367.html.

Green, Michael. 2010. "Golden Gate Corner." *Online Nevada Encyclopedia*, October 18, 2010. http://www.onlinenevada.org/articles/golden-gate-corner.

Green, Michael. "Shades of Trump." January 27, 2016. http://vegas-seven.com/2016/01/27/shades-of-trump/.

Harris, Martin. 2016. "U.S. Presidents who played poker." *PokerStars*, August 2, 2016. https://www.pokerstars.com/en/blog/2016/us-presidents-who-played-poker-162602.shtml?no_redirect=1.

Hawthorne, Christopher. 2014. "How Arcadia is remaking itself as a magnet for Chinese money." *Los Angeles Times*, December 3, 2014. https://www.latimes.com/entertainment/arts/la-et-cm-arcadia-immigration-architecture-20140511-story.html.

History.com Editors. 2009. "Bugsy Siegel opens Flamingo Hotel." *History.com*, November 24, 2009. Last updated December 21, 2020. https://www.history.com/this-day-in-history/bugsy-siegel-opens-flamingo-hotel.

History.com Editors. 2009. "Las Vegas." *History.com*, December 2, 200p. Updated December 4, 2020. https://www.history.com/topics/us-states/las-vegas.

HobbyDB. "TWA." https://www.hobbydb.com/marketplaces/hobbydb/subjects/twa-airline.Hochman, Gene, Tom Dawson, and Judy Dawson. 2000. *The Hochman Encyclopedia of American Playing Cards*. Stamford, Connecticut: U.S. Games Systems.

Holden, Stephen. 1998. "Frank Sinatra Dies at 82; Matchless Stylist of Pop." *New York Times*, May 16, 1998. https://www.nytimes.com/1998/05/16/movies/frank-sinatra-dies-at-82-matchless-stylist-of-pop.html.

Holloway, Chad. 2014. "Game Security: Borgata Introduces State-of-the-Art Poker Chips After January Scandal." *PokerNews*, April 9, 2014. https://www.pokernews.com/news/2014/04/game-security-borgata-introduces-state-of-the-art-chips-17985.htm#:~:text=HomeNews-, Game%20Security%3A%20Borgata%20Introduces%20State%2Dof%2Dthe%2DArt, Poker%20Chips%20After%20January%20Scandal&text=Back%20in%20January%2C%20the%20Borgata, ultimately%20charged%20with%20the%20crime.

Holzwarth, Larry. n.d. The Eccentric Mogul: 8 Facts About the Strange Life of Howard Hughes." *History Collection*. https://historycollection.com/fabulously-wealthy-strange-howard-hughes/3/.

https://lasvegassun.com/news/people/bob-stupak/.

http://thecitizensvoice.net/?p=13339.

http://thecitizensvoice.net/?p=13815.

http://www.lvstriphistory.com/ie/barb.htm.

https://www.newspapers.com/newspage/148266602/

Hudson, Berkley. 1989. "Laura Scudder Was More Than a Name: Monterey Park Will Honor 'Pioneer, Instigator, Doer' Who Helped Create Snack-Food Industry." *Los Angeles Timesi*, April 9, 1989. https://www.latimes.com/archives/la-xpm-1989-04-09-ga-1646-story.html.

Hurley, Lawrence. 2020. "U.S. Supreme Court deems half of Oklahoma a Native American reservation." *USNews*, July 9, 2020. https://www.usnews.com/news/top-news/articles/2020-07-09/us-supreme-court-deems-half-of-oklaho-ma-a-native-american-reservation.

IMF (International Monetary Fund). "World Economic Outlook Database, October 2019." https://www.imf.org/external/pubs/ft/weo/2019/02/weodata/weorept.aspx?pr.x=53&pr.y=1&sy=2017&ey=2021&scsm=1&ssd=1&sort=country&ds=.&br=1&c=546&s=NGDPD%2CPPPGD-P%2CNGDPDPC%2CPPPPC&grp=0&a=.

Janson, Donald. 1983. "Atlantic Condominiums Bought for Fun and Profit." *New York Times*, August 28, 1983. https://www.nytimes.com/1983/08/28/realestate/atlantic-city-condominiums-bought-for-fun-and-profit.html.

Jason. 2017. "Reno Nevada Gambling History." *Legit Gambling Sites*, April 27, 2017. https://www.legitgamblingsites.com/blog/reno-nevada-gambling-history/#:~:text=Reno%20found%20this%20in%201860, took%20a%20stand%20against%20gambling.&text=In%201869%20the%20law%20makers, unchanged%20for%20another%2040%20years.

Juipe, Dean 2004. "Tapit gives Las Vegas a Derby connection." *Las Vegas Sun*, April 30, 2004. https://lasvegassun.com/news/2004/apr/30/columnist-dean-juipe-tapit-gives-las-vegas-a-derby/.

Kantowski, Ron. 1984. "Remembering Las Vegas' first national basketball champions. *Las Vegas Review-Journal*, April 1, 1984. https://www.reviewjournal.com/sports/sports-columns/ron-kantowski/remembering-las-vegas-first-national-basketball-champions/.

Kelly, Howard D. 1959. "Showboat Hotel and Casino, Fremont Street, looking north." *Kelly-Holiday*. https://calisphere.org/item/a8ba66649854d20db9795e73e86d6061/.

King Arthur Wiki. "Excalibur (Hotel)." https://kingarthur.fandom.com/wiki/Excalibur_(Hotel).

King, Larry, host. 2002. *Guests Discuss the Late Howard Hughes.* Aired January 20, 2002, on CNN. http://edition.cnn.com/TRANSCRIPTS/0201/20/lklw.00.html.

Knightly, Arnold M. 2007. "Casino business: Blink and you'll miss him." *Casino City Times*, February 26, 2007. http://www.

casinocitytimes.com/article/casino-business-blink-and-youll-miss-him-55406.

———. 2009. "Partners create new look for Golden oldie." *Las Vegas Review-Journal*, September 26, 2009. https://www.reviewjournal.com/business/partners-create-new-look-for-golden-oldie/.

———. 2009. "Station parcels offered for sale." *Las Vegas Review-Journal*, April 18, 2009. https://web.archive.org/web/20090424042607/http://www.lvrj.com/business/43218452.html.

Koch, Ed. 2008. "Desert Inn, Stardust chief helped integrate Las Vegas Strip." *Las Vegas Sun*, September 1, 2008. https://lasvegassun.com/news/2008/sep/01/desert-inn-stardust-chief-helped-integrate-las-veg/.

Koch, Ed, Mary Manning, and Dave Toplikar. 2008. "Showtime: How Sin City evolved into 'The Entertainment Capital of the World.'" *Las Vegas Sun*, May 15, 2008. https://lasvegassun.com/news/2008/may/15/evolution-worlds-entertainment-capital/.

La Ganga, Maria L. 1987. "Borden Buys Laura Scudder to Get Bite of State Market." *Los Angeles Times*, September 23, 1987. https://www.latimes.com/archives/la-xpm-1987-09-23-fi-6144-story.html.

———. 1987. "Laura Scudder Owed a Lot to Peanut Butter." *Los Angeles Times*, September 23, 1987. https://www.latimes.com/archives/la-xpm-1987-09-23-fi-6165-story.html#:~:text=It%20was%20peanut%20butter%20that, Clough%20in%201881%20in%20Philadelphia.

Las Vegas 360. 2012. "Alpine Village Inn Las Vegas-Remembered." Published October 25, 2012. https://www.lasvegas360.com/2262/apline-village-inn/.

Las Vegas 360. 2018. "On this Date September 3, 1954, The Showboat Hotel & Casino Opened on Boulder Highway." Published September 3, 2018. https://www.lasvegas360.com/3491/on-this-date-september-3-1954-the-showboat-hotel-casino-opened-on-boulder-highway/#:~:text=Skip%20to%20content-, On%20this%20Date%20September%203%2C%201954%2C%20The%20Showboat%20Hotel%20%26, Casino%20

Opened%20on%20Boulder%20Highway&text=n%20 1998%2C%20Harrah's%20Entertainment%20bought, fit%20with%20the%20company's%20strategy.

Las Vegas Blog Staff. 2013. "Caesars Palace Adds European Roulette to Its Repertoire." *Las Vegas Blog*, March 4, 2013. http://blog. caesars.com/las-vegas/las-vegas-hotels/caesars-palace.

Las Vegas Country Club. "Our Story." https://www.lasvegascc.com/ Our_Story#:~:text=Established%20in%201967%2C%20 our%20Club, to%20be%20and%20be%20seen.

Las Vegas Historical Site. http://www.lvstriphistory.com/ie/world70. htm.

Las Vegas Online Entertainment Guide. "History of the Desert Inn." https://www.lvol.com/hotels/history/h-di.html.

Las Vegas Sun. "Timeline." https://lasvegassun.com/history/ timeline/.

Levitan, Corey. 2008. "Gritty City." *Las Vegas Review-Journal*, march 2, 2008. https://www.reviewjournal.com/life/gritty-city/.

Lewis, Dan. 2014. "The mystery Vegas casino you can only visit once every two years." *BoingBoing*, September 3, 2014. https:// boingboing.net/2014/09/03/the-mystery-vegas-casino-you-c. html.

Lo, Andrew. 2009. "The game of leaves: An inquiry into the origin of Chinese playing cards." *Bulletin of the School of Oriental and African Studies* 63, no. 3 (January): 389–406.

Luv-It Custard. http://www.luvitfrozencustard.com/.

McCracken, Robert D. 1996. *Las Vegas: The Great American Playground*. University of Nevada Press.

McKee, David. 2006. "Station plans Latin flavor for Castaways site." *Las Vegas Busines Press*, October 9, 2006. https://web.archive. org/web/20090424022340/http://www.lvbusinesspress.com/ articles/2006/10/09/news/news02.txt.

Merlan, Anna. 2020. "After the end of the world: the eerie silence of the Las Vegas Strip." The Guardian, April 4, 2020. Last modified July 1, 2020. https://www.theguardian.com/world/2020/ apr/14/las-vegas-strip-closed-coronavirus.

Moehring, Eugene P., and Michael S. Green. 2005. *Las Vegas: A Centennial History*. University of Nevada Press.

Mok, K. M., and K. I. Hoi. 2005. "Effects of Meteorological Conditions on PM10 Concentrations—A Study in Macau. *Environmental Monitoring and Assessment* 102 (2005): 201–223. https://link.springer.com/article/10.1007/s10661-005-6022-6.

Monterey Park California. "History of Monterey Park." https://www.montereypark.ca.gov/721/History-of-Monterey-Park.

Montero, David, Richard Winton, and Ruben Vives. 2017. "In the solitary world of video poker, Stephen Paddock knew how to win. Until he didn't." *Los Angeles Times*, October 9, 2017. https://www.latimes.com/nation/la-na-vegas-shooting-gambler-20171009-story.html.

Moreno, Richard. 2008. *Nevada Curiosities: Quirky Characters, Roadside Oddities & Other Offbeat Stuff*. Globe Pequot.

Murderpedia. "Benjamin 'Bugsy' Siegel." https://murderpedia.org/male.S/s/siegel-bugsy.htm

Murray, Robert K., and Tim H. Blessing. 2004. *Greatness in White House*. Pennsylvania State University Press.

Cirque Wiki. "Mystere." https://cirquedusoleil.fandom.com/wiki/Myst%C3%A8re.

National Indian Gaming Commission. 2011. "Gaming Tribe Report." July 6, 2011. https://web.archive.org/web/20130220134916/http://www.nigc.gov/LinkClick.aspx?fileticket=0J7Yk1QNgX0%3d&tabid=943.

National Indian Gaming Commission. n.d. "NIGC Tribal Gaming Revenues.2011." https://web.archive.org/web/20121010012057/http://www.nigc.gov/Portals/0/NIGC%20Uploads/Tribal%20Data/GamingRevenues20072011.pdf.

Needham, Joseph. 1954. *Science and Civilisation in China*. Vol. 1, *Introductory Orientations*. Cambridge University Press.

———. 1962. "Part 1, Physics." In *Science and Civilisation in China*. Vol. 4, *Physics and Physical Technology*. Cambridge University Press.

———, and Tsuen-hsuin Tsien. 1985. "Science and Civilization in China: Volume 5, Chemistry and Chemical Technology, Part

1, Paper and Printing." The China Quarterly 108 (December): 733–735. https://doi.org/10.1017/S0305741000037309.

Nevada Resort Association. "History of Gaming in Nevada." https://www.nevadaresorts.org/about/history/

Newton, Michael. 2009. *Mr. Mob: The Life and Crimes of Moe Dalitz*. McFarland.

Norm. 2020. The 1968 Stardust 7-11 Off-Road Race. *The Norm*, May 5, 2020. https://vegas-to-you.com/TheNorm/the-1968-stardust-7-11-off-road-race/.

Nunberg, Geoff. 1986. "Resolution: English Only." *Linguistic Society of America*, December 28, 1986. https://www.linguisticsociety.org/resource/resolution-english-only.

Oldest.org. "11 Oldest Casinos in Las Vegas." https://www.oldest.org/entertainment/casinos-in-las-vegas/.

Online Blackjack. "Card Marking." https://www.onlineblackjack-realmoney.org/faq/card-marking.

Online Nevada Encyclopedia. "Guy McAfee." http://www.onlinenevada.org/articles/guy-mcafee.

Online Nevada Encyclopedia. "Las Vegas Strip: The First Boom." http://onlinenevada.org/articles/las-vegas-strip-first-boom.

Online Nevada Encyclopedia. "Meadows Club." http://www.online-nevada.org/articles/meadows-club.

Online Nevada Encyclopedia. "Red Rooster." http://www.onlinenevada.org/articles/red-rooster.

Online Nevada Encyclopedia. "Pair-O-Dice Club and Early Las Vegas Strip." https://www.onlinenevada.org/articles/pair-o-dice-club-and-early-las-vegas-strip.

Oxford Dictionary Lexico. "die." https://www.lexico.com/definition/die.

PacerMonitor. "Trump Entertainment Resorts." https://www.pacermonitor.com/view/QGLEBUY/Trump_Entertainment_Resorts_Inc__debke-14-12103__0001.0.pdf.Painton, Priscilla. 1989. "Atlantic City, New Jersey Boardwalk of Broken Dreams: The hometown of the con job may now be the victim of one." *Time*, September 25, 1989. http://content.time.com/time/subscriber/article/0,33009,958614,00.html.

Pang, Kevin. 2015. "72 Hours Inside the Eye-Popping World of Cardistry." *Vanity Fair*, April 21, 2015. https://www.vanityfair.com/culture/2015/04/cardistry-con-2015.

Parlett, David. 2015. "Chinese Leaf Game." *Games and Gamebooks*, 2015. https://www.parlettgames.uk/histocs/leafgame.html#top.

Parry, Wayne. 2013. "Atlantic City's Trump Plaza goes for bargain $20M." *New York Times*, February 14, 2013. https://www.nydailynews.com/sdut-atlantic-citys-trump-plaza-goes-for-bargain-20m-2013feb14-story.html.

———. 2014. "Trump: Plaza and Taj Mahal too shabby to bear his name anymore." *The Philadephia Inquirer*, August 5, 2014. https://www.inquirer.com/philly/business/20140806_Trump__Plaza_and_Taj_Mahal_casinos_too_shabby_to_bear_his_name_anymore.html.

PBS. "Guy McAfee (1888–1960)." In *Las Vegas: An Unconventional History*. https://www.pbs.org/wgbh/americanexperience/features/lasvegas-mcafee/.

PeoplePill. "Laura Scudder." https://peoplepill.com/people/laura-scudder/.

Pew Research Center. 2013. "Second-Generation Americans." Published February 7, 2013. https://www.pewsocialtrends.org/2013/02/07/second-generation-americans/.

Pew-Templeton: Global Religious Futures Project. "Religions in Macau." http://www.globalreligiousfutures.org/countries/macau#/?affiliations_religion_id=0&affiliations_year=2010&region_name=All%20Countries&restrictions_year=2016.

Pokerchipmania. https://www.pokerchipmania.com/.

Pollack, Andrew. 2000. "MGM Grand to Acquire Mirage Resorts for $4.4 Billion." *New York Times*, March 7, 2000. https://www.nytimes.com/2000/03/07/business/mgm-grand-to-acquire-mirage-resorts-for-4.4-billion.html.

Pop Culture Wiki. "Viva Las Vegas." https://pop-culture.fandom.com/wiki/Viva_Las_Vegas.

Potempa, Philip. 2012. OFFBEAT: Las Vegas MGM Grand Hotel and Casino Losing Trademark 'Live' Lions." *The Times of Northwest*

Indiana, January 5, 2012. Updated June 8, 2017. https://www.nwitimes.com/entertainment/columnists/offbeat/offbeat-las-vegas-mgm-grand-hotel-and-casino-losing-trademark-live-lions/article_4465b977-33b6-5607-9a2d-29c63cbd5d5b.html.

Prabook. "Virginia Hill." https://prabook.com/web/virginia.hill/1772383.

Price, Michelle L. 2020. "Nevada to reopen casinos June 4, welcoming tourists again." *ABC News*, May 26, 2020. https://abcnews.go.com/Health/wireStory/us-warns-nevada-governor-person-worship-limits-70890031.

Quan, Douglas. 2007. "Some in Chino Hills nervous about ethnic shift." *Press-Enterprise*, February 7, 2007. https://web.archive.org/web/20070403025010/http://www.pe.com/localnews/inland/stories/PE_News_Local_D_asian07.25558b4.html.

QuickFacts. "Monterey Park city, California." https://www.census.gov/quickfacts/montereyparkcitycalifornia.

Radke, Brock. 2014. "How New is New? First Impressions of The Cromwell." *Las Vegas Weekly*, April 30, 2014. https://lasvegasweekly.com/column/incidental-tourist/2014/apr/30/first-impressions-cromwell-how-new-is-new/#/0.

Ravo, Nick. 1991. "Redd Foxx, Cantankerous Master of Bawdy Humor, Is Dead at 68." *New York Times*, October 13, 1991. https://www.nytimes.com/1991/10/13/nyregion/redd-foxx-cantankerous-master-of-bawdy-humor-is-dead-at-68.html.

Ray, Alyssa. 2020. "Molly Sims Shares Behind-the-Scenes Memories From *Las Vegas* Ahead of E! Marathon." *E!* June 24, 2020. https://www.eonline.com/ap/news/1164539/molly-sims-shares-behind-the-scenes-memories-from-las-vegas-ahead-of-e-marathon.

Resorts Casino-Hotel. "Atlantic City's First Casino." https://resort-sac.com/history/.

Rosenfeld, Everett. 2018. "Steve Wynn is out as CEO of Wynn Resorts." *CNBC*, February 6, 2018. Updated February 7, 2018. https://www.cnbc.com/2018/02/06/steve-wynn-is-out-as-ceo-of-wynn-resorts.html.

Rotten Tomatoes. The Only Game in Town. https://www.rottento-matoes.com/m/the_only_game_in_town.

Reid, Ed, and Ovid Damaris. 2010. *The Green Felt Jungle*. Ishi Press.

Reinhold, Robert. 1989. "Las Vegas Transformation: From Sin City to Family City." *New York Times*, May 30, 1989. https://www.nytimes.com/1989/05/30/us/las-vegas-transformation-from-sin-city-to-family-city.html.

Reno Gazette-Journal. https://www.newspapers.com/newspage/1480 91655/.

Richard, Brendan. 2018. "Las Vegas: past, present and future." *Journal of Tourism Futures*, September 7, 2018. https://www.emerald.com/insight/content/doi/10.1108/JTF-05-2018-0027/full/html

Riviera Hotel. https://www.rivierahotel.com/.

Sagrev, Sal. 2018. "The Flamingo on the Sal Sagev NCN7 Strip." May 20, 2018. https://www.geocaching.com/geocache/GC7PZF0_the-flamingo-on-the-sal-sagev-ncn7-strip?guid=4e4d5d26-a97e-494f-9775-0e92cffe6fc6.

Chinatown Report. "San Gabriel Valley." http://chinatownreport.com/san-gabriel-valley/.

Sawyer, Kathy. 1980. "MGM Executives Defend Hotel's Fire Safeguards MGM Aides Defend Hotel's Safety Provisions." *Washington Post*, 1980, November 24. https://www.washingtonpost.com/archive/politics/1980/11/24/mgm-executives-defend-ho-tels-fire-safeguards-mgm-aides-defend-hotels-safety-provisions/a2a3ccb9-e81a-4515-9084-bdda5a6031c4/.

Schwartz, Benjamin S., and Christina Schwarz. 1999. "Going All Out for Chinese." *The Atlantic*, January 1999. https://www.theatlantic.com/magazine/archive/1999/01/going-all-out-for-chinese/305473/.

Schumacher, Geoff. 1997. "'Rise and Fall of Bob Stupak' a towering addition to limited Vegas bookshelf." *Las Vegas Sun*, May 15, 1997. https://lasvegassun.com/news/1997/may/15/rise-and-fall-of-bob-stupak-a-towering-addition-to/.

SEC (Securities and Exchange Commission) Database. "Wynn Resorts LTD., Form 10-K, Filing Date March 1, 2013." http://

edgar.secdatabase.com/736/119312513087674/filing-main.
htm.

SEC (Securities and Exchange Commission) Info. "Borden Chemical
Inc.—'10-Q' for 6/30/94." http://www.secinfo.com/dsVS7.
bPm.htm.

Segaloff, Nat. 2013. *Final Cuts: The Last Films of 50 Great Directors.*
Bear Manor Media.

Semple, Kirk. 2009. "In Chinatown, Sound of the Future Is
Mandarin." *New York Times*, October 21, 2009. https://www.
nytimes.com/2009/10/22/nyregion/22chinese.html.

Shamus, Short-Stacked. 2013. "The Top Five Poker-Playing
Presidents." *Betting.Betfair*, August 9, 2013. https://betting.
betfair.com/poker/news/the-top-five-poker-playing-presi-
dents-070813-77.html.

Shearer's Foods, Inc. Acquires Snack Alliance, Inc. (2010, March 31).
https://web.archive.org/web/20110716052829/http://www.
shearersfoodsinc.com/Newsroom/NewsReleases/2010/033110_
SnackAllianceAcquisition.aspx.

Sheehan, Jack. 1997. *The Players: The Men Who Made Las Vegas.*
University of Nevada Press.

Sheng, Mingjie, and Chaolin Gu. 2018. "Economic growth and development in Macau (1999–2016): The role of the booming gaming
industry." *Cities* 75 (May): 72–80. https://www.sciencedirect.
com/science/article/pii/S0264275117308995?via%3Dihub.

Simon, Bryant. 2004. *Boardwalk of Dreams: Atlantic City and the fate
of urban America.* Oxford University Press.

Simpson, Jeff. 2003. "Castaways loan approved." *Cacino City Times*,
June 27, 2003. http://www.casinocitytimes.com/news/article/
castaways-loan-approved-136104.

———. 2003. "Castaways on verge of bankruptcy." *Cacino City
Times*, June 27, 2003. http://www.casinocitytimes.com/news/
article/castaways-on-verge-of-bankruptcy-136093

———. 2004. "Historic casino: Castaways closes." *Las Vegas
Review-Journal*, January 30, 2004. https://web.archive.org/
web/20050703074823/http://www.reviewjournal.com/lvrj_
home/2004/Jan-30-Fri-2004/news/23111924.html.

Skytamer. "Overview—A Little History About Laura Scudder and Laura Scudder Potato Chips." https://www.skytamer.com/F331.html.

Sloca, Paul. (1998, January 18). Missouri's 'Boats in Moats' Get That Sinking Feeling. Retrieved from https://www.latimes.com/archives/la-xpm-1998-jan-18-mn-9506-story.html

Smith, John L. 1999. "Bob Stupak." *Las Vegas Review-Journal*, February 7, 1999. https://www.reviewjournal.com/news/bob-stupak/.

Smith, Rod. 2004. "Acquisitions: Station snaps up Castaways." (2004, October 2) *Las Vegas Review-Journal*, https://web.archive.org/web/20041010165241/http://www.reviewjournal.com/lvrj_home/2004/Oct-02-Sat-2004/business/24891914.html.

———. 2004. "Vestin reaches deal for casino." *Las Vegas Review-Journal*, April 9, 2004. https://web.archive.org/web/20040710160007/http://www.reviewjournal.com/lvrj_home/2004/Apr-09-Fri-2004/business/23601977.html.

Snyder, John P. 1969. *The Story of New Jersey's Civil Boundaries: 1606–1968*. Bureau of Geology and Topography: Trenton, New Jersey. https://www.state.nj.us/dep/njgs/enviroed/oldpubs/bulletin67.pdf.

Stafford, Jeffrey. 2016. "A Brief History of Poker Chips." *Spinnetis Gaming Supplies*, August 22, 2016. https://spinettisgaming.com/blogs/casino-gaming-history-news/a-brief-history-of-poker-chips.

Stafford, Jeffrey. 2016. "Evolution of a Casino from the Marina to the MGM Hotel & Casino." *Spinnetis Gaming Supplies*, September 3, 2016. https://spinettisgaming.com/blogs/casino-gaming-history-news/evolution-of-a-casino-from-the-marina-to-the-mgm-hotel-casino.

Stanwick, Michael. n.d. "Chinese Money-Suited Playing Cards." *The Mahjong Tile Set*. https://www.themahjongtileset.co.uk/money-suited-playing-cards/.

Starr, Michael Seth. 2011. *Black and Blue: The Redd Foxx Story*. Applause.

Steve Wynn's Vegas Vision Turned Into Reality. (2009, February 9). Retrieved from https://abcnews.go.com/Nightline/Story?id=3650310&page=1

Stutz, Howard. (2006, January 12). Casino sinks into history. https://web.archive.org/web/20061025113103/http://www.reviewjournal.com/lvrj_home/2006/Jan-12-Thu-2006/news/5303102.html

Stutz, Howard. 2007. "Investors group sues Archon over stock redemption price." *Las Vegas Review-Journal*, September 4, 2007. https://www.reviewjournal.com/business/investors-group-sues-archon-over-stock-redemption-price/.

————. 2007. "Luxor's New Look: Farewell to Egypt." *Las Vegas Review-Journal*, July 12, 2007. https://web.archive.org/web/20071212201120/http://www.lvrj.com/business/8451727.html.

————. 2008. "Commission approves sale of 50 percent stake in Golden Gate." *Las Vegas Review-Journal*, March 21, 2008. Retrieved from https://www.reviewjournal.com/business/commission-approves-sale-of-50-percent-stake-in-golden-gate/.

————. 2012. "Bill's Gamblin' Hall to close Feb. 4 for renovations." *Las Vegas Review-Journal*, November 29, 2012. https://web.archive.org/web/20121202034632/http://www.lvrj.com/business/bill-s-gamblin-hall-to-close-feb-4-for-renovations-181392651.html.

————. 2012. "Gaughan offers link to days of old Vegas." *Las Vegas Review-Journal*, October 28, 2012. https://web.archive.org/web/20140313001601/http://www.reviewjournal.com/inside-gaming/gaughan-offers-link-days-old-vegas.

————. 2014. "The Cromwell latest name for former Barbary Coast on the Las Vegas Strip." *Las Vegas Review-Journal*, January 31, 2014. https://www.reviewjournal.com/business/the-cromwell-latest-name-for-former-barbary-coast-on-the-las-vegas-strip/#:~:text=announced%20Friday%20the%20new%20name, Courtesy%2FCaesars%20Entertainment%20Corp.)&text=So%20long%20Bill's%20Gamblin'%20

Hall%20and%20good%20riddance%20Gansevoort%20
Las%20Vegas.

Sun Staff. 2000. "Off-Strip location made Hilton one of LV's biggest gambles." *Las Vegas Sun*, July 12, 2000. https://lasvegassun.
com/news/2000/jul/12/off-strip-location-made-hilton-one-of-
lvs-biggest-/.

Sylvester, Ron. 2013. El Cortez joins National Register of Historic
Places. *Las Vegas Sun*, February 25, 2013. https://lasvegassun.
com/news/2013/feb/25/el-cortez-joins-national-register-his-
toric-places/.

The Casino Chip & Gaming Token Collectors Club, Inc.
(CC&GTCC), d/b/a Casino Collectibles Association (CCA).
http://www.ccgtcc.com/ccgtcc_history.pdf. The Cromwell Las
Vegas. http://www.sweetbet.com/the-cromwell-las-vegas/.

The Cromwell. https://www.codagroupinc.com/portfolio/the-cromwell/.

The Culture Wiki. "Trans World Airlines." https://culture.fandom.
com/wiki/Trans_World_Airlines. The Editors of *Encyclopedia
Britannica*. 1998. "Pearl River Delta." *Britannica*, July 20,
1998. Revised December 30, 1999. https://www.britannica.
com/place/Pearl-River-Delta.

The Ed Sullivan Show. "About Ed Sullivan." http://www.edsullivan.
com/about-ed-sullivan/.

The Elvis Newspage. https://the-elvis-newspage-tcotoe.mn.co/feed.

The Strat. "Attractions." https://thestrat.com/attractions.

Thompson, Gary. 1999. "Harrah's sells LV Showboat." *Las Vegas
Sun*, July 21, 1999. https://lasvegassun.com/news/1999/jul/21/
harrahs-sells-lv-showboat/.

Triposo. "Atlantic City, New Jersey, History." https://www.triposo.
com/loc/Atlantic_City2C_New_Jersey/history/background.

Triposo. "MGM Grand Las Vegas." https://www.triposo.com/poi/
MGM_Grand_Las_Vegas.

Triposo. "Vegas Vic." https://www.triposo.com/poi/Vegas_Vic.

TV Database Wiki. "Red Foxx." https://tvdatabase.fandom.com/
wiki/Redd_Foxx.

TV Guide. "TV Guide Magazine 60 Best Series." https://www.tvguide.
com/news/tv-guide-magazine-60-best-series-1074962/.

United States Census Bureau. "DP-1: Profile of General Population and Housing Characteristics: 2010 for Atlantic City, Atlantic County, New Jersey. https://archive.today/20200212103750/http://factfinder.census.gov/bkmk/table/1.0/en/DEC/10_DP/DPDP1/0600000US3400102080.

Vegas.com. "The Beatles in Las Vegas." https://www.vegas.com/beatles/.

Vegas World.

Velotta, Richard N. 2001. "Stupak proud, but not notably nostalgic about Stratosphere." *Las Vegas Sun*, May 4, 2001. https://lasvegassun.com/news/2001/may/04/stupak-proud-but-not-notably-nostalgic-about-strat/.

Victor, Adam. 2008. *The Elvis Encyclopedia.* New York City: The Overlook Press.

Vinson, Mike. 2015. "'Mop Heads' vs. 'High and Tight': Most famous haircut since the Beatles!" *Murfreesboro Post*, April 5, 2015.   https://www.murfreesboropost.com/opinion/mop-heads-vs-high-and-tight-most-famous-haircut-since/article_a19a81ea-e1c2-5d65-97d2-ccf84b03e125.html.

Vintage Las Vegas. https://vintagelasvegas.com/tagged/91-Club.

Wechsler, Philip. 1978. "Atlantic City opens its first casino in 1978." *New York Daily News*, May 27, 1978. Updated May 25, 2015.   https://www.nydailynews.com/news/national/casino-atlantic-city-opened-1978-article-1.2228123.

Waymarking. "The Cromwell Hotel and Casino." https://www.waymarking.com/waymarks/WMQEV7_The_Cromwell_Hotel_and_Casino_Las_Vegas_NV.

Wikiwand. "Castaways Hotel and Casino." https://www.wikiwand.com/en/Castaways_Hotel_and_Casino

Wikiwand. "El Rancho Hotel and Casino." https://www.wikiwand.com/en/El_Rancho_Hotel_and_Casino.

Wikiwand. "MGM Grand Fire." https://www.wikiwand.com/en/MGM_Grand_fire.

Wikiwand. "New Frontier Hotel and Casino." https://www.wikiwand.com/en/New_Frontier_Hotel_and_Casino

Wittkowski, Donald. 2013. "Carl Icahn won't approve sale of Trump Plaza for $20M." *Press of Atlantic City*, April 23, 2013. https://pressofatlanticcity.com/news/press/atlantic_city/carl-icahn-won-t-approve-sale-of-trump-plaza-for/article_6bf05244-abb4-11e2-97a7-0019bb2963f4.html.

ABOUT THE AUTHOR

Eric P. Endy is the third and youngest son of Paul Endy. He received his bachelor of science degree from the University of Nevada, Reno, and his master's degree in audiology from Cal State, Los Angeles. In addition, he received his MBA from the University of Nevada, Las Vegas, in 2007. Eric is married to Hsiaochin (Cathy) Endy and has three adult children: Daren, Nevin, and Celine Endy. He is proud to have worked in the gaming supply industry and to have been part of the history of fabulous Las Vegas. Lastly, Eric would like to thank Mrs. Karen Constantine in Las Vegas for her contributions to his father's book.

CPSIA information can be obtained
at www.ICGtesting.com
Printed in the USA
LVHW071601300422
717323LV00004B/10

9 781637 102381